The *Fast,* The *Fraudulent,* & The *Fatal*

The Dangerous and Dark side of Illegal Street Racing, Drifting and Modified Cars

First Edition

Michael Bender

authorHOUSE®

AuthorHouse™
1663 Liberty Drive, Suite 200
Bloomington, IN 47403
www.authorhouse.com
Phone: 1-800-839-8640

First published by AuthorHouse 3/13/2009

ISBN: 978-1-4343-0146-8 (sc)

Printed in the United States of America
Bloomington, Indiana

This book is printed on acid-free paper.

About the Author and this Book

I attended my first auto theft seminar in 1974 and was intrigued by the methods used to steal cars. Over 30 years later, and thousands of investigations later, I am still intrigued by the methods used. It has, and will continue to be, a cat and mouse game. The automotive industry and others will devise systems to prevent theft and detect fraud, and the auto thieves will find ways to circumvent those new systems.

My career in auto theft and fraud began as a police officer in California. After several years in patrol, I worked as a training officer, a school resource officer, a SWAT team member, a child abuse detective, and finally as an auto theft detective. After leaving the police department, I worked for the National Auto Theft Bureau (which later became the National Insurance Crime Bureau) and continued my career in auto theft and fraud detection, prevention, investigation, and identification. During this time (1995) I created VINtrack software to assist in the identification of stolen vehicles along with other tools to assist law enforcement, the automotive industry, and the insurance industry (For more information on these tools visit Bender Enterprises Inc. at: www. VINtrack.com).

During this journey, I have learned a lot from everyone involved in the industry (including auto thieves). Today I continue in investigations, consulting and training with auto theft task forces, insurance companies, automobile manufacturers, and law enforcement throughout the world and continue to evolve in auto theft and fraud detection and prevention.

This book will include much of the information I present at my auto theft and fraud training sessions and workshops across the country. Over the years, we have received thousands of questions, calls, and emails regarding auto theft and fraud as it relates to the modified sport compact scene and illegal street racers. I have attempted to answer the most requested of these questions within this book. Sport compacts (for purposes of this book) are smaller cars with added performance or enhanced style options (Sport Compacts have also been referred to as SpoCom at car shows). A stock Toyota Camry would be considered a compact, while a Honda Civic Si could be considered a sport compact; the differences can be very subtle to non-enthusiasts. Included in the sport compact category will be heavily desired or modified compacts. Initially, Scion vehicles (a division of Toyota) were highly successful in this category with enthusiasts because of all the styling that could be accomplished more than for the performance options. Sub-compacts are also emerging with similar interests, with such cars as the Honda Fit, which was embraced and modified before it officially came to America.

It has been my goal and belief that each person that reads this information will identify theft and fraud that would have otherwise been missed. This awareness, understanding, and knowledge will benefit investigators as well as protect those from becoming victims.

While there appears to be an epidemic amount of fraud related to the sport compact and modified vehicle scene, always remember that for every fraudulent scenario presented here there are also legitimate reasons for the situation to happen.

Throughout this book, I will use the word "We" instead of "I"; without the constant collaboration between all disciplines involved, my experience and knowledge would be limited. One of our best tools in the fight against auto theft is our network of auto theft and fraud professionals, associations such as IAATI, WSATI, AATIA, CATI, TAVTI, DELMARVA, IMPACT, MD-DC ACT, NOTFEA, VA-Heat, FATIU, RATT, RATTE, RATTLER, VIPER, and IASIU, along with the personal contacts we have all developed over the years.

We welcome your comments. If you would like to recommend areas of this book to be expanded, deleted, or corrected, drop us a line. If your contribution is significant, we will send you the second edition free. We can be contacted via our websites: www.ProtectOurStreets.org, or www.VINtrack. com.

While every attempt has been made to insure accuracy in this book, there may be additional factors relating to the subject matter presented that could have other meanings or inaccuracies. The information presented should be independently verified before taking any action.

Acknowledgement

Writing this book was a culmination of many years of auto theft investigations and associated crimes. Along the way I have encountered many helpful and devoted professionals who included me in their operations. I would like to express my appreciation to the investigators and officers that have paved the way and assisted in attacking this dangerous scene. Some of the people who played a vital role along the way include Mark Stowell, Ed Clair, John Rosetti, Todd Brown, Brian Farnsworth, Phil Ens, Mark Hoerrmann, Greg Sloan, Tim Coyle, Joe Nannery, Mike Meulemans, Tommy Hansen, Bob Jagoe, Skip Showalter, Michelle Rodriguez, Jeff Higbee, Rob McClandish, Thomas O'Dell.

Dedicated

To Mikali and Cynthia for their patience, love, and support.

Table of Contents

Introduction

For the record, we want to acknowledge that the majority of tuners, car clubs, and enthusiasts around the world work hard for the money it takes to customize their vehicles and are not recklessly endangering lives on our city streets. Most insurance claims and reports of theft are legitimate. Motorsports and car clubs have many positive and beneficial contributions to our society. Remember, we are focusing on the *Fast and the Fraudulent* side of these motorsports and know that the overwhelming amount of activities in sanctioned events serve a great purpose and are legitimate and honest. In fact, Motorsports have the highest attendance rates of any spectator sports today.

This book concentrates on the dark side of the modified vehicle scene as it relates to the theft, fraud, and illegal street racing, as well as other related activities. Understanding the principals in this book will give you the necessary tools to recognize – and stop – fraudulent and dangerous activity.

Most of the people we see who are heavily involved in the sport compact street scene have more money tied up in their vehicle than they could ever hope to recover if sold. The average return on investment can be as little as 30 cents on the dollar (This is not the case with classic customized vehicles and other similar vehicles that can appreciate and become a good investment). Personalization and customization does not just happen with the sport compacts and is prevalent in many of today's vehicles.

We have seen numerous fully customized, trophy-winning vehicles offered for sale at a great loss over what had been invested in them. One owner at an Arizona car show was advertising that he had $25,000 plus invested in his show car and was selling it for $7,000 or best offer. Putting $20,000 into an 11-year-old Honda bought for $1,800 is not unheard of. It was reported that to equip a 2009 Honda Fit with all available Mugen parts would cost an additional $20,000 over the $16,000 sticker price of the Fit.

Many of these enthusiasts only recover one-third of what they spend on their cars. These losses in investment are a motivating factor for many to commit insurance fraud in order to recover the money they have spent.

To build a car from parts can be extremely expensive, particularly if one adds high-performance and customized parts. A 2000 Honda Accord LX may have cost over $22,000 new, but if it had been built from the cost of the individual parts, the cost could have been as much as $68,000.

I started specializing in the illegal street race and modified vehicle fraud and auto theft scene in 1997. Nighttime illegal street racing was rampant in many areas throughout the country at that time. Law enforcement agencies, responding to calls of illegal street racing, would arrive to find several hundred to over 1,000 street racers and spectators at a single location. Several years later, street racing appeared to have run its course and died out in the most popular cities, but in 2006, it appeared to have made a comeback. However, a new decade of enthusiasts were calling these races or events by other names. The outcome was the same, however; speed exhibitions on our streets that are unsafe and illegal. For those of us that have been around long enough, we know how important it is to keep these "new" problems and trends from getting out of hand.

The information presented in this book will never be outdated regarding theft, fraud, and human behavior. You might have to dust it off in 5-10 years but hold on to it, because chances are good you will need it. Trends seem to come and go, but if you travel the country or world, you will find they just move or resurface. A variety of theft and fraud scenarios will be presented throughout this book with real-life cases and methods of operation as examples. Where appropriate, I have combined some cases together to provide a more thorough example of how to detect and deter certain crimes. While these investigative solutions may be offered for a specific type of theft, applying these principals to all theft and fraud investigations when appropriate is recommended.

This book addresses several primary factors that contribute to the theft and fraud related to sport compact cars, primarily the Street, Show, Drift, Stunt, and Drag scenes. These are general categories that can apply to similar trends that involve heavy modifications and aggressive or stunt-type driving. Frequently the enthusiasts that build and modify these cars are called "tuners" because they are tuning (to make run better/faster) up their car. The majority of those who participate in theses scenes also use their cars on a daily basis for work and general transportation, thus the term "daily driver" is used often to further describe the owner. The brief descriptions that follow on Street, Show, Drift, Stunt, and Drag will be explained in detail throughout the book and in Chapter 3. When speaking of drag racing, we are primarily talking about the *illegal* street drags, or *illegal* cars that are mentioned in this book, not the legitimate sport of drag racing.

"**Street**" will refer to those who modify their vehicles to increase power and performance and frequently engage in illegal street contests such as illegal street racing and varying degrees of exhibition of speed. They may set up illegal eighth-mile to quarter-mile drag races on sections of our roads (the quarter-mile often referred to as the 1320 and the eighth-mile as the 660, representing the amount of feet traveled).
They may have all-out races on the freeways from point A to point B, or they may take over parking lots or intersections (commonly referred to as Side Shows).

"**Show**" will refer to those who modify their vehicles inside and out to show them off. They could have a $5,000 custom paint job, custom interiors, graphics, and gauges – the types of cars where the engine compartment is so clean you could eat off it. We have seen $75,000 in accessories in some show cars. They may display them at shows or just on the street. Some show cars are also street, drift, and drag cars. Some are referred to as lifestyle cars, Show and Go, or Drag, Drift, and Drive cars.

"**Drift**" is the art of driving vehicles into a turn, or a series of turns, at high rates of speed while sliding (drifting) into, through, and out of, the turns instead of steering through the turns. Drifting into a turn at 80 mph with the rear tires spinning and smoking is common. Generally, rear-wheel drive vehicles are favored.

"**Drag**" will refer to quarter-mile drag races seen historically at many NHRA (National Hot Rod Association) events. Typically, a stock car may take 19-seconds to travel a quarter-mile from standstill. Some of these sport compact cars have been modified to such a degree that they can now travel that quarter-mile in eight seconds and less. We have seen many street-driven "daily drivers" that can travel the quarter-mile in ten seconds. Drag racing at sanctioned tracks is a legitimate and respected sport and should not be confused with the illegal sport compact drag activity we discuss in this book. We will focus on the Fast and Fraudulent crowd that uses theft and fraud to compete at these events.

"**Stunt**" or Stunting most often involves sport bikes but can include vehicles involved in sideshow and ghost riding type activities. Riding a motorcycle on one wheel while splitting lanes on a freeway at over 100 mph could be one example. Sideshows can involve taking over intersections and doing figure eights with a vehicle, while ghost riding would involve jumping out of a moving vehicle and jumping on top of the hood and car surfing down the highway.

Vehicles today have become second homes, second recreation rooms, and second offices. They are generally the second largest investment an individual will make in his lifetime. This book focuses primarily on sport compact cars as they have accounted for much of the theft and fraud we see. Honda and Acura are mentioned frequently due to their early popularity among the modified compact scene. However, numerous vehicles make up the scene today due to the accessibility of aftermarket parts and emerging trends.

The difference between street racing "back in the day" and today's scene is the unacceptable percentage of vehicle modifications that are underwritten by insurance fraud and the increased danger that is posed to society in terms of injuries to innocent victims and lost lives.

By cracking down on the auto theft and fraud aspects, as well as providing continuous and updated education, it is our firm belief that lives will be saved. By reading and understanding the information contained in this book, the reader will be better prepared to recognize the theft and fraud involved in the Fast and the Fraudulent scene.

Chapter 1: The Fast and Fraudulent Scene

Our streets, highways and canyons come to life at midnight with the distinctive sound of heavily modified vehicles transforming our streets into the Wild West of the 21ˢᵗ Century. While parents are asleep, their children are out looking for their next rush. The vehicular addiction of speed and personalization brings with it an enormous amount of theft and fraud, along with injuries and deaths. Throughout many parts of the world, there is an epidemic of young adults defrauding the insurance industry and using law enforcement to initiate false reports in order to fund their passion. It can be very expensive for teens to compete with their peers in this modified vehicle scene.

The need for speed and a fine looking ride supersedes the budget for many of these participants. The Fast and the Fraudulent crowd will steal cars to obtain a faster engine, transmission, or better tires. Many commit insurance fraud to achieve their desired vehicle. A lot of cash may change hands at an illegal nighttime race and often times, in lieu of cash, participants will bet vehicle parts such as tires and wheels. If they lose, they may part out their own vehicles and then make a false theft report to initiate a fraudulent claim to buy replacement parts. Many somehow come to believe that it is "okay" to make a false report or false claim of theft or vandalism in order to get the insurance companies to pay for their modifications and fix their problems.

Today's society is a fast paced, have to have it now group. Our youth see a car on television, at a show or in a magazine and they "have to" have one better. To some, having the best looking, fastest, loudest, most powerful car is more important to them then relationships, education, and employment.

Generation Y: Income vs. Expenses = Fraud

Our youth are driven to be defined by and noticed for the vehicles they drive. Generation X (born between the 1960s and 1970s) made the Honda Civic the must-have compact car during the 1990s. Generation Y, also known as Gen Why, Millenniums/Millennials, Net generation and Echo Boomers (born between the 1980s and 1990s), represent close to 1/3 of the U.S. population at 75 million strong. They have been reported as the largest consumer group in the history of the U.S. They are responsible for spending $150 to $200 billion a year and many do not even have fulltime jobs. They love and embrace technology and prefer new over used, including cars and accessories; they are the Lifestyle Generation. We must understand and study Gen Y in order to prevent dangerous trends from evolving.

We must understand this and future generations and use that knowledge accordingly. This group is seen most in the sport compact type vehicles as there has been a move towards small cars. Money and jobs are not as important as social ideas and time to this generation. This generation relies on peer feedback, and they are a very interactive group with a sense of community.

1

The 20-something age group has been emerging as a new second phase of adolescence that further delays adulthood and feeds this vehicle modification desire longer. Generation Y has expensive tastes and little disposable income of its own. Those who are going to college may be graduating with twice the debt as the previous generation; by graduation, students have already incurred an enormous amount of student loan and credit card debt. When a new student receives the orientation package at college, it frequently is full of credit offers, further driving the student into debt. This debt has a direct correlation to the increase in theft and fraud. The majority of the sport compact car participants of the street, show, drift, stunt, and drag scene are 16-27 year-olds driving heavily modified vehicles that are often times paid for and insured by their parents. Many of these car owners want to immediately personalize their vehicles with modifications or customization to make them uniquely their own or to keep up with their friends, as well as their sports and music idols.

The print and news media frequently report on the flashy side of illegal street racing, car shows and drifting. However, too often the media does not address the issue of how many of the participants in this scene do not have an income that can support its high cost. Where does an unemployed or minimum wage student, living at home, come up with thousands of dollars in expendable income? Fraud is too often the answer and will be explored in depth in this book. In a June 2004 issue of a Sport Compact magazine, they advised their readers that if their income were $35,000 per year, it would be reasonable to dedicate $4,000 to invest in the car. For many impatient tuners, that amount is not nearly enough. They may spend that much on a complete engine swap without any other modifications.

In 2006, SEMA (Specialty Equipment Market Association) conducted a survey and the average household income for sport compact enthusiasts was $47,000. Nearly 20% reported income of less than $25,000 and another 20% reported income between $25,000 and $45,000 (for more information go to www.sema.org). The average income of many of the tuners we have investigated is far below $35,000. According to several experts, the average disposable income for Gen Y is only $100 per week.

There are many sport compact magazines reaching hundreds of thousands of sport compact enthusiasts. Many of them are supported entirely by a young readership. Magazines such as DSport have listed their circulation and demographics similar to what we see at the various sport compact events we attend. In 2008, DSport listed their total audience at 675,000 per month. Of their readership, 95% were males under the age of thirty-five, of which 67% were involved in college or had graduated (http://dragsport.com). This is a male-dominated activity, but the female enthusiasts certainly have their role in the Fast and the Fraudulent side of things with all-girl racing clubs in both street racing and drifting.

Whether a car is built to race at a legally sanctioned venue or illegally on our highways, the financial cost can be high. Too many enthusiasts have paid for their modifications with money obtained through theft and fraud. It can take a lot of money to create and maintain a tuner, super-tuner, show, drift, or lifestyle car. Enthusiasts tend to drive their cars much faster and tend to put more stress on their cars than the average car owner. This "enthusiasm" has demonstrated a higher percentage of insurance claims than the same vehicle not involved in "the scene."

Aftermarket Parts Industry and Vehicle Trends

The Specialty Equipment Market Association (SEMA) first tracked the sport compact performance market in 1997, when retail sales of accessories and products for this automotive market sector totaled $295 million. A record $38.11 billion worth of specialty automotive products were purchased in 2007. These types of products are used to modify the performance, appearance, or handling of the vehicle and are part of discretionary spending, unlike parts that are required for automotive repair.

Of the sales, 58% went to accessories and appearance, 24% to wheels, tires, and suspension, and nearly 18% was spent on racing and performance. The Street-performance niche grew 64% in 2006 and the performance-related products of the compact-performance niche grew *416%* between 2000 and 2006. Nearly $7 billion was spent on the sport compact performance market in 2007.

SEMA sponsors an aftermarket exhibition with over 100,000 industry professionals every November in Las Vegas. Power, Performance, Customization and Personalization were the trends being set for the 2006 season during the 2005 SEMA show, and they were right on target with their prediction. During that show, the Honda Civic Si won the "2005 Vehicle Manufacturer of the Show," the first time a non-domestic manufacturer was named. In 2008, the 2010 Chevrolet Camaro won the vehicle of show award, which fits the trends of muscle cars' increased involvement in the street scene. In 2007, the Honda Civic, both new and used, was the most popular car among teens. Automakers watch the aftermarket industry closely to identify trends in design and products, as should we as investigators. SEMA is strictly a business-to-business event.

Toyota took a unique approach in marketing to the younger generation with the Scion. In the same price range as a Civic, owners got some additional features. Initially Scion attended up to 70 events per month around the country and had the youngest buyers, with an average age of 31 years (the industry average was 46).

Contributing to the growth of the $38 billion automotive specialty equipment aftermarket industry is the amount of time Americans now spend in their vehicles. Long commutes to work, road trips, and urban sprawl have also helped mobile electronics become one of the fastest growing categories of the SEMA show.

The aftermarket parts industry shows no signs of slowing. Studying SEMA is a great predictor of what we can expect to see on the streets and thus, where the most theft and fraud will occur in the upcoming year. In addition to watching trends from the SEMA show, the Tokyo Auto Salon Tour sets the theme for activity in North America. U.S. citizens will travel to Japan and then report on new and emerging trends in the Japanese Domestic Market (JDM). This event is generally held in January of each year.

Automobile manufacturers have seen how lucrative the aftermarket parts industry has become and have been scrambling to build cars to fill this demand for personalization, customization, performance, and speed. They have also begun making aftermarket parts of their own for this generation as well as making sure that their vehicles are accessory friendly for those owners wanting a personalized look.

The median age for many automotive buyers has been dropping for sport compact cars. This scene is more than a fad; it is a lifestyle and an attitude. Their vehicles represent their personalities. Studying marketing trends can help to identify emerging trends that are more than a fast fad. These are, however, very trend-conscious enthusiasts, and we must consistently study the constantly changing trends in order to keep a handle on the potential for theft and fraud. Vehicle manufacturers are designing new cars to fill the desires of our youth. In the auto theft and fraud world, this relates to at least five years of a particular model vehicle -- five years of potential theft and fraud issues that should be addressed with each new change.

The part of the country in which one resides will dictate which automotive trends should get the most focus. In many parts of the country, trucks and SUVs far outnumber sport compact vehicles. In some sections of cities, there may be large number of lowered vehicles while other cities may face issues with raised trucks. Remember, any significant modification trend is a factor to be considered in fighting theft and fraud.

We have been tracking and investigating modification trends since 1997. Ten years later, we were still getting reports of how the modified vehicle scene is just now emerging and taking off in some areas of the country. We continue to track global trends in this scene as it may take five to ten years for a trend to travel the globe. Monitoring trends will assist in the prevention of theft and fraud. Our industry needs to pay attention to these trends to prepare and prevent emerging fraud trends.

GM, Ford, and Chrysler were considered the "Big 3" for decades. In 2004, the Japanese Big 3 (Toyota/Lexus, Honda/Acura and Nissan/Infiniti) outsold the Big 3 domestic brands in the United States. This change in American interest has increased the number of sport compact cars in many cities. In 2006 Japanese exports to the United States increased 36%, making one in eight light vehicles sold in America being manufactured in Japan. According to Automotive News, the export increase in 2006 was at its highest point since 1989.

The economy also plays a big role in what is desired. In 2008, the United States experienced it largest trend to date in moving from large, gas-guzzling vehicles to compacts and sub-compacts. For the first time, sales of vehicles with four-cylinder engines represented more than 50% of all sales, while six and eight-cylinder engines declined over the past year. The move towards fuel efficiency is dominating the automotive industry in North America, with the production of light trucks, SUVs, and minivans being replaced with small and mid-sized vehicles. Ford announced the biggest quarterly loss, $8.7 billion, in its 105-year history. Of the top five automobile manufacturers, only American Honda had a sales increase the first quarter of 2008 (but finished down only 8% by the end of the year compared to 20-30% declines for GM, Ford, and Chrysler). In June 2008, the Honda Civic dethroned the Ford F-150 pickup to become the best selling car in the United States. The F-150 also fell behind the Toyota Corolla/Matrix, the Toyota Camry, and the Honda Accord.

In June 2008, there were 202 million licensed drivers and 251 million registered cars and light trucks in the United States, with the Honda Civic still in the top ten stolen vehicles. Due to the shortage of new fuel-efficient cars, a one-year old used 2007 Civic was running approximately $1,000 over the sticker price of a new 2008 Civic. Mid- to small-size cars represented approximately 40 percent of the registered vehicles.

Today's young car owners are very much into restyling their vehicles to make them an extension of who they are and what they like; from music to style to attitude. With the influx of sport compacts there will be an ever-increasing desire to customize vehicles and make them unique. Personalization and customization can increase substantially in a down economy, because consumers are holding on to their used vehicles and want to update them.

Fraud Costs

Fraud hurts everyone. Not just the insurance companies affected but every citizen. The FBI estimates that non-health related insurance fraud costs the average U.S. family $400-700 per year with a total yearly cost of $40 billion. Think about that figure and how it relates to other devastating costs. To put this in perspective, some of our most costly disasters (prior to hurricane Katrina) cost less than fraud costs every year (hurricane Andrew reportedly cost $25 billion). Hurricanes are predictable but not preventable; fraud is predictable *and* preventable in many cases.

Fraud costs are handed down to every citizen that pays insurance. Fraud not only costs in monetary payouts but it wastes a lot of time (which equals money) that could otherwise be spent on services that are more productive. Fraud wastes *everyone's* time and money. Additional fraud costs information can be found at the Coalition Against Insurance Fraud's website, www.insurancefraud. org, the Insurance Information Institute, www.iii.org, and at the National Insurance Crime Bureau www.nicb.org.

Auto theft and fraud varies greatly throughout cities and states. Too often, auto theft is considered a "victimless" crime – until one becomes a victim. Overcoming this idea takes some work. We are all victims of auto theft and fraud in a variety of ways, particularly by paying higher insurance premiums.

In a report prepared by the Insurance Information Institute, it was reported that auto insurance fraud amounted to $14 billion in false claims (per year) by the end of 2004. Conservative estimates of fraud costs just for vehicle and homeowners insurance premiums are $250 per year per household. Other estimates indicate that 15% of our Auto and Homeowners insurance payment goes towards paying fraudulent claims. That is over $2.5 million being wasted for every 10,000 households in your city each year. Combating insurance fraud is tough enough without considering the apathy that is frequently involved when it comes to insurance in general. According to the report, one in four U.S. adults say that overstating the value of a claim to an insurance company is acceptable, and more than one in ten say they approve of submitting insurance claims for items that were not lost or damaged or for treatments that were not provided. Commonly those who commit insurance fraud commit other types of fraud such as workers' compensation, welfare, credit card, mail order, and many other types.

It has been suggested that more big screen TVs have been reported stolen than have ever been produced. False reports of property losses to law enforcement and subsequently to the insurance industry are particularly heavy around tax time. People make false reports of theft to take additional tax write-offs and get money from the insurance industry.

In addition to theft, collisions are common in the sport compact scene. In 2003, the Insurance Research Council found that 26.4 out of every 100 claims for vehicle damage nationwide were accompanied by bodily injury claims. In California the number was 29 (down from 35 in 2002) and in some counties such as Orange and Los Angeles the number rose to 50 and 60 out of every 100 claims in 2002. At that time, the Insurance Research Council found that two-thirds of such claims in Los Angeles appeared to involve fraud. (The Insurance Research Council is a non-profit division of the American Institute for Chartered Property Casualty Underwriters and the Insurance Institute of America www.ircweb.org). In 2006 seven of the top ten cars with the most expensive collision losses were sport compacts, with the Mitsubishi Lancer Evolution at number one, the Dodge SRT-4 at number three, the Subaru Impreza WRX at number four, the Lexus IS 300 at number six, followed by the Honda S2000, Acura RSX and Nissan 350z.

If you know someone who is thinking of committing insurance fraud, remind him or her that with the hundreds of thousands of legitimate claims, it becomes easy for insurance investigators and law enforcement to spot the false ones. Thousands of people have learned this the hard way after being arrested for felony insurance fraud.

Modified Vehicles; Theft and Fraud Costs

One of the first questions we get from the news media relates to the cost of sport compact theft and fraud. Sport compact vehicles that are involved in theft and fraud, as well as street racing in general, do not have their own reporting category. They generally get reported as the crime itself. For example, a traffic collision on the streets will be reported, but there may not be a check box on the collision form that indicates that a "street race" was involved; we have to rely on additional reporting or narratives to get those details.

Several studies have been conducted by various insurance companies over the years regarding sport compact cars. One insurance company reported that Honda took five of the top ten spots of vehicles that were reported vandalized and Acura came in tenth. Another insurance company reported that in Northern California alone they paid out $6.3 million in miscellaneous comp claims, $1.1 million in partial theft and stereo, $6.1 million in vandalism, $3 million in fire losses, and $22 million in total thefts.

Several years ago, members from a large national insurance company in Virginia attended a sport compact drag event. They identified 12 of their policyholders racing at this event. Of those policyholders, 100% of them had submitted insurance claims within the past 18 months and 85% of those claims were suspicious. They had averaged five accidents in the previous year. Those 12 people had cost this company more than $224,000 in first- and third-party claims in the previous 18 months. For a comparison, the insurance company took a sampling of similar sport compact cars that were not involved in the street, show, drift, stunt, and drag scene. The 12 sampled were responsible for only $6,000 in claims, versus the $224,000 in claims the drag race attendees had (not twice or 10 times as much; but 37 times more). This company and many others like it are taking great losses from a small book of business.

Another insurance company took a proactive stance in identifying sport compact insurance fraud. They initiated training and education of their employees and customers and their claim losses dropped from over $4 million to $1.6 million. Since data supports that insureds that are interested in the street, show, drift, stunt, and drag scene have a substantially greater potential for claims related to theft and fraud, it is imperative that insurance companies and law enforcement scrutinize claims that involve the types of vehicles and circumstances that are discussed in this book. Through education, training, and policy implementation, insurance companies can avoid these types of losses in the future, enabling them to pass the savings on to their customers.

In addition to the obvious vehicle claims that arise with sport compact cars, we noticed that each of these insured owners and the vehicles had a long claims history involving different types of losses. One street racer we were investigating also owned a performance shop; that shop had a claims history of multiple losses and thefts, as well as workers compensation claims.

Frequently we run vehicle identification numbers of cars featured in a street racing magazines, car shows, drift and drag events, and illegal races. For the past 10 years, we have seen similar theft and collision claims for these types of vehicles. In addition, we have seen increased worker's compensation claims, vandalism, and comprehensive claims, as well as other types of losses associated with the insured. We have also been able to relate additional claims back to other performance shops, additional insureds, and their cars.

Many scams and claims coincide with events that cater to the street, show, drift, stunt, and drag scene. Being aware of these events can help in the prevention and detection of fraudulent claims and auto theft. Preparing to enter a car in a race or show can be expensive. Parts are frequently broken at races and need to be fixed. Will the enthusiast have the money to fix the car, or will they look at theft and fraud as an option?

Both parents and investigators do not realize how much money is going into these modified vehicles. They may assume a stereo loss is several hundred dollars instead of the several thousand dollars often claimed. We have seen stereo systems that range from $10,000 to $50,000 and more at some of these shows; this scene is costing billions of dollars in theft and fraud claims. A SEMA study reported in 2007 indicated that 56% of people surveyed would spend more than $2,500 on modifications and 13% would spend $10,000 or more (The Introduction lists additional examples of modified vehicle costs that can lead to fraud).

Global Influences

Throughout this book, we will mention popular cars with which you may not be familiar. When automobile manufacturers build a vehicle, its name frequently changes depending on what country it is destined for. Some of these vehicles have greater horsepower and fewer restrictions than those destined for the United States or other countries. These different models are desired by the drivers in countries that do not have them, and enthusiasts will not stop until they can get their hands on one.

An Acura Integra in the United States is a Honda Integra in Japan. It may have rectangular headlights in Japan, where in the U.S. it has round headlights. A Honda Fit in the U.S. is a Honda Jazz in the U.K. A Nissan Silvia in Japan may be called a Nissan 240SX in the United States, and a Toyota in Japan may be a Lexus in the United States. As it goes in America, many want what they can't or don't have. It can be too costly to import these Gray-Market vehicles into the states through the proper channels; instead, our citizens may convert their vehicles to look like the Japanese model, commonly referred to as Japanese Domestic Market (JDM).

A Nissan 240SX with its new Japanese front clip will now be referred to by the owner as a Nissan Silvia. Knowing this should tell the investigator that the vehicle's owner/driver might be drifting, as Silvias are popular drift cars. It is also important to be aware of these conversions, as some of them may violate safety standards laid down by the Department of Transportation (DOT), the National Highway Traffic Safety Agency (NHTSA), and the Environmental Protection Agency (EPA). Some of these conversions also void warranties, which have lead to more insurance fraud. For more information on theses types of vehicles, refer to JDM in Chapter 5, and Gray-Market Vehicles in Chapter 7.

Vehicle Theft statistics

According to the latest Uniform Crime Reports (UCR) theft data for the United States, a vehicle was stolen in the United States every 26.4 seconds. With approximately 1.2 million thefts per year for the last five years running, auto theft is the largest and most expensive property crime committed, costing an estimated $7.9 billion in 2006, based upon the FBI using $6,649 per stolen vehicle (If we used the actual costs involved, the loss would be much greater. Including finance charges, the total cost of buying an average-priced light vehicle was $29,400 in 2006. In 2008, the average wholesale price of a used truck or car was over $9,300. SUVs averaged between $10,000 and $13,000 depending on size, far above the $6,649 figure the FBI uses).

The nationwide recovery rate for stolen vehicles is consistently below 70% (motorcycles are less than 25%). This equates to hundreds of thousands of stolen vehicles on our streets at any given time, compounded year after year. In the West, where many automotive trends start or are heavily participated in, auto theft increased 4.5% in 2005 while the nation overall decreased 11.4% (in 2006 there was a 7.6% reduction). Only 12.6% of the vehicle thefts were cleared by arrest. According to the California Highway Patrol, 247,896 vehicles were stolen in California in 2006, which is approximately one stolen vehicle for every 48 homes, almost double that of the rest of the nations average of one for every 98 homes.

The vast majority of vehicle theft is committed by 18-25 year-old males. This same age group is also heavily involved in the "Fast and the Fraudulent scene." Additionally, theft from motor vehicles and theft of motor vehicle accessories occurs, and costs more, than any other property crimes including robbery, burglary, and shoplifting.

Every 3.1 seconds a property crime occurs in the United States. While auto thefts dropped in 2004, theft of automobile parts and accessories shot up over 29%. For more information regarding the Uniform Crime Reports, visit www.fbi.gov. (The U.S. Department of Justice, Office of Justice Programs, and Bureau of Justice Statistics have useful statistical information also http://www.ojp.usdoj.gov/bjs).

In 2004, an estimated 57,497 felony cases were filed in the state courts of the nation's 75 largest counties (there are 3077 counties in the U.S.). The highest felony conviction rates were for motor vehicle theft (74%), followed by a driving related offense (73%), murder (70%), burglary (69%), and drug trafficking (67%).

These 75 counties accounted for 37% of the nation's population and 57% of all auto thefts. 45% of the motor vehicle theft defendants and 40% of burglary defendants had prior arrests or convictions when arrested. In 2005, they reported that property crimes (burglary, theft, and vehicle theft) made up slightly more than three-quarters of all crime in the United States. These statistics are important to remember to combat the stereotyping of auto theft as a victimless or minor crime because stolen vehicles are more often used in serious crimes, and those who commit the thefts are more likely to have a criminal record.

Heavily modified vehicles continue to lead the pack in claims and thefts, costing the insurance industry millions of dollars each year. Questionable body shops contribute to millions of dollars in fraud, both directly and indirectly. Additional costs affect law enforcement in time and inflated stats, as many of the reports for theft and vandalism are false. Fictitious claims estimates range from 10-25% on average and 50% or more in certain areas or class categories such as the Fast and the Fraudulent sport compact scene. This epidemic of false claims is fueled by the Street, Show, Drift, Stunt, Drag, and modified vehicle scene, as depicted in popular movies, which tend to glorify this lifestyle and culture.

There is consistent data showing the increase in theft and fraud related to sport compact cars and the modified vehicle scene. Each year throughout the country, one can see the rise of these trendy vehicles on the top ten stolen lists. Throughout the last decade, several studies were conducted relating to the sport compact scene. During one sport compact peak, CCC Information Services Inc. (www.cccis.com) reported that California had the highest theft volume, with 21 of the top 25 vehicles stolen being imports. Of the four domestic vehicles that made California's top 25 list, three of them were sport compacts. In the same year, 23 of the 25 top stolen vehicles in New York were imports. In their 2005 report, tuner cars were well represented and the Acura Integra took eight of the top 25 spots based on years represented.

According to the most recent report from the National Crime Information Center (NCIC), the top ten cars stolen in the United States for 2007 were dominated by sport compact cars:

1.   1995 Honda Civic
2.   1991 Honda Accord
3.   1989 Toyota Camry

4.   1997 Ford F-150 Series Pickup
5.   1994 Chevrolet C/K 1500 Pickup
6.   1994 Acura Integra
7.   2004 Dodge Ram Pickup
8.   1994 Nissan Sentra
9.   1988 Toyota Pickup
10.   2007 Toyota Corolla

Vehicles are frequently the target of theft and fraud based on model or because of their particular parts. The Cadillac Escalade also made top marks, which we can attribute to ease of theft coupled with desired accessories, particularly tires and wheels. Nissan Maximas were heavily targeted for thefts because many tuners wanted their High Intensity Discharge (HID) lights for their own cars. At one time in San Diego, California, it was reported that 80% of the street racers with whom law enforcement came in contact were driving Honda or Acura vehicles. A study by a large insurance company in Oregon during the same period showed that 64% of their total losses were Honda and Acura, with 25% of the Acura total losses having a multiple theft history. The cars we are seeing on this scene are also the same cars that have the highest injury, collision, and theft losses, according to the Insurance Institute for Highway Safety (IIHS). Keeping abreast of current trends in your area can help to control epidemic fraud.

We continually provide information to automobile manufacturers regarding theft and fraud trends so that they can design future cars that are more theft-resistant. Contact us if you have information that could assist manufacturers and enlighten us as to what you are seeing. (Visit www.ProtectOurStreets.org for tips and trends regarding vehicle theft).

Contributing Factors in Theft and Fraud

Predicting trends involves the consideration of many facets and can assist in the prevention of theft and fraud trends. Knowing what the automotive and aftermarket industry is doing, or planning to do, will allow you to make policy changes before a problem can occur. Watching popular shows such as those on MTV or the Speed channel can lead to responsible decision making. Knowing which top ten vehicles have poor customer satisfaction could explain why a particular car is continually getting reported as "stolen." Knowing what type of financing was obtained on the car can explain a spike in theft reporting at the end of leases. The fact that bankruptcies or foreclosures are on the rise should be an indicator that so too will stolen vehicle reports begin to rise.

A shortage of cars is created due to bombings and other destruction when we have long-term wars or conflicts going on in other countries. When this occurs, we see spikes of vehicles being exported to these countries. Unfortunately, many of these cars are our stolen vehicles being used to replace their losses or to help fund war and terror related activities. Since many in the military are involved in the sport compact scene, we may see an increase in stolen vehicle reports when they are deployed overseas. Deployment can mean financial devastation for some of the families involved, and unfortunately, we have seen an increase in fraudulent reports of vehicles being reported stolen during the time of deployment.

Higher interest rates along with other economic issues have a tendency to increase the number of leased vehicles, longer-term loans and zero-percent financing. 72-month loans can be hefty and troublesome for many, and in 2007, they accounted for nearly two-fifths of all new-vehicle loans, according to Power Information Network. The average new vehicle loan in 2007 was 64 months, and there was a 20% increase in 73- to 84-month loans. Longer financing terms means that more customers are upside-down on their vehicles, owing more in payments than they have in equity. According to the American Bankers Association, auto loan delinquency in the United States hit a 17-year high in the fourth quarter of 2007.

Edmunds.com estimated that nearly a fourth of borrowers were "upside-down" in their car loans. Frequently these upside-down balloon payments are responsible for owner give-ups (allowing or causing your car to be stolen) and a multitude of additional fraud schemes. According to Kelley Blue Book, in the first quarter of 2007, 29% of consumers were upside-down on their vehicles. Additionally, on average, people traded in cars on which they still owed more than $3,600. According to Automotive News, the average loan-to-value rate was 105% in September 2008; meaning vehicle buyers were borrowing more than the car was even worth. Factor in the immediate loss in value when a vehicle drives off the lot, and the upside-down factor keeps increasing.

In certain parts of the country, leases can account for 60-80% of a dealership's business, particularly in Detroit and northeastern cities. Leasing is the choice among young professionals, those into the newest technology, and those that are upside-down in their trade-in vehicle.

In July 2008, many banks and automakers started to tighten up or pull out of the leasing business with GM/Chrysler/Ford due to the poor economy and increased risks. Industry experts predicted these cutbacks would increase the number of 72-month and longer loans which, at the time, represented over 43% of dealership loans.

Some insurance companies have been faced with the unfortunate situation of having to pay off a lien holder even when they can prove the claim was false. This type of mandate is wrong and further victimizes the insurance industry, which in turn victimizes every citizen. Policy language should be allowed to indicate that the lien holder would not be paid if the claim were proven fraudulent. The criminal attempted to defraud the insurance company should be held responsible for their actions, not the insurance company. Requiring the insurance company to pay for a criminal's misdeeds only gets the cost passed on to every citizen that pays for insurance.

With no money down and 84-month payment plans, GAP coverage is soaring (Guaranteed Automotive Protection or Guaranteed Asset Protection). Some auto theft suspects that have been arrested talk about the increased use of GAP insurance. GAP insurance has been increasing dramatically. GAP insurance essentially pays off a loan, or pays a significant portion of a loan, if a vehicle is totaled or stolen and not recovered. GAP providers put limits on what they will pay; lenders are paid the difference between what the GAP policyholders owe on their vehicle loans and what they receive from their vehicle insurance companies. GAP is included in the cost of most leases but is typically an option for vehicle buyers. Some estimates were that about 20% to 30% of new- and used-vehicle buyers who finance through a dealership buy GAP policies – that compared with less than 5% the three years prior. Sales of this GAP insurance have soared in the past few years.

We work with investigators throughout the world in order to predict and prevent upcoming scams. Prior to the Internet, it could take seven years for a theft trend to reach across the United States. With the Internet and today's mobility, cross-country theft trends have gone from seven years to seven seconds. What is a problem in one country, state, or city may not be in another. Saturn thefts were popular in various parts of the country for several years. A city in Florida had a juvenile suspect who was responsible for many Saturn thefts. During that same period, Las Vegas was not experiencing an unusual amount of Saturn thefts – until the Florida suspect moved to Las Vegas. Within two months, hundreds of Saturn's were stolen. It turned out that the Florida suspect shared the ease of stealing Saturn's with his new high school friends and they went to town. This type of spike in theft happens frequently, and if looked at closely, a cause and solution can be found quickly. Identifying a potential problem and taking preemptive corrective action can save millions of dollars every year.

Understanding and paying attention to automotive trend predictions can have profound affects on an insurance company's bottom line, both in profit and fraud costs. When an automotive magazine lists the next five automotive trends worth watching, we should all pay attention. Some of these trends cost a lot of money and the current target customer may be of a generation who will not wait for income to catch up with expenditures.

The Fast and the Fatal

In April 2007, the World Health Organization reported that road traffic injuries are the leading cause of death worldwide among young people aged 10-24 years. Out of the 1.2 million people that die in car crashes each year, nearly 400,000 people under the age of 25 die on the world's roads, an average of more than 1,000 deaths a day. More than 5,000 teens die every year in the United States. (More information on the WHO report is discussed in detail in their report "Youth and Road Safety," www.who.int/roadsafety/en).

According to NHTSA, 31% of the 15-to 20-year-old drivers involved in fatal crashes in 2007 did not have valid operator's licenses at the time of the crash nor had previous license suspensions or revocations. Additionally, 31% of the drivers who were killed had been drinking.

In 2006, some police agencies estimated that well over 300 people are killed as a result of illegal street racing in the United States each year. The California Office of Traffic Safety (OTS) reported that there were 607 fatalities in California related to unsafe speed in 2005; how many of those were related to street racing is not known. In 2008, the OTS estimated that street racing contributed to over 100 fatalities in California. That figure was significantly underreported, as there is no specific reporting field for street racing related casualties.

According to the Insurance Institute for Highway Safety, Highway Loss Data Institute (HLDI), the crash rate for 16-19 year-olds is four times the risk of that for older drivers, with 16 year-olds being the highest risk. The crash rate for 16 year-olds is twice as high as it is for 18-19 year-olds.

According to AAA Foundation for Traffic Safety, more 16-18 year-olds die in car crashes then the next five leading causes of death combined: homicides, suicides, drowning, poisonings, cancer, and heart disease; with 18 year-olds being at the highest risk. Two additional people die in each teenager involved fatal collision (such as other drivers, passengers, or pedestrians).

Teenagers in the past used to receive their first car via the family hand-me-down on a limited basis. Many teenagers today are driving their own cars and don't have to share it. Parents are still the major financial contributor in vehicle purchases and are in the perfect position to protect their children and our streets. *If a parent buys a teen a fast car, that teen will be driving fast.*

National Highway Traffic Safety Administration 2005 statistics indicated that drivers between 15 and 20 years old make up 16% of all drivers involved in crashes and 12% of all drivers involved in fatal crashes. This problem appears greater when you consider that this age group makes up only 8.5% of the population.

The US Department of Transportation's Fatality Analysis Reporting System (FARS) reported that 84% of teenage motor vehicle crash deaths in 2005 were passenger vehicle occupants. Of all motor vehicle crash deaths among teenagers in 2005, 54% occurred on Friday, Saturday, or Sunday. Midnight to 3 a.m. on Saturdays and Sundays proved to be the deadliest three-hour periods throughout 2004, adding credence to the saying, "Nothing good ever happens after midnight."

Speeding is one of the most prevalent factors contributing to traffic crashes. The economic cost to society of speed-related crashes was estimated by NHTSA to be $40.4 billion per year. In 2004, NHTSA estimated that highway crashes cost our society more than $230 billion a year. Speeding was a contributing factor in 30% of all fatal crashes, and 13,192 lives were lost in speed-related crashes. For drivers involved in fatal crashes, young males are the most likely to be speeding. The relative proportion of speed-related crashes to all crashes decreases with increasing driver age. In 2004, 38% of the male drivers' age 15 to 20 who were involved in fatal crashes were speeding at the time of the crash; 68% of speed-related fatalities occurred on roads that were not interstate highways. Also in 2004, 26% of the speeding drivers under age 21 who were involved in fatal crashes had a blood alcohol content of 0.08% or higher. For drivers between the ages of 21 and 24 who were involved in fatal crashes in 2004, 49% of speeding drivers had a blood alcohol content of 0.08% or higher. NHTSA also estimates that aggressive driving behaviors are responsible for one-third of injury crashes and two-thirds of highway fatalities.

More information can be obtained through HLDI, NCHS (National Center for Health Statistics), and NHTSAs Fatality Analysis Reporting System (FARS) at: http://www.iihs.org/research, http://www.cdc.gov/nchs, and http://www-fars.nhtsa.dot.gov.

In California, teen drivers' rate of speeding violations per mile traveled is triple that of drivers 30 years and older, according to the Insurance Institute for Highway Safety. According to NHTSA, there were 41,059 fatalities for 2007 and nearly 2.5 million injuries resulting from highway crashes nationwide, down nearly 4% from 2006. However, motorcycle rider fatalities continued their 10-year increase, reaching 5,154 in 2007 with 103,000 injuries. Motorcycle rider fatalities accounted for 13% of total fatalities, exceeding the number of pedestrian fatalities for the first time since

NHTSA began collecting fatal motor vehicle crash data in 1975. The average age of a supersport motorcyclist fatality was 27 in 2005 (more on motorcycles in Chapter 3).

According to AAA, between 2000 and 2003, citations for driving faster than 100 mph increased more than 25% in California. Also in California, from 2000 through 2006, drivers plead guilty to illegal speed contests in about 50,000 cases, according to the Department of Motor Vehicles. Since speed is a factor in 29% of all fatal crashes in the United States, we should question why our youth need to change that stock 110hp engine into 200hp and above.

Like drunk drivers who are involved in collisions, street racers place more than their own lives at risk. In many cases, passengers, pedestrians, and other motorists are killed for being in the wrong place at the wrong time and the driver escapes such peril (as previously reported, 84% of teenage motor vehicle crash deaths in 2005 were passenger vehicle occupants). When things go wrong, the causes are common: driver inexperience, excessive speed, and variables such as traffic and road conditions.

As hard as it may be, parents who make their teenagers wait to start driving may decrease the likelihood of their children being involved in a serious accident. Many states that have initiated graduated driver licensing expect to see a decrease in deaths, injuries, and collisions involving our youth. States that have enacted graduated licensing requirements report that the benefits far outweigh any costs. According to HLDI, in Oregon, the administrative costs were estimated at $150,000 while the benefits were estimated at nearly $11 million. Maryland and California also reported life-saving and injury-reducing benefits well in excess of administrative costs. According to a AAA Foundation Research Report, Graduated driver licensing for teens can reduce fatal crashes by 38%.

Awareness, education, and enforcement save lives. To reduce injuries and fatalities, billions of dollars are invested every year to repair and construct safer highways, enforce traffic safety laws, and educate users of the nation's highway system on safe driving practices.

From December 16, 2004, to January 2, 2005, the California Highway Patrol (CHP) ran Operation Holiday Wish List, a program designed to reduce the number of people killed in traffic collisions as compared to the number killed in the same period in previous years. The CHP worked with the media to get out three messages: "Obey Speed Limits," "Click It or Ticket," and "You Drink, You Drive, You Lose." They put 80% of their uniformed personnel on the streets. During that effort, there were 26% fewer fatalities than the previous year, 184 versus 247 deaths. Unfortunately, many agencies are short-staffed and cannot keep up such enforcement tactics (Information obtained from the September 2005 issue of Westways magazine, put out by Auto Club of Southern California). The amount of street racing reported deaths that come across my desk every week astounds even me. In 2002, RaceLegal.com reported that for every 1,000 people participating in illegal street racing in California, 49 were either killed or seriously injured; in contrast, the national fatality rate due to drunk driving was 15 per 100,000!

With the high rate of deaths from illegal street racing, the problem was looked at as a public health issue. Armed with a grant from The California Office of Traffic Safety (OTS) the San Diego Police Department's Dragnet team used innovative tactics to nearly stop illegal street racing. In 2002, San Diego was faced with an "epidemic" of illegal street racing activity. They documented 16 deaths and 31 serious injuries directly attributed to illegal street racing. Due to Dragnet's proactive and innovative operations, no lives were lost the first eight months of 2003, and in 2005, they had an unprecedented 94% improvement with only three serious injuries and no deaths. This decrease took place when the rest of the state and country were having increases. *In 2007, Dragnet disbanded, and there were subsequently 12 street race related deaths and four injuries.* Statistics like these should speak volumes about why a department needs to continue programs after their stated goal is accomplished.

In conjunction with San Diego's enforcement program, RaceLegal's track alternative provided a safe place for enthusiasts to drag race. During this time, RaceLegal.com commented that racers were 100 more times more likely to be killed while street racing in San Diego than they were to die in an alcohol related crash. (Several programs exist throughout the globe to help get street racers off the streets and onto a safe track environment such as www.RaceLegal.com and www. BeatTheHeatInc.org; more on these programs are discussed in Chapter 8, as well as legislation stemming from street race related fatalities).

In Ontario, California, street racing-related deaths went from seven in 2004 to one in 2006 due to similar proactive enforcement actions the agencies Dragnet team took. The San Diego Dragnet Team and Ontario's Team (San Bernardino County Regional Street Racing Task Force) were both funded primarily by the California Office of Traffic Safety.
Canada has also had its problems with street racing-related deaths from early 2000 through 2007. In 1996, the York Regional Police Department, along with the Peel Regional Police and the Ontario Provincial Police, created "Operation Dragnet" in the Toronto area. This later evolved into Project E.R.A.S.E. (Eliminate Racing Activity on Streets Everywhere). Officers from 12 different police agencies, the Ministry of Transportation, and the Ministry of Environment worked collaboratively to target illegal street racing. From 1999 to 2005, they reported that 34 people had been fatally injured in the Greater Toronto Area as a result of street racing activities.

Enforcement, in my opinion, saves more lives than education, but they are equally important. Remembering my adolescence, I refrained from doing certain activities due to fear of getting caught more than from the knowledge of whether or not it was right or wrong. In an April 2007 article from USA Today, Sharon Jayson reported on a study by Temple University psychologist Laurence Steinberg regarding the adolescent brain. The research suggested that society was wasting billions of dollars on education and intervention programs tying to dissuade teens from dangerous activities. The research indicated that the teen brains were not yet capable of avoiding risky behaviors. This certainly fits with the "I am invincible" or "It won't happen to me" attitude we see with illegal street racers. The research indicated that, since teens don't have full capacity to control themselves, parents (and in my opinion, law enforcement) need to do some of the controlling. Jayson reported that studies by Steinberg and others have found that the mere physical presence of peers increased the likelihood of teens taking risks.

Michael Bradley, a Philadelphia-area psychologist and author specializing in teenagers, says U.S. culture tends to view teens as small adults when, neurologically, they are large children. Flaura Winston, MD, scientific director of the Center for Injury Research and Prevention at the Children's Hospital of Philadelphia reported similar findings indicating that the ability to control impulses is not fully formed in the teenage years. Laurence Steinberg's review can be read in the April 2007 issue of Current Directions in Psychological Science.

One case that I use in my seminars typifies most aspects of the Fast and the Fraudulent scene involving illegal racing, collisions, hit and run, false reports, and insurance fraud. During the movie release of "2 Fast 2 Furious," the California Highway Patrol saw a group of six cars racing on a freeway in the San Francisco Bay area, driving well over 100 miles per hour, weaving in and out of traffic (more information on Freeway Racing is in Chapter 3). They successfully stopped all the vehicles, arrested the drivers, and impounded the cars. The drivers had ticket stubs in their pocket indicating that they just came from watching the movie "2 Fast 2 Furious."

During the booking process, one officer discovered a video tape in an arrestee's sock. The officers viewed the video, which depicted numerous illegal and unsafe racing activities on various freeways and city streets in the bay area of California. One portion of this clip that I play in my seminars shows the speedometer displaying 135mph while this vehicle and several others are weaving in and out of traffic, nearly colliding with innocent motorists. On one segment of the video, a female passenger got out of the vehicle while it was parked on the shoulder of a freeway. The video showed that this vehicle had sideswiped another vehicle, disabling it in the number two lane. As fate would have it, another vehicle came along and rear-ended the disabled vehicle. The street racing passenger videotaped the collision damage on the disabled vehicle, and on the vehicle she was riding in. The driver discusses with her whether they should commit a hit and run, which they did.

Another segment of the video shows the suspect vehicle parked inside a residential garage. The vehicle has now been "keyed" on every panel, including the lights. The video shows detail of the keying and the words that were keyed into the paint, as well as the aftermarket parts that had been striped off the car (more on keying vandalism in Chapter 2). The suspect and his girlfriend discuss further actions they should take to vandalize and cover their tracks from the hit and run. In particular, the suspect was worried about the car club decals he had on his vehicle that might connect him to the scene. Other subjects join them in the garage while someone uses a hammer to break the windshield glass to further the vandalism claim. The girlfriend advises them not to damage the windshield too much as they still need to drive it away from the house (to make a false theft/fraud claim).

What started as attending a street-racing movie concluded with reckless freeway racing, a hit-and-run collision, vandalism fraud, auto theft fraud, and a false insurance claim. Unfortunately, the actions depicted in this video are not unique and happen on a daily basis.

Movies Blamed for Street Racing Deaths

The National Highway Traffic Safety Administration said that connecting fatal crashes to illegal drag racing is difficult, but the year the first Fast and the Furious movie came out in June 2001, at least 135 people died in accidents from possible races. That was almost double the number recorded the year prior (there were 72 possible street racing deaths in 2000). Many more deaths may have slipped under the radar, as tracking deaths attributed to street racing has been neglected or under-reported. During the time of this first movie, reports came in from several cities specifically relating street racing deaths to the film. Some were on their way to see the film and others had just seen it. In 2003, street racing crashes were reported on or about the same date as the release of the sequel, titled *2 Fast 2 Furious* in a several cities, and in 2006, as soon as the third installment came out, *The Fast and the Furious, Tokyo Drift* was released, drifting crashes were reported across the country. The fourth installment of the *Fast and Furious* franchise has an April of 2009 release date.

Proactive police departments stepped up traffic patrols around some theaters to help prevent drivers from trying to imitate the stunts shown in the movie *2 Fast 2 Furious*. In Texas, the police in Plano, near Dallas, posted extra officers on stretches of a highway close to two big multi-screen theaters where the movie was playing. Police said the extra manpower succeeded in preventing many accidents. Police in Boca Raton, Florida, stepped up patrols outside a theater as well and issued 52 tickets for speeding and reckless driving on the movie's opening night.

If it is predictable, it is preventable. My partner and I flew to Texas to assist the Houston Police Department in indentifying stolen vehicles at a car show. We wanted to get a feel for the street scene while there, and knew if we went to the local movie theater, playing *2 Fast 2 Furious*, we could just follow cars out of the theater to find illegal street racing. As soon as the show let out, we followed a group of cars that led us to an illegal race site on a city street. We filmed several races and gathered information while waiting for the local authorities.

Many personal tragedies from around the United States were shared in the news and print media in an effort to have teens listen and learn from others during these movie-induced crashes. Some died while racing to see the movie and others died while racing on the way home. Others died several weeks later. This is not Universal Studios fault; it just shows the effect that movies and games can and do have on our youth.

The sad fact is that most of these deaths and injuries are preventable. We cannot just blame movies and games. We all have a role in making our streets safe and protecting our youth. Parental vigilance is one factor that can and does help reduce these preventable deaths. Parents could help by limiting the number of passengers their children are allowed to have in the car with them, making seat belt use automatic, counseling on alcohol, being discriminating about the models of cars they drive and the modifications they add, and setting curfews for driving at night. The risk of being involved in a fatal traffic accident increases with the number of passengers in the vehicle. Teens need to learn and practice car control. Many driving programs are available to teach our youth to handle dangerous and stressful situations.

Chapter 2: Common Types of Fraud and Theft

Over the years many different scams have come, gone, and come back again. Each decade new names appear for the types of theft and fraud scams, but the principals remain the same. We will concentrate on the typical scams we see in the auto theft and fraud realm as it relates to modified vehicles. Enthusiasts have different goals in mind; they may start with a stock car or want to change the theme of their already-modified car, but the scams they use to get there are very similar.

Keying Vandalism

Keying is a general term for scratching the paint on a car with a key but the damage may in fact have been caused by a knife, screwdriver, a nail, or similar sharp metal object. In a real key vandalism claim, we typically see the vandal walk down one side of the car while holding the key against the paint. When the vandalism is finished, the damage is generally inflicted upon one or two sections of the vehicle in a line. In some cases, the scratch will run the entire length of the vehicle. The suspect(s) may know the individual who owns the vehicle and have a motive for the keying, but other times it is just a random act. Some vandals may have animosity toward the style of vehicle, and key it for that reason alone.

If a dishonest enthusiast wants a new paint job, graphics or body kit (body kits generally consist of restyled front and rear bumpers as well as side skirts), they may vandalize their own car by keying it. During the commission of fraudulent keying, the motive is usually that they want a new paint color, new graphics, or a new body style. They don't just run the key down one side of the vehicle like a real key job, because the insurance company may only have to repair the particular body part instead of the entire car. They methodically scratch every panel of the vehicle, including the hood, trunk, and roof. Sometimes, if they want new head or tail lights, they will scratch the glass or lens covers also. Many times, they will scratch a profane word or some type of gang insignia (tag) into the paint as well. They believe this gives them credibility in their false claim, wanting the investigator to believe that "someone" was after them.

When dealing with the potential of gang involvement, the investigator should show a picture of the gang tag to a gang detective or expert to determine if it was real or staged, as is the case with fraud. Additional questions to ask of the gang expert would be, "Have there been any other instances of that gang tagging in the area of this reported vandalism?" "Are their gangs known for using another gangs tag to implicate them and divert the investigation from the real suspects?"

Typically, when a gang member tags a vehicle, he does so while seated inside the car (because he just stole it). The majority of any tagging is then done from the drivers or passenger seats and may be seen on the headliner, center console, or visors. If a vehicle sits unattended in a gang-ridden area, one may see tags on the outside in addition to some other vandalism or thefts.

It becomes obvious in many keying vandalism claims that fraud was the motive when one compares the before and after pictures of the vehicle. The vehicle transforms from a stock model to one with custom paint, added or new body kits, and/or graphics.

The insured is not always the one who does the dirty work; sometimes it is the insured's friend or family member acting on behalf of the insured. Other times a body or repair shop will scratch the car or give advice on how to scratch it. We have listened and watched while dirty shops instruct the insured how to scratch the paint and glass if they want new paint, body panels, windshields, or after market lights. They instruct not to scratch too light or the paint will just be color sanded and polished out, and not to scratch too deep or it makes their job more difficult to make the scam worthwhile and allowing less money for other upgrades.

One shop owner's advice was to scratch it deep enough so you can feel it with your finger. Some shop owners request that they be allowed to scratch the vehicle so as not to cause too much damage. Some shops have added damages to vehicles to assist the insured in more modifications or to get more money from the insurance company. During one sting, the shop owner took the undercover officer into his shop and keyed an older car to show how fraudulent keying should be done. He advised him to key every panel except the roof, (see Body Shop Fraud for more information later in this chapter). Some shops will give advice on how to key the car and remove additional items such as the radio, airbags, or rims in order to get a larger insurance payment (they can, and have, re-installed these items later).

One dirty shop owner was caught on tape describing how he would write the false estimate for repairs by putting down prep time and repair of the panels. On the false estimate under "repair hood," he put down five-tenths of an hour to indicate that there was damage but avoided stating the car was keyed or scratched (which it wasn't).

Many successful law enforcement stings have addressed the fraudulent activity at body or repair shops. These shops gain from the insurance payment for the repairs they gave an estimate on. They sell the fraud scheme to the insured, indicating they can have a custom car without having to pay any money. Not only do these shops offer a new paint scheme but also they will use the insurance fraud money to replace fenders, add body kits, lights, and other accessories or modifications.

Many suspects we have interviewed throughout the years think that this type of body shop fraud is easily prevented. If the insured was required to maintain the vehicle as stock and not have any enhancements made after a key job, such as custom color paint, there would be no personal gain and the shop owners would not be tempted to commit the fraud. (See Chapter 9, Insurance Company Issues, for suspect quotes regarding insurance fraud and the keying of vehicles).

Owner Give-Ups

When an insured wants his car to be stolen and takes steps to make it happen, he has committed an "owner give-up." He may never want to see it again and hopes the insurance company will pay him for the loss and pay off his loan to the lien holder. Mechanical problems, high gas prices while owning an SUV, high mileage on a leased vehicle, traffic collisions, and cash flow problems are all factors to consider in owner give-ups.

There are many factors at varying times that influence theft trends. Some commit an owner give-up when they can't handle the payments anymore. In the early 2000s, some vehicle manufacturers offered 0 down, 0 payments for the first year on some models. When that first year was up, many customers decided they did not want to start making those high payments on a used car and committed an owner give-up.

Creative financing has also led to problems when the loan comes due. To get out of the lease, too many vehicle owners have decided to commit insurance fraud by burning their own car, then claiming that someone stole it and caused the fire. Forensically, these recovered stolen vehicles did not show any of the typical signs that the vehicle's anti-theft systems had been bypassed, compromised, or that the car was actually stolen. These owners hopes that the insurance company would pay off the lien holder fell short when the fraud was discovered. Not only did they get arrested for felony insurance fraud but also they were still responsible to make payments on a car that no longer existed.

In Cerritos, California a Finance and Insurance (F&I) employee participated in owner give-up insurance frauds in order to make sales by assisting the customer in getting out of their current payments. He would advise the customer to leave their car keys in the glove box of the vehicle they needed to rid of along with $300.00, and someone would come pick it up. After it was missing a certain amount of time, it would be reported stolen. The suspect who picked up the car would abandon and burn it, knowing this would result in a total loss by the insurance company and the lease or loan would be paid off. The customer would then return to the dealership to close that new car deal.

Investigations proving fraud in these cases should address the previously-mentioned motives as well as other financial situations, such as whether or not the insured was behind in their payments and if there were business, financial, or marital problems.

Often a low credit score can be an indicator of a potential of fraud. Low credit scores that occur due to being overextended, having maxed-out credit card balances, only making minimum payments, being behind in payments, or making delinquent payments are all factors to consider in an owner give-up. (However, with the credit crises in 2008, many credit card companies lowered credit limits for their customers automatically maxing out their cards and negatively effecting credit scores.)

Cities close to the Mexican border have a unique problem; the owner drives his vehicle across the border and sells it or gives it up through abandonment or trade. Frequently they have family or friends that live in the country and have made previous trips or phone calls into Mexico. After the car is safely across the border, they return and report the car stolen. Some insureds will have friends or associates drive the vehicle across the border with instructions to mail the keys back to the insured so they can produce them for the insurance company when asked. In some American border cities, there are areas where it is common knowledge (among thieves) that if you leave your car there it will be taken and driven across the border. Most of these main crossings have a variety of technologies, including license plate readers (LPR), and law enforcement is able to determine how many stolen or questionable vehicles are crossing the border or if the vehicles crossed the border prior to the vehicle being reported stolen. These types of fraud cases are easily detected, much to the owner's surprise.

Every theft recovery should be examined to determine how and why the car was stolen. Inspect the car when it is recovered for any signs that the theft/ignition systems were bypassed. Were those factors consistent with how that particular make of vehicle can be stolen? Did the insured have all sets of keys, including the valet key? (See Chapter 4 for details on auto theft methods of operation).

In some states like California, enforcement of smog law violations or illegal vehicle modifications by police have led to owner give-ups. I worked a case in which a Mitsubishi Eclipse was reported stolen, then recovered completely burned. While inspecting the vehicle, it was determined that the ignition was not defeated, causing further suspicion as to the validity of this claim.

A look at the insured's driving record showed that he was cited for smog law violations (27156 b CVC) and was ordered to take the vehicle to the California Bureau of Automotive Repair (BAR). When this happens, the owner may be required to put the car back together as stock or bring it within compliance with smog laws, depending on the particular county or state's emissions laws. This can be quite costly and has been a motivating factor for insureds to "get rid" of their vehicles instead of fixing them. By committing an owner give-up, the insured is hoping not to have to fix the car, and that the insurance company will pay off the loan, allowing the insured to purchase a new vehicle.

In this case, the insured had reported to the insurance company that his vehicle had an aftermarket turbo installed when it was "stolen" (see Chapter 5, Turbochargers and Superchargers for more information). As part of the claim, he wanted to be reimbursed for the $1,150.00 that the turbo had cost him. I questioned the insured about his citation to the Bureau of Automotive Repair, and he advised me that he returned his vehicle back to stock condition prior to the theft. He said he put the stock turbo back on the vehicle and sold the aftermarket turbo to a friend. With this new information, we were able to prove insurance fraud against the insured, as he was requesting the insurance company pay him for the aftermarket turbo when in fact it was not missing.

When someone reports a loss to an insurance company, they are generally required to complete some form of "proof of loss" or "affidavit of theft" form. These are usually completed under penalty of perjury. In this case, the insurance company's proof of loss form had a question asking the insured if the vehicle was ever used for racing or speed contest. The insured stated "no" to this question. When I inspected this vehicle there were markings on the hood indicating that he was sponsored by a car dealership for racing purposes; lying on a proof of loss form can be a perjury violation, and if the statement is material to the claim, it may violate a felony insurance fraud law. Based on the insured's misleading statements, an investigation was opened regarding the discrepancies. The insured was arrested for felony insurance fraud and was still responsible for the payments on this burned Eclipse.

These types of false auto theft and insurance fraud claims happen many times every day. These seemingly small $30,000 claims add up quickly, and we as consumers all pay a significant price in increased premiums due to insurance fraud. Through training and education, we can make a difference.

Arson

One must consider arson in every vehicle fire. While often times an electrical issue causes a vehicle fire, when it comes to the modified vehicle scene, we often see arson – and most times, it is committed by the insured or with his knowledge. When it doesn't involve mileage or payment issues as mentioned previously, we look at other motivating factors, such as the owner trying to cover up evidence of a hit and run or other crime.

We investigated a vehicle fire in which the insured reported his vehicle stolen, stripped, and burned. During the investigation, we learned that the insured's son had previously asked for a new car but his parents told him no. The son's friend suggested that they burn the car and then the parents would get a new car from the insurance settlement. However, the friend decided that they should strip the aftermarket parts off the car prior to burning it and sell the parts on eBay. It wasn't long before their involvement was discovered, and they were arrested for arson, false reporting, and theft by false pretenses.

Arson may be common in certain areas when it comes to auto theft. I have worked several cities in which it is common for the car thieves (usually juvenile joy riders) to burn the cars after use to try to cover up fingerprints. Recovering a target car in these areas is not as suspicious in cities were arson is usually committed by the insured. With gas price hikes throughout the years and enthusiasts' passion for large cars, we saw a big spike in arson to vehicles the months following the hikes. When gas prices spiked in 2006, some fire departments responding to car fire calls would arrive to find multiple vehicles burning at one location. In June and July 2008, gas averages were over 4 dollars per gallon and people were unsuccessfully trying to sell their gas-guzzlers. In August 2008 Ford F-150 sales dropped 42 percent compared to August 2007 and dealerships were hesitant to buy used SUVs.

Tires and Wheels; Trends, Thefts, and Frauds

The Specialty Equipment Market Association estimates that the sale of custom tires, wheels, and aftermarket suspension systems was nearly $9 billion in 2006. Aftermarket wheel packages can cost from a few hundred dollars to tens of thousands of dollars. Some installers have charged as much as $20,000 for wheel and tire combinations and labor.

Frequently wheels (also referred to as rims) and tires are the target of theft as well as insurance fraud. For a time the 1995, Acura Integra was listed as one of the most stolen vehicles throughout areas of the United States. In researching why that particular model year was so desired, we learned it was most frequently stolen for the stock wheels. (Over a decade later, the Acura Integra still makes most states top-ten stolen lists, but this is due to its popularity in the street, race, show, and drag scenes). Thin, non-drive tires for racing at the track were desirable, and many in the scene knew that the Ford Thunderbird Turbo coupe spare tires had desirable alloy wheels, as did third generation Mazda RX7 vehicles (1993-2002). Knowing this type of information can help to explain why a vehicle is targeted and who the suspect(s) may be.

According to Highway Loss Data Institute (HLDI), for several years in a row the Cadillac Escalades EXT made many most-stolen lists. The last year before this publication it was reported that the EXT had overall theft losses that were 16 times higher than average. The reason? Once again, it was a vehicle with desirable tires and wheels. (It didn't help any that the EXT was easy to steal). Too frequently, when cars reach the top ten stolen lists, we forget to step back and ask why. Knowing why a vehicle was targeted can lead you to the suspect and allow for quicker preventative solutions for the future.

While there is always a certain percentage of insurance fraud occurring, there are individuals, groups, and rings that are more organized who specialize in stealing whatever is desired by others. Many auto thieves who specialize in parts thefts have a car parts shopping list with them (hit list). When they are driving the streets and see an item they want, they will make a note of the vehicle's license/tag number to acquire the address for a later theft. (Many suspects have had friends and contacts within motor vehicle departments that would sell or give them the address of a registered vehicle that was targeted, which is unlawful and easily detected). Several suspects have been arrested and their hit lists obtained. The hit lists typically contain the type of vehicle, its license/tag number, the address where it could be located, what type of accessory that could be stolen, and any security information, such as gated communities, gate codes, and other things to look out for.

Sometimes thieves follow the victim home to acquire his address. Some crews attend car events to scope out their next victim, while others work in the aftermarket parts businesses or service shops and obtain the addresses there. When an order comes in from the street, body shop, or performance shop, the suspects sells the address for $50-$100.00 or steals the desired item for more profit. Several performance shops we have investigated over the years would install a nice set of wheels and tires (or any aftermarket part) and then steal them back from the customer to resell and reinstall them on yet another potential victim. We had a victim drive from Blythe, California to Phoenix, Arizona to a speed shop to buy some tires and wheels he wanted. After the installation, he returned to his home in Blythe and three days later, his tires and wheels were stolen. After the insurance settlement, he returned to the Phoenix speed shop to buy another set, only to find his tires and wheels back on the showroom floor for sale.

Many thieves specialize in stealing particular parts of cars and become very proficient in it. One such group was called the "Lug-nut Bandits." They operated in Arizona, specializing in stealing tires and wheels from new as well as private-party vehicles. They were seen on surveillance video buying floor jacks to use in their heists. They would rollup to a car dealership, shoot out lights with pellet guns, and just like a pit crew, and they would jack up the vehicle and remove the tires and wheels they wanted. They would leave the floor jacks with the vehicle; their $120.00 investment resulted in thousands of dollars in stolen goods. They were subsequently caught and convicted.

When an insured desires an aftermarket part for his vehicle but does not want to pay for it, he may stage or arrange a theft of that item or items. Many individuals report tires and wheels stolen that they never owned in the first place. These individuals use fake receipts or invoices and fake pictures to perpetrate fraud. In the mid 1990s, one of theses types of scams was referred to as "Black-outs," as owners would remove their stock hubcaps exposing the black steel wheels. (In 2005, some referred to the black stock tires as "Black-eyes"). They would then make a false theft report to law enforcement and their insurance company, claiming expensive aftermarket tires and wheels were stolen and the suspect, or their friends, replaced the missing wheels with the stock tires then on the vehicle. We have also worked cases in which the shop provides old rollaway tires for the insured to use to complete his "theft" scam with law enforcement and the insurance companies.

Frauds like these can be easily identified. One suspect reported his tires and wheels stolen to local law enforcement. When the officer came out to the house to investigate, the insured was there with his friend. The officer was told that unknown suspects came in the middle of the night and removed his expensive tires and wheels, leaving his car tireless and resting on its brakes. The insured's friend stated that he brought over four extra stock tires and wheels and put them on his friend's car after the theft. The insured's vehicle had been previously modified, making it lower to the ground (this was commonly referred to as Slammed).

When the officer asked the insured how they placed the friend's tires on the vehicle, they stated that they used their floor jack to put them on. The officer confronted the insured and his friend with the fact that the vehicle was slammed too low for the jack to fit under the car in order to lift it up and place the tires on it. Even with the stock tires and wheels that were currently on the car, the jack would not fit under it. Through persistent questioning by the officer and other investigative techniques, the insured and his friend admitted that the tires currently on the vehicle were the insureds and no theft had occurred. Cases such as these qualify under most felony insurance fraud statutes, and the insureds and their accomplices are frequently shocked when they get arrested and convicted of a felony.

To perpetrate frauds like these, a variety of scams is employed by the suspects. Once the insured makes a claim for a "stolen" item, the insurance company is going to ask them to complete the previously mentioned "Proof of Loss" or "Affidavit of Theft." In cases such as the tire and wheel losses, the insurance company may ask for proof that the items were purchased and installed. This may include receipts, invoices, and/or photos of the items that are listed on the proof of loss. This type of information is an invaluable asset to law enforcement.

We have seen individuals post pictures of their cars on the street racing sites, requesting someone with photo editing software to integrate the desired tires and wheels onto the photo of their vehicle. If the photo editing is good enough when the picture is printed on photo paper, it appears as if the car was equipped with those items. The insured may then provide the insurance company with this edited photo in support of the false claim. A good investigator with knowledge of this scheme and using thorough investigative questioning may be able to determine that such photos are altered.

Several companies have come into existence who now rent tires and wheels to those who can't afford to buy them. Make sure that the "victim" in a tire claim actually owned his pictured tires and wheels and was not just renting or borrowing them for the sake of making a false claim.

Sometimes when insureds report tires and wheels stolen that they do not own but want to buy, dishonest performance shops may have provided false receipts or invoices to the insured so they can "show" an insurance company that they had the items. Some dishonest speed or performance shops have conspired to assist insureds to commit this type of fraud. Several cases have occurred where the insured goes into the shop and lets the owner or friend/employee know he wants a specific brand of tires and wheels. The shop will write them out a receipt or invoice for the item, back date it, and tell the insured to report them as stolen to the insurance company. When the insurance company requests receipts to the 'stolen' items, the insured supplies the false receipt or invoice provided by the shop. They are further advised that when the insurance company settles the claim, that the insured bring the money to the shop and purchase the items. The shop benefits from the sale and the insured has the set of tires and wheels he wanted without having to pay for them out of his pocket.

All documentation needs to be verified when processing these types of claims. Examine the receipt or invoice closely. What is the invoice number? Is it in order of other invoice numbers from that same date and time? Did the item listed exist on the date of purchase? Do the sales tax and other information match what is on record for that area? Does the shop have a purchase order and invoice they received from buying the listed item prior to the "sale" to the insured? Does the item listed on the receipt or invoice fit on the insured vehicle? Did the invoice list the method of payment? Sometimes it may be necessary to go to a questionable shop and purchase a small item to determine the normal procedure they use in giving out invoices.

We have seen 5-lug rims listed on the receipt or invoice when the insured's vehicle only accepts 4-lug wheels, and there was never a lug conversion done on the vehicle. If the insured did provide a real picture of the "stolen" items, are they the real deal? There are numerous imitation or knock-off items in the marketplace whose value is far lower than the real item. Check the lug-nut plate and brake area front and rear. There may be evidence that the tires currently on the vehicle have never been off. There could be caliper fluid drip marks running from the rear of the brakes over the tire that have been there for weeks or months.

Some dishonest shops will buy the desired item the insured wants in order to obtain a real invoice from the manufacturer. Once the insurance company does the initial investigation as to whether the item was in fact purchased, the suspect shop returns the items for a full refund. Competent insurance companies learn about this fraud by contacting the original equipment manufacturer or wholesaler after a claim is paid, to determine if the shop returned the item.

Chargeback's are common in this industry. Several shop owners and suspects have described numerous scenarios regarding scamming the industry. One online shop owner reported that some suspects would order expensive products, receive them, and then falsely state that they never ordered or received anything. The owner then will receive a chargeback from the credit card company and is out the merchandise. One shop owner reported that he was stiffed for $1,000 in parts from one subject on eBay, and he is said to have around $100,000 in parts he owes to other vendors. He also heard of a wheel company stiffing an international buyer out of close to $100,000. This owner described the amount of theft in this industry as "out of control." *Follow the paper trail as far as possible to determine the truth.*

Investigative Clues; Tire Codes, Dates, and Speed Ratings

When examining parts thefts, look for additional clues that could help verify the legitimacy of the claim. Items such as parts, tires, and wheels have quite a bit of useful data listed on them. Something insurance companies could do if they suspect a fraudulent tire claim is to check the DOT (Department of Transportation) code of the tire. The DOT code may list the week and year the tire was made. A sample DOT code is HDPA DJRX 0900. The last 3-4 numbers indicate the week and year. In this case, 0900 equals the 9th week of the year 2000. Photo 1 depicts code: DOT HNXF HEWX 1603, which would indicate that the tires were made in the 16th week of 2003.

Photo 1

Using the DOT date code may help to show that the reported tires were made after the date of theft. Some stores place the DOT code on the receipts or invoice. Check with your insureds documentation to ensure the correct codes are listed.

In one case, an insured had his tires stolen and a possible suspect was named. The insured had purchased the car used, and the prior owner had provided him with the Costco receipt. Using this receipt and examining the suspect's vehicle, the investigators learned that they had the same DOT code and were able to prove the suspect was lying regarding how and when he acquired them.

In another tire case, an insured suspected a neighbor of stealing his tires. The suspect was interviewed and stated the tires came stock on his vehicle and he had not replaced them. The date code of these tires matched the year of the victim's vehicle and not his. They were also manufactured after the suspect's vehicle was made and could not have been stock.

In cases like the one where the insured's friend stated he brought over his old stock tires for the insured to use, compare the date codes. If the date code on the tires matches the insured's vehicle and not the friend's vehicle, you may want to investigate further. In another case, an insured stated that his tires and wheels were stolen and the suspect replaced the "stolen" tires with someone else's. However, the DOT code was "coincidentally" the same as insureds year of vehicle.

In addition to the DOT date code, the sidewall of every U.S. tire has information about tire size, maximum load rating, maximum inflation pressure, and tire construction and performance standards. The tire rating system on your tires may look like 205/60R15 102V. The 205 is the tire width in millimeters; the 60 is the Aspect Ratio; R stands for Radial Construction; 15 is the diameter of the wheel in inches; 102 is the Load Index indicating the vehicle has a load carrying capacity of 1874 pounds, and V is the speed rating for 149 mph plus as depicted in photo 2. Z rated tires were initially rated to exceed 149 mph but were not specific, so they added a W rating for 168 mph and a Y rating for 186 mph.

Photo 2

In the unlimited speed category, you may see something that looks like P275/40ZR17 93W. In this case, the P stands for Passenger car and the ZR in combination with the W speed rating would indicate that tire is rated at 168 mph. In the case of P275/40ZR17 93Y, the ZR with the Y speed rating indicates it is rated at 186 mph. For tires having a maximum speed capability above 149 mph, a "ZR" **may** appear in the size designation. For tires having a maximum speed capability above 186 mph, a "ZR" **must** appear in the size designation.

Additional examples:

225/50ZR16 in excess of 149 mph
205/45ZR17 88W 168 mph
285/35ZR19 99Y 186 mph

Many other examples exist, so it is always best to check with the tire manufacturer on the exact meaning and design. (Google "tire speed rating" for more information).

Speed ratings can assist in determining the use of a tire on some vehicles. If the car you are inspecting has a speed rating that is far above what the car was designed for, this can be a clue that they are either heavily involved in street racing or just want a tire of that quality. Adding all of the factors together helps to paint a complete picture.

We have seen cases in which the car owner does not want anyone to know what the speed rating is, so the owners have shaved off the speed-rating letter from the tire. Many tires are designed for a specific use and have useful information that you should consider when investigating a claim. Some tire manufacturers tout themselves as a good tire for drifting, others are made for speed, and some advertise that their tires are good for Drift, Drag, and Drive. Conduct research on what the manufacturer had in mind, what the common use is for the tire. Using an Internet search engine is always a good start.

A vehicle that is used for a particular sport compact event such as drifting, drag racing, street racing, or burnouts will show different wear patterns on the tire, indicating such use or misuse. Other evidence could be the rubber that flies off a tire and onto the inner fender wells and quarter panels from spinning the tires excessively. There are companies that sell burnout guards, and some enthusiasts may tape the inner fender wells or spray them with WD-40 or PAM to minimize the caked on rubber.

One insurance company was investigating a claim on a sport compact owner who made a claim regarding a blown engine. The SIU investigator noticed that the front tires were bald (front wheel drive car) and the rear tires still had plenty of tread. The date codes on the tires were the same, so he knew the tires were from a matched set. There was a lot of rubber on the inner fender well and some on the quarter panel. Based on the evidence and insured's statements, the investigator was able to prove that the blown engine was caused by the insured doing burnouts or donuts and not from some other defect.

Tire and Wheel Warranty Issues

In the beginning of the big tire and wheel trend, some automakers were saying that oversized tires and wheels could spell big trouble. That was especially true if the tires and wheels were exceedingly heavy or strayed from the manufacturer's specification for size, load-bearing capacity, or width. Once the owner starts to deviate from what the manufacturer had designed for the vehicle, they go outside the boundaries for what the vehicle is warrantied. Several vehicle manufacturers indicated that fitting aftermarket tires and wheels on their car would invalidate any claims over wheel related breakages.

Larger wheels are not advantages for sport compacts that are into speed because they tend to be heavier and slow the car down; 17-inch wheels are sufficient. Bigger tires and wheels offset factors such as handling, steering, and stopping and could pose safety hazards. Several shop owners have seen vehicles in for repairs because the aftermarket tires and wheels that the insured installed were too big for the wheel well. There have been reported issues regarding the 20-24-inch wheels, and some tire and wheel modifications may void a vehicle manufacturer's warranty. Larger wheels such as 24-30 inches are prevalent on older sedans (that have been excessively lifted to fit the tires) such as a 1970s to 1980s Buick Regals that have custom paint, interiors, and accessories. These are typically referred to as Donks, Slabs, Dunks, Boxes, or Bubbles. More than $70,000 can be spent on these otherwise valueless cars. Fraud and theft are just as ripe for this group of modified vehicles as it is with our sport compacts.

Still, big, flashy aftermarket tires and wheels have become status symbols, despite warnings against modifying beyond reasonable limits. They often leave it to dealers and consumers to decide wheel size. Wheel companies market their tire and wheel products as must-have car jewelry, also known as shoes. Shoes (as tires) are very important to enthusiasts.

Stereo, Audio-Visual, and Electronic Losses

In Car Entertainment (ICE) is a huge industry. The primary consumers of these systems are once again our 16-24 year-old sport compact enthusiasts. According to SEMA, electronics and software represent more than 20% of the cost of today's vehicles. It is estimated that auto electronics sales will reach more than $50 billion by 2012, up from $38 billion in 2006.

The quality of some of these in-car audio-visual systems is better and more expensive than many in-home systems. We have become accustomed to the DVD screens in the back of every headrest in many SUVs, particularly those who transport young kids. In the sport compact show scene, not only do we see DVD and video game screens in every headrest, but they are often found in the side panels of doors, within the mirrors, and there are even large video screens in the trunk. Many hardcore enthusiasts have more money invested in their audio-visual systems than they do in the original purchase price of their car.

Theft of these desired systems has skyrocketed over the past few years. Some manufacturers are losing systems when the vehicles are off-loaded from the docks and while awaiting delivery to the dealerships. Not only is theft and fraud a problem with these video systems, but the increase in DVD and video game players in vehicles become dangerous distractions. A National Highway Traffic Safety Administration (NHTSA) study conducted by the Virginia Tech Transportation Institute (VTTI) found that 80% of crashes and 65% of near crashes involved driver inattention within three seconds of the onset of the event.

Nationwide Mutual Insurance conducted a survey of 1,200 drivers regarding dangerous driver behavior in January 2007. They found that 73% of those surveyed talk on cell phones while driving, and cell phone use was highest among young drivers. 19% of the drivers polled stated that they text message while driving. For detailed information regarding Cell Phones and Driving, see the Insurance Information Institute's update from October 2007 at www.iii.org.

Although statistics are hard to come by, several fatalities have been attributed to drivers who were watching DVD players while driving. Law enforcement citations for watching videos while driving have been increasing in vast rates. Varying degrees of murder and manslaughter charges have been filed in those cases involving fatalities while driving with a DVD playing in the vehicle. Strict enforcement of violations regarding these systems is imperative, as mobile video sales are a huge growth industry showing no signs of slowing. During our investigations of collisions, investigators need to be more aware of potential contributory factors as well as what can be done to prevent future related collisions. GPS systems on the dash may be helpful for the drifter who is approaching a mountainous hairpin turn at night, but it does not display any of the potential road hazards and still requires them to take their eyes off the road while already driving in an unsafe manner.

While many legitimate thefts of these systems occur every day, we must still be mindful of the fictitious thefts. We have worked several cases in which unscrupulous body, tire, upholstery, and stereo shops work together in providing fictitious invoices to the insured, indicating he had purchased a stereo or tires and wheels that were subsequently reported stolen. To boost the false claim value, in addition to the fictitious invoices for system losses, they may indicate that damage to the vehicle had also occurred during the "thefts" and requires additional repairs. After the false invoice is prepared, the insured would then report this "theft" and "damage" to his insurance company. The insurance company would pay the invoice, not knowing it was false. As explained in the fraudulent tire losses, some of these shops would sell a fictitious invoice to the insured while others would advise the insured how to make the false theft look legitimate. Some enthusiasts have been known to steal invoices from various shops without their knowledge to submit to their insurance company.

While conducting several investigations involving body shops that cater to the sport compact scene, we saw shop owners give unsolicited advice on how to remove the car stereo, make it look like it had been stolen, and falsely report it as stolen. In one sting we conducted, the shop owner advised us how to scratch the paint for new paint and body work, how to break the lights so we could get new sporty clear lighting, and how to remove our stock radio in order to get the insurance company to pay for all of it. To complete this sting, we took the car back to our warehouse and scratched the car and broke a light but did not remove the radio.

When we returned with the car, we told the owner that we did not know how to remove the stereo. He advised us that he would take care of it. When we sent in an undercover adjuster the following day to take pictures, the radio was mysteriously missing, the fraud complete. The owner of this shop was subsequently arrested for felony insurance fraud. During the subsequent arrest and search warrant service, other frauds were discovered in his shop, such as billing the insurance company for new items when they were repaired and not replaced.

During another sting, an undercover investigator went into a stereo shop and advised the employee that he wanted his insurance company to buy him a new stereo system. He advised the employee that he needed a receipt for a system under $2,000.00 and needed it backdated. The employee stated it would cost $20.00 for a false receipt to which the undercover officer agreed. The backdated receipt was made out for $1,861.22 for an amplifier, stereo speakers, and the wiring cable. He even included a $50.00 installation fee. It was listed as a cash transaction so it would be harder to trace.

In cases such as this, follow the money trail. If the insured indicated they paid cash for the item, find out where that cash came from. Back it up with bank statements showing a large withdrawal or interview the "person" that supposedly "lent" him the cash.

There may also be evidence that the system was not installed and the receipt or invoice numbers will not be in sequential order because they were backdated. Make sure the system under scrutiny could have fit in the opening and that supporting evidence is available to prove that the system was in fact installed and that the vehicle could have accommodated the wiring and additional power usage. Frequently, a thorough inspection of the vehicle will reveal that there was no wiring or mounts to support that the alleged stolen items were ever installed in the vehicle. Follow up with the shop may reveal that the shop never sold or installed the system and that the invoice the insured provided has been falsely modified.

Some stereo systems are not compatible with certain years or makes of vehicles. Generally, when stereos or similar components are stolen from vehicles, damage occurs to the dash area and wires are cut. During fraudulent reports of stolen stereos, the shop or insured carefully removes items so as not to damage the dash or wiring harnesses. In real thefts, the thieves are not so careful.

There are stereo stores that will not allow the insured to return a stereo because it did not fit. They advise the insured up front that they must verify from their list that it will work prior to purchase. If an insured is faced with this type of situation, they may be tempted to make a false report.

To identify dirty shops, undercover investigators pay them a visit and offer the employees and owners "stolen" stereo systems for sale. The ones that buy the stolen property will install them in customer's cars, generally without their knowledge. If it was an insurance claim, the shop will bill the insurance company for a new system and provide them with a false invoice if requested. On one occasion while serving a search and arrest warrant at a dirty body repair facility, we observed a car leaving the shop that was affiliated with a stereo store. Further investigation revealed that the body shop was buying stolen stereo systems and selling them to the stereo store to install in customers' vehicles without their knowledge.

Some insureds who want to upgrade their car stereo system but cannot afford the $3,000 system they desire may sell their existing system to a friend or on an Internet site such as eBay or Craigslist. They will then file a false police report and an insurance claim for the stereo system. After they receive the insurance check for the "stolen" equipment, added to the money they made for selling their previous system, they will start shopping for the new system. We have worked countless cases that involved the insured selling his "stolen" items on the Internet.

Just as with tire and wheel thefts, or any component part theft, many insureds commit fraud by over-valuing the equipment that was stolen. Instead of claiming the real $400 system that was stolen, they claim that a state-of-the-art CD changer and speakers valued at over $2,000 were stolen and provide a "borrowed" receipt from a friend to support their claim that they owned this equipment. We have caught insureds soliciting others on Internet sites for stereo boxes and receipts or invoices to use as false verification to the insurance company that they had purchased the items. Photo 3 is a screen shot from an insured seeking proof of purchase supporting documents that he can supply as his own to an insurance company for a theft claim.

Photo 3

Another type of fraud committed involves the insured removing his stereo to make it look like theft, then falsely reporting the system stolen. After receiving the insurance claim payment, he then reinstalls his original system. Numerous methods can be used to determine if the insured has reinstalled his radio. Depending on the system, the investigator can use the serial number, radio code, or vehicle electronics to verify if the original radio was installed back in the same vehicle. Some systems require a radio code be entered to activate the security system, and we can use that code to help determine if the "stolen" stereo was reinstalled.

When an insured reports his system stolen, it should be confirmed if they, or the shop they purchased it from, had registered it for warranty purposes. This can be good confirmation that the radio was in fact owned and registered by the insured. Warranty cards can provide useful data regarding when and where the item was purchased, price paid, and original owner information. If the insured gives you paperwork with a serial number to the "stolen" item, contact the manufacturer of that item to determine who registered it.

Perhaps the insured did purchase the system but it was obtained through fraudulent means. Their credit card or check may have been used and later cancelled. If this is the case, then the system the insured is claiming as stolen does not belong to him in the first place, as he did not yet pay for it. There is a large amount of merchant account fraud, where systems are purchased by fraudulent means. Sometimes, just like other accessories, they are purchased to get a real receipt and invoice, but the item is later returned for credit. Always consider how much they paid for the system versus how much expendable income they have. How does someone pay for a $10,000 sound system on a $7,000 per year income?

Car clubs are a very tight knit group. They are passionate about their cars and share common interests. If your suspect or insured has a loss, you may be surprised to find out that several of his team members have had a very similar loss. We went to a show in Arizona to view several hundred sport compact cars on display. A week after the show we learned that the majority of a Neon car clubs members had reported stereo losses after the show. The activity appeared highly suspect at the time, as the losses were reported to a variety of different carriers within multiple states.

There have been cases in which a particular radio installed in new vehicles has had many reports of being defective soon after the typical year warranty expires. Check Internet forums for chat regarding issues such as this to look for other motivating factors in false radio/stereo reports.

Several dirty shops have given us advice on which insurance companies to stay away from because their fraud fighting tactics were too difficult to overcome. Other shops openly talk about which insurance companies are easiest to take advantage of when committing insurance fraud. Don't become an easy mark. When investigating a stereo or other high dollar loss, make sure you verify all information. Does the receipt actually belong to the insured or did he borrow it from a friend? Did he produce it on his home computer? Do the amounts add up? Is the sales tax the correct percentage for the county it was sold in? Did the insured buy it then return it for credit? Was there a charge back after purchasing it? Does the same shop name come up often in stereo losses? Was the stereo torn out or carefully removed? Were there other items of value in the car that were not taken?

Headlight Theft

Once again, wanting what they don't have, enthusiasts love the look of the high-intensity discharge (HID) lights, also referred to as Xenon lights. That blue glow (Xenon gas) coming down the street is something they desire. Many of these HID lights from new-model vehicles will fit older models if there has not been a significant body style change, making those new lights a high theft item. Manufacturers that consider this type of fraudulent activity will design the new model so its parts and options will not fit directly onto the older vehicle. These manufacturers keep their cars safer from attack and their new owners happy. Unfortunately, this reprieve from theft may only last a few years until the new model has inundated our streets and the demand for the new parts is once again there.

For example, in 2004 the Nissan Maxima thefts and claims rates increased eightfold. The primary reason was that in 2002 the Maxima came equipped with HID lights that were desired by other car enthusiasts. Maximas were particularly targeted in New Jersey during this time. In 2004 the Maxima was redesigned with new HID lights that would not fit in older models, thus the theft rates dropped dramatically for the fifth generation Maxima (2000-2003 model years). Lexus implemented a program to retrofit certain RX models to help prevent theft, and in 2006, they included those changes at the factory.

In Florida, during this same period, Porsches were being targeted for their headlights. Unless you have been a victim of a car or parts theft, you may not realize the impact it has. Walking out to get into your new car and observing your headlights missing is bad enough, but it's not just the theft of the part that is disturbing; it is the collateral damage that is caused by the thieves in trying to get the part off the vehicle in a hurry. Damaged body panels, scratched paint, broken parts, and cut wires cause a multitude of problems. The theft of one hundred-dollar item can cause thousands of dollars in damage and much grief. Design changes, parts markings, and theft deterrent systems will help to bring these thefts down in the future.

Interior Scams

Customizing a stock interior can be one of the top priorities for many enthusiasts. They may start with changing the seats by installing custom racing seats or reupholstering the stock seats. They may use matching material on the door panels, headliner, and dash. Some enthusiasts replace the steering wheel with a racing wheel (which does not include an airbag). They may add specialized gauges to the dash area and in some cases replace the stock ones. Frequently we see racing tachometers with a shift light as depicted in photo 4. (a shift light flashes at the driver, reminding him to shift at the proper time). These shift lights can also be seen at night and be used as a clue on who to monitor for unsafe driving (more on interior modifications in Chapter 5).

Photo 4

For those who commit insurance fraud, an all too common scam to upgrade one's interior is to slash the seats and claim that they were vandalized. Many times the insurance payoff just for seats is enough for the insured to have his entire interior reupholstered. Another scam we have seen all too often is to report their leather seats as stolen, make a false theft report and insurance claim, then sell the falsely reported "stolen" seats, and take the insurance payoff to pay for a complete custom interior.

We have also seen paint or other substances poured on the seats the insured wants to replace instead of slashing the seats. In cases such as this, the insured/suspect is careful not to get the damaging liquid on any items he wants to keep. Most times in a true vandalism, the damaging liquid will not be scattered in a particular area of the vehicle but scattered everywhere. In cases where the insured no longer wants his vehicle and wants the insurance company to total his car due to extensive damage, he may trash the majority of his vehicle by trying to make it appear as a real vandalism.

During one body shop sting, we witnessed a dirty upholstery shop owner give an estimate for non-existent damage to help with the commission of insurance fraud. He wrote on the invoice that the seats were slashed top, bottom, front, back and sides. The shop owner indicated to the undercover officer that with the insurance company settlement money he would be able to give us a complete custom interior without any money out of pocket. Another dirty shop owner we spoke with indicated he was going to stop doing upholstery scams because there was more money to be made in body shop fraud. He indicated three false bumper repairs were equal to one false interior repair and he could get them done in half the time. He also indicated there was too much competition in interior repairs and the pricing was too competitive.

If the insured indicates possible gang involvement, as discussed in the keying section of this chapter, make sure the tags (graffiti markings) used are real and not imitation. Generally, when a real gang member steals a car, they may tag the inside of the vehicle while driving and riding. Tags would be on the interior of the roof, visors, dash, center console and other similar areas one would access while sitting and waiting.

Engine Scams

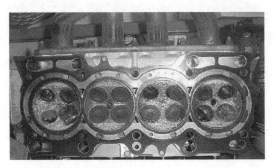

Internal Engine Damage

The need for speed and power will always be a factor for the automotive enthusiast. The need to have a visually appealing engine is great in the modified sport compact scene. For some of the show car enthusiasts, speed might not be as important as having a visually appealing engine. Both of these desires, performance and looks, are costly and contribute greatly to sport compact fraud. For those who drag, drift, and race on the street or track, engine problems are guaranteed. To transform a stock 160hp engine into a 500hp engine can cost a lot of money and create many problems. These problems can range from small component failures to blowing the engine beyond repair. This costly damage drives many to theft and fraud. Blowing out an engine per week is not unheard of, particularly when running nitrous oxide.

Some enthusiasts would rather change their engines than modify them. Complete engine replacements, commonly referred to as swaps, transplants, and hybrids, are desired and bring their own set of problems. Many swaps void the vehicle manufacturer's warranties. Some times only part of the engine is replaced such as a VTEC head on a non-VTEC engine, also may be referred to as a Frankenstein. (See chapter 5 for additional engine and VTEC information).

Very few enthusiasts have sponsors with deep pockets to help them build their dream car. To fund a Street, Show, Drift, Stunt, or Drag car can take a lot of money. The fraudulent subjects that do not have the disposable income to fund this passion have turned to duping the insurance industry and law enforcement.

We have seen numerous vehicles blow their engines and damage their drivetrains while racing. We have seen many of those participants turn to fraud to repair or replace their engines or transmissions. One common scam is to take the disabled vehicle, (whether it is damaged from a collision or mechanical failure), and park it away from the track or the owner's house. The owner then falsely reports it stolen to law enforcement and their insurance company. Once the police recover it (sometimes the insured coincidently "finds" it themselves), the owner will claim that the thieves damaged the car's engine when they stole it (see Appendix A, Internal Clues or Causes of Racing and Modification Damage, for associated damage).

On the other hand, if they are worried about being discovered, they may remove the engine and transmission before reporting it stolen and then accuse the "suspects" of stealing the parts. They will hope this false report goes undetected and the insurance company will buy them a new engine. We have found evidence in some "recovered" vehicles that show the car had been racing at a sanctioned track event in the days prior. Paying a visit to these tracks showed that the vehicle had been racing at the track, the insured had been driving it, and the engine was blown during its last race. Compression tests or leak-down tests can help determine engine failure causes.

You don't need to be an enthusiast or mechanic to identify fraudulent indicators regarding engines. Once you have looked a few stock engines, the modified engines will stand out (See Engine Modifications in Chapter 5 for additional information).

Body Shop Fraud

Body shop fraud has negatively affected the insurance industry for decades. In addition to the everyday fraud that occurs at these shops, insurance companies that look closely at the claims being paid out involving sport compact and modified vehicles have seen a dramatic increase in payments related to this scene. As mentioned in Chapter 1 under "Modified Vehicle Theft and Fraud Costs," one company compared twelve street racing vehicles with twelve similar non-racing vehicles and the claims payout was a $224,000.00 vs. $6,000.00; that is a thirty-seven times greater payout in claims per vehicle!

Keeping up with the trend of personalization, customization, power and performance demands exterior work much of the time, whether it is to change the color scheme, add a body kit or fix damage from a collision while racing. Some insurance companies have estimated that two out of every three claims dollars spent goes to body shops. A disproportionate number of body shops that specialize in the sport compact car scene have engaged in questionable business practices involving these types of vehicles.

I went to one shop to gather some background information and observed many sport compact cars under varying degrees of repair. While I was there a black Civic was driven in and I spoke with the owner. He mentioned that the car was going to have a complete transition from "stock to shock." The paint was keyed but the taillights were in good condition. The owner mentioned that they were going to report non-existent damage so he could get the insurance company to buy him some nice aftermarket lights. I looked around the parking area and noticed another street racing vehicle that had its taillights broken out and noticed that the broken lens glass was lying directly below the car.

One of the most successful stings in combating these questionable sport compact body shops was a joint operation conducted by the Regional Auto Theft Task Force (RATTF) of Santa Clara County and the Department of Insurance in California. This sting was led by Todd Brown of the California Highway Patrol while he was assigned to an insurance fraud task force. *Sgt. Brown was the perfect candidate for this operation, as he had successfully finished assisting in the prosecution of a large operation involving body shop fraud.*

We called this operation "The Fast and the Fraudulent." We knew from investigating cases and interviewing suspects that body shops were assisting insureds in filing false claims when it came to improving the look of their vehicles. One sting we were involved in showed that 76% of the body shops that we contacted were either willing to commit fraud or referred us to a shop that would commit fraud when it came to having our car repainted through fraudulent means.

As part of this sting an undercover officer (UC) drove a mostly stock Honda Civic into numerous body shops, upholstery shops, and stereo stores. The task force obtained a pretext insurance policy for the sting vehicle from a large insurance carrier. The UC told the shop owners or managers that he wanted a new paint job. There was nothing wrong with the current paint job – no scratches, dings, or other blemishes. Keying fraud was so rampant at the time that as soon as the UC would advise them that he wanted to go through his insurance company to get a new paint job, some shop owners would immediately respond with, "Oh, so you're going to key it?"

The UC would tell the shops that he had already falsely reported to the police department and insurance company that his car had been keyed. He told them that he needed them to fax over an estimate to his insurance company indicating that the car had been keyed. Many of the shops gave advice and demonstrated how to key the car so that he could have his new paint scheme. One owner showed the UC examples of key jobs in his shop waiting for repairs. One shop owner noticed that the windshield was old and advised the UC to scratch the glass as well. Another advised the UC to scratch the headlights and taillights to get the insurance company to pay for clear aftermarket lenses. One dirty shop explained how he would pad the false estimate he was going to prepare. He indicated he would put down five-tenths of an hour for repair to the hood to get the "key" scratches out. He also stated he would indicate the antenna was broken and charge for a new one. Some shop owners even offered to scratch the car while he waited to assist in the false vandalism claim.

To conclude this sting, it was decided that the next time an owner offered to key the car at the shop he would be allowed to do it. The vehicle was taken to a large, well-known auto body repair facility and, sure enough, the owner insisted on scratching the paint to assist in the fraud. Some suspect shops prefer to do the damage themselves to make certain that just the right amount of damage is caused – not too much and not too little. They want to get their share of the fraudulent insurance money without doing too much work. The owner had the UC drive the vehicle behind the shop, out of public view. He had a sharp object in his hand and very casually walked around the vehicle while scratching the paint. He was finished in less than ten seconds. When the UC said that he wanted new lights, the shop owner scratched the lights. He then wrote up and estimate for the damage he had just caused and faxed it to the insurance company. The false claim was approved and the shop owner kept the car for the repairs.

In many of these types of false claims, the insured hopes to get a completely new look to his car without having to pay any money out of pocket. In this case, the insurance payoff was enough to have the sting vehicle completely repainted as well as replace the stock front quarter panels with Z3 type vented quarter panels, install a rear wing, and add some new lights. When the UC went back to pick up his car, the shop owner gladly had his picture taken with the officer in front of his new car, funded by fraud, probably hoping the UC would send even more fraudulent business his way.

In addition to faxing over the false invoice, other crimes were taking place during this sting. The UC had a trunk full of body repair tools and stereo systems that he represented as stolen property. Several of the various shop personnel willingly purchased these items thinking they were stolen. In those cases, additional charges of attempt possession of stolen property were filed with the District Attorney's Office. Some employees had extensive criminal backgrounds from committing fraud in shops in which they had previously worked.

This sting was concluded and 41 complaints were issued for insurance fraud and attempted possession of stolen property. Twenty-five different body shops had charges filed against them. The arrest warrants were served, and 32 of the suspects were arrested at their shops. An additional six suspects were arrested for other insurance fraud cases that involved staged accidents and false thefts. Out of the 65 shops that were contacted as part of this sting, 25 provided a false estimate. Six more agreed to go along with the insurance fraud but asked the undercover officer to go key it and bring it back. Four referred them to a shop other than their own that would do the fraud. One shop owner stated he could not print the false estimate at the time. Some of the shops that declined to participate had previously been caught involved in fraudulent activity and apparently had learned their lesson.

One shop did not participate only because he was part of that insurance companies Direct Repair Program (DRP) providing the insurance policy for this sting (see Chapter 9 for more on DRP). Two shops were not open and two shops did not paint cars (which was part of this sting). Out of 65 shops contacted, only 15 wanted nothing to do with fraud or had no record of fraudulent activity. Of those 15 that said no and had no previous fraud history, seven of them were stereo stores. The fraud rate was close to 76% regarding percentage of body shops that were willing to commit the fraud or give advice on how to complete the fraud.

The Employment Fraud Task Force also assisted in the sting and cited several shops for not having Workers' Compensation Insurance or for making cash payments. This resulted in over $100,000 in fines and the temporary closure of 10 shops. In states that have agencies that oversee auto repair, such as California's Bureau of Automotive Repair (BAR), they are generally included in these types of operations as their authority allows the inspection of business records to ensure the proper repairs are being completed and there is not fraud involved in billing.

The press was invited along during the service of the arrest warrants in this sting. This case made most of the local papers and radio stations. Coincidently, no vandalism claims consistent with sport compact fraud were reported to the local insurance companies the following weekend. After all of the media attention, some body shops called insurance companies and asked that the vandalism estimates that they had previously sent in be rescinded, stating there were some "clerical" errors.

After the trials and convictions, I interviewed one of the shop owners involved in this sting while he was serving his time. He had been in the repair business for over 20 years and thought many of the shops he had worked for or was aware of commonly committed insurance fraud with *and* without the vehicle owner's knowledge. Whenever he could sneak something by an insurance company or insured, he would attempt to. If the damage being claimed was not enough to make a descent profit on repairs, he would enhance it. If the scratches were not deep enough, he would go over them again with a key. If a part were broken, he would bill the insurance company for a new part but would only repair the damaged part. He would pad the invoice regarding time required to fix a part, adding tenths of hours, which over time added up to a substantial increase in money. If he could list non-existent damage he would, and then he would charge to "repair" it. On one fraudulent invoice, he added a $685 tow bill for a car that had been driven to the shop, not towed.

Another common scheme insureds try to commit involves failing to repair the damage to their vehicles after the insurance company pays to have it repaired. After the insurance claim payment check is issued for the damage repair, the insured may then cancel his insurance policy with that company and insure it with another. After a month or two, the insured then claims the vehicle was involved in a collision and presents the previous collision damage as new, trying to be paid again for the same damage. Other dirty insureds may obtain insurance policies on one car from multiple carriers and then submit a claim for the same damage to multiple companies at one time. Both of the above scenarios are felonies in most states and are easily caught by such insurance databases as ISO. The ISO database contains more than 175 million claims and represents more than 91% of the private passenger premium volume (see http://iso.com/ for more information).

Insureds learn quickly which shops are most likely to assist in committing insurance fraud and will travel many miles to take their vehicles there, which is one of the many investigative tactics we use to locate dirty shops. If an insured drives 50 miles and passes hundreds of shops to get his vehicle repaired, frequently we find a dirty shop. Some insureds will shop around and find out which shop charges the highest hourly rate. If the rates are $70.00 per hour in one city and $35.00 per hour in another city, they want an estimate from the $70.00 per hour shop. The estimate will be higher and they will be able to get more customization completed to their vehicle. Additional fraud occurs when body shops waive the insurance deductibles, initiate fraudulent repairs, list damage that is non-existent, or enhance damage with or without the insureds knowledge.

Some states have organizations such as California's Bureau of Automotive Repair that will spot check repairs completed to ensure the consumer is not being taken advantage of. They will also send "documented" cars into a repair facility. A documented vehicle has been damaged in a controlled environment and the agency has documented every aspect of the vehicle's damage all the way down to each bolt that would have to be removed to fix the damaged part. Undercover agents then leave these vehicles with repair facilities to be repaired. The undercover agents return after the repairs are completed and take the vehicle back to the Bureau of Automotive Repair for re-inspection and documentation. As you can imagine, they find all types of fraud and fraudulent repairs.

It is easy to spot the shops that cater to sport compact modification and repair. Generally, there are street racer-type vehicles parked out front and several inside the shops in various states of repair. If the shop is into installing wide-body kits, you may see mountains of front and rear stock bumpers at the repair facility. When we conduct business inspections at these shops, we examine these piles of stock parts. We have found most of them without damage, which indicates that the owner is just changing the look of his car. However, when we look at the insurance claim, we find the shop or the insured reported a front or rear collision or a "key" vandalism claim. We have also discovered that many of these parts were reported "stolen." When body parts like fenders, doors, and bumpers are reported "stolen" from a vehicle, we may suspect two main causes. One is the insured, who makes a false report of theft because he wants to add a wide-body kit or any other popular fad to make his car customized; the other is a dirty body shop that has a similar vehicle in for repair and he needs the parts to repair it but does not want to pay for them.

Once we learn about a questionable shop, we look into the prior activity that has taken place over the years. We have found that when shops are willing to commit one type of fraud, they will also commit others. In researching some of these shops, we have found some of them to be involved in false burglary claims from their own businesses, such as reporting the theft of expensive tools that they never owned.

If the damage to a car is too extensive to be cost effective to fix, then the insurance company may declare it a total loss. The car will then be moved from the repair facility and taken to an auto auction company for sale. We have had reports from tow truck drivers that some dirty shops will strip the vehicle of parts they can use prior to the car being transferred to the auction/salvage company. We have also seen further unlawful stripping of the vehicle while at the auction yard prior to sale. This is more money taken from the insurance company, for which we all pay in higher premiums.

We have found dirty shops to be involved in staged accidents, both at their facility and away from the shop. One shop had a large pole cemented into the ground that they used to crash cars into in order to enhance the damage. Others had cars they kept to cause collisions with an insureds car. To catch a dirty shop, compare the damage of the vehicle before it was taken to the shop to damage that the shop gives an estimate for. Surprise visits prior to repair are also beneficial to catch shop fraud.

Owners of a vehicle sent in for repairs should review the invoice that the shop sends to their insurance company. Fax or email the invoice, in plain English, to the insured to verify that the repair claimed by the shop is justified and that when the car is returned, that the repairs were made.

Since some insurance companies have reported paying two out of every three dollars to repair facilities, body shop fraud such as those mentioned above need to be identified and stopped.

Chapter 3: Events that Drive Theft and Fraud

Thousands of events are held each year involving the sport compact scene – events such as car shows, drifting competitions, time attacks, and sanctioned drag races. Many enthusiasts compete in several different sport compact categories. Each event brings with it a potential rise in theft and fraud for this Fast and Fraudulent crowd. Sometimes fraudulent claims are submitted before an event in an effort to gain additional money to modify their vehicle. Other times claims are submitted after the event to fix the problems that arose from competing, or to make a style change that will help them win more trophies next time.

Some may describe their car as "Show and Go," referring to a good-looking modified car that can also go fast. "Street to Strip" refers to a daily driven car that can drive right on to a drag strip and compete with little change. The expression "Drag, Drift and Drive" throws racing, drifting, and daily driving into the mix of what a particular car or club can do. When attending any of the sport compact events, law enforcement and insurance companies periodically run the VINs and license plate numbers through several databases. Some events we have attended have shown as many as 25% of the show cars having long history of multiple claims consistent with theft and fraud associated with this scene (Enforcement operations regarding these events are discussed in Chapter 7).

Sanctioned Drag Events: Legal and Safe, but ripe for Theft, Claims, and Fraud

Sanctioned drag events generally involve two vehicles racing side by side in a straight line from a dead stop to the finish line, generally for a quarter-mile. The first one to cross the finish line wins; however, many race wins come from beating a particular elapsed time or E.T. (how many seconds it takes them to travel a quarter-mile). For many of the daily driver enthusiasts, a 10-second E.T. is a goal. A visit to the NHRA's website at www.nhra.com provides useful and enlightening information about drag racing and the various classes. The NHRA and other organizations contribute to getting the illegal racers off the streets by having "Street Legal" races. This allows our youth to bring their daily driven cars, as well as more modified vehicles, to the track instead of the street. Several programs exist throughout the globe to help get street racers off the streets and onto a safe track environment such as www.RaceLegal.com and www.BeatTheHeatInc.org. (Refer to Track Alternatives in Chapter 8 for more information).

The Fast and the Fraudulent group does not represent the typical Motorsports audience when it comes to drag racing. They are younger and typically, there are many more sport compacts and imports versus the American muscle cars seen at a standard NHRA event. With millions of enthusiasts around the globe, each drag event also becomes a lifestyle show with parking lot displays and plenty of vendors. In the mid-2000s the IDRC (Import Drag Racing Circuit) differentiated the import drag audience from the NHRA type audience as younger, indicating that 67% of the

IDRC audience was less than 25 years-old and that 92% were under 35-years old (NHRA average age was 41 years).

Experience has taught many competitors that parts are going to break and systems are going to fail during a stunt, drag, or drift event. Because of this, it can become a very costly hobby. Many unscrupulous competitors turn to theft and fraud to fund their passion and assist in these costly repairs. One way many insurance companies combat the inevitable damage that occurs during these competitions is to exclude such activity in the policy coverage. When the insured violates this clause in their contract, the policy is voided and no coverage occurs. Some fraudulent insureds know about this clause, and if their car is damaged during one of these events, they will tow it off site, abandon it, and make a false report for the damage. Looking for tow marks on the vehicle can help to verify the reported circumstances.

The insured then calls the police and reports the car stolen and notifies their insurance company. When the car is recovered, the insured maintains that the suspects must have damaged the vehicle or engine when they stole it. The insured then turns to the insurance company for repairs. Many insureds who have tried to commit this type of fraud have found out the hard way that evidence of their racing may be at the track or on the Internet. In addition, with video cameras installed practically at every corner in America, there always exists multiple ways to catch this type of fraud. Every adjuster, law enforcement officer, and investigator needs to evaluate all aspects of the claim.

For example, what is not missing on the vehicle at time of recovery can be just as important as to what *is* missing. The Acura Integra pictured in photo 6 was reported stolen shortly after a sanctioned drag race was held. When the vehicle was "recovered" there was only one headlight missing.

When evaluating this claim, other factors became apparent that this vehicle was modified to fit the drag race scene. Knowing that the vehicle could have been used for drag racing would explain why the right headlight was missing. Serious drag racers want to allow as much air as possible into their intake system because that can increase the speed of the vehicle (see chapter 5 for more modification information).

Photo 6

In photo 6, this Integra's air intake is located behind the right headlight. Removing the headlight allows more air to travel into the intake and increase the vehicles speed (with some additional factors involved). Armed with this knowledge, an investigator could easily put the pieces together that this vehicle was racing at a track when the engine blew. In this case, the insured did not want to pay for the costly repairs, so he towed the car off track and dumped it, making a false theft report in hopes to get the insurance company to pay for the damages.

Tech Inspections

When a sport compact participant attends a drift or drag event, they usually drive the car to the location; very few cars are brought in by trailer. To compete in a drag race, most tracks require that the driver show proof of insurance prior to racing, and the vehicles go through what is referred to as a tech inspection. Track officials go through the car and make sure everything is bolted down and that the car is safe to race; there are at least 50 items a tech inspector may be looking at. Knowing what is involved in your track's tech inspection process can help to determine if the car was racing on a track or on the street.

There are many classes of competition that a driver can enter based upon the type of car and its modifications. Naturally (or normally) aspirated, turbocharged, supercharged, and nitrous oxide are common modifications within classes of vehicles. Some vehicle modifications are different depending on the speed the vehicle can or has traveled (E.T.). These modifications can be clues to an investigator as to what the vehicles primary purpose is.

The following tech inspection knowledge could assist you in your investigations:

- Vehicles are required to have all windows in good condition as they may be required to run with them up.
- There must be easy access for track officials to get into a car, so shaved door handles may not be allowed.
- Vehicles with batteries that are relocated from the stock location may be required to have an external master cutoff switch on the outside rearmost portion of the vehicle. This switch must kill all electrical functions including the engine. The OFF position of this switch must be labeled for the safety crew. (There may be additional requirements for relocated batteries).
- The carburetor must be covered.
- If the vehicle has no hood, the mechanical fan must be removed, but an electric fan is OK.
- All hubcaps and trim rings must be removed, unless bolted on.
- If a rear-wheel-drive vehicle is capable of running quicker than 13 seconds in the quarter-mile, a driveshaft loop is required (these are metal loops bolted to the vehicle in which the drive shaft runs through. In case of U-joint failure, the drive shaft will not fly from the vehicle and injure someone).
- Vehicles running 11.99 or faster must have a roll cage.

♦ There must be at least one working tail light and tires must be in good condition with at least 1/16 inch of visible tread remaining and no cord showing. Slicks must have visible wear indicators showing. (There could be obvious tire wear signs that allow an investigator to know if a vehicle was involved in Drifting vs. Dragging).

Photo 7

If the car passes the tech inspection, it is issued a number, which is used to track its progress throughout the day. These numbers are applied to the windshield or side glass of the vehicles as seen in photo 7. Many racers like to keep this number on their car for as long as possible after an event to show others on the street that they were drag racing. Many tracks keep a record of this data and post race results on the Internet with names, vehicle types, dates, and times.

Since racing for time can void many policies, some insurance companies have decided to allow their insureds to be up front about their drag racing passion and participation. Generally, companies that insure this type of activity charge a higher premium to help cover the inevitable losses that will occur.

The first sanctioned event I attended as an investigator was in 1997 at the Sears Point Raceway in Sonoma California (now Infineon Raceway). Several hundred cars were lined up at seven in the morning, waiting for the gates to open so they could race. These daily-driven vehicles went through tech inspection and got in line to race the quarter-mile. Many tracks allow spectators full access to the pit areas and tech inspection lines giving them – and investigators – access to the vehicles about to race.

We started browsing the cars, and it didn't take even five minutes to see our first stolen vehicle. Within 30 minutes, investigators had located vehicles with stolen engines, transmissions, and altered vehicle identification numbers. As these vehicles were pulled to the side, word spread like a wild fire that law enforcement was checking for stolen vehicles and parts. Vehicles were making u-turns and fleeing the park to avoid detection, impound, and arrest. Ten years later, investigators still attend these events and are hard-pressed not to locate stolen vehicles and parts. As an investigator, you owe it to your city or company to pay a visit at least once to any of these types of sport compact events.

There have been several investigations involving insurance fraud and false theft reports that were shaped due to the data that appeared on street racing related Internet sites, particularly if a crash was involved. Sometimes photos of your suspect or insured's car are posted on the promoter's site or on the area chat boards. By monitoring several sites, you can stop some of the fraud before it starts or before it costs too much. Since websites come and go so very often, it is best to use search engines to locate the appropriate tracks and forums when looking for information. Key words and search terms applicable to your city may help to identify a site, as can the many sport compact magazines found at bookstores, convenience markets, and newsstands. Chapter 6 has a section on Internet Websites that may be useful in locating local information.

If an insurance company does not have a policy that restricts drag racing, they may want to consider implementing limits for this type of activity. I have seen daily driven and insured cars that, when purchased new, would run a quarter-mile race in 19 seconds, but after heavy modification, they would then run the quarter-mile in the 10-second range. Unfortunately, many of these insureds are still paying premiums based on a stock car instead of a high-performance sports car. Past experience has shown that these highly competitive cars have a history of insurance claims far above the average vehicle.

Drifting

Drifting is the art of taking turns sideways at speeds up to 100 mph, sliding sideways into a turn, going into and out of a series of left and right turns, keeping the car pitched sideways, tires spinning and rubber burning the entire time. Imagine off-road rally racers sliding their cars around dirt corners, only place that image on asphalt instead of dirt roads, in parking lots, city streets, or preferably on an asphalt racetrack.

Drifting's popularity in Japan was strong for over a decade before it caught on in the United States. Drifting has been gaining popularity in the United States steadily since 2000, because it requires more technical mastery over a car than simply mashing the gas pedal to the floor. Drifting has also increased the age demographic by approximately 10 years, to the 18-to-34 age group. Drifting was initially considered more affordable than the Show and Go scene, but the potential for additional fraud activity is just as great.

In the mid 2000s, the "Drifting" phenomenon was the "new" trend, which would most likely result in an increase in claims for vehicles and individuals associated with compact racing activities. We have been tracking and accurately predicting the affect sport compact trends have on insurance claims for many years. Drifting was the latest trend in this increasingly popular and quickly changing cultural phenomenon and needs to be a top consideration in present and future claims and underwriting practices. Drifting in 2004 was where import drag racing was in 2000, but it added a new variety of cars, primarily front engine vehicles with rear-wheel drive, commonly referred to as FR.

Before you say you don't have a drifting problem, look around your city. In preparation to speak in any city, I contact the local enthusiasts to see what the scene is like in that particular area. When drifting was fairly new to the United States (into the third year of the Formula D series), there were several cities throughout the country in which I was speaking where the audience had not heard of drifting. However, in my preparation, I had visited local drift shops and local drift forums documenting how alive and well it was in that city. After my training sessions, many people in each audience came forward to discuss how they had been seeing the claims and activities but did not know it was associated with drifting. Frequently during the breaks of our training sessions, investigators are on the phone calling their co-workers with pertinent information regarding current claims and cases that they had just realized were part of the dark side of this scene. Many of the vehicles involved in the sport of drifting are driven daily and insured by unsuspecting carriers throughout the U.S.

Legal drifting contests may be held at sanctioned racetracks, closed mountain sections, or at car shows in the parking lot. The primary consideration for an event's location is making sure there is a straightaway that allows a build up of speed in order to navigate a series of left- and right-hand turns. At some organized events, there is tandem drifting, in which the cars will enter a turn side-by-side, just inches apart.

On June 15, 2003, American Drifting achieved new status when the D1 Grand Prix US Driver's Search came to the Irwindale Raceway in California. Nine professional D1 drivers flew in from Japan to participate. This was in preparation for the D1 Grand Prix USA. On Sunday August 31, 2003, the D1 Grand Prix (D1GP) was held at Irwindale Speedway. This was the first time that competitors from outside of Japan were invited to compete in this type of event, which included 18 Japanese compact racecars and teams who came to California to compete. According to promoters, this was the largest D1 drifting event ever held in the world and the first time it had been held in the United States. Irwindale Speedway officials stated it was the largest motorsports event ever held at their track. Approximately 10,000 spectators were present for this inaugural race.

U.S. drivers came from as far away as New Jersey. Vehicles involved in this event were photographed, as were the many collisions that occurred on site. On December 16th and 17th Irwindale held what was pegged as D1 Grand Prix U.S. versus Japan. Japan brought their best to compete against America's best.

When D1GP held its U.S. versus Japan exhibition event in 2005, Maryland's Vaughn "JR" Gittin beat Japan's elite drifters to become the first win for an American in any D1GP while driving a Ford Mustang. However, in 2006 the Japanese regained their reign and swept the D1GP. Many drift events are held throughout the United States today. The D1 Grand Prix and Formula D are very well known, but there are also many smaller events such as the Drift Showoff and various Drift Days at local tracks. In 2008, the D1GP did not host any events in the United States but had four scheduled for 2009. Unfortunately, in order to prepare for many of theses contests, the participants take it to the streets and too frequently, endanger lives.

At exhibitions or professional events, drifters are judged subjectively on a number of areas. Not only do they have to show their skill in sliding the car into and out of a corner but they must also have the ability to get the crowd and judges excited. The judges want the slide to be fast, with the wheels locked into counter-steer (steering into the drift), with the car at the most extreme angle possible without loosing control. They want to see that the driver can hold the throttle, steering and braking steadily through a drift. For tandem drifts, there are two cars within a few feet of each other, sliding in and out of turns. Since points are awarded for style and technique, *not based on a timed event*, insurance companies should review their policy verbiage to make sure that events like these are excluded or declared. Although drifting may not technically be racing, to the novice watching an event, it looks like an awful lot like a race.

How to Drift

Understanding the principals involved in drifting can assist in evaluating related insurance claims and losses. There are a couple of main ways to start a drift. One is by popping the clutch to get the wheels spinning (also referred to as Clutch Kicks). Just before entering the turn, the driver will push in the clutch and shift the car into a lower gear. He then revs up the engine, turns slightly away from the turn (counter or over-steering), and quickly cuts back into the turn while popping the clutch and causing the rear tires to lose traction and start to spin. (This frequently used technique is hard on the drivetrain). If done correctly, the vehicle will lose traction and begin to slide around the curve while maintaining control; staying in control while sliding is the hard part.

With a series of tight turns in close proximity, the driver should hold the drift (slide) until the next turn in competition. To do this, the driver must keep his or her foot on the accelerator while at the same time adjusting the steering wheel to avoid spinning out. Once the drifter reaches the end of the turn and approaches the next turn (which is hopefully in the opposite direction), they must repeat the above sequence if they want to keep the tires spinning and the car drifting. As you can imagine, drifting in control takes a lot of practice, and there are many spinouts throughout one's career. Heel-and-toe driving is used frequently in drifting, which allows the driver to have one foot on both the gas and brake pedals at the same time they are using the clutch with their other foot. This technique is commonly used in performance driving as it smoothes out the shifting process.

Using the parking or emergency brake, also referred to as the e-brake, is another technique used to start a drift. While this method is used by a few drifters in rear-wheel drive cars, this technique is really the only way one can drift in a front-wheel drive car. A front-wheel drive vehicle cannot whip its rear end out as easily because all of the power is going to the front tires as opposed to the rear, so when approaching a turn, the driver will pull the e-brake, which causes the rear tires to lock up and the traction loss of the rear end starts the slide. It is also much harder to take consecutive turns with a front-wheel drive. The Front engine and Front drive vehicles are typically referred to as FF. Common clues that a front-wheel drive car is involved in drifting (besides the decals and bumper stickers that say "I love to Drift") would be excessive rear tire wear.

Visualize the process of drifting and the way in which the rubber would be worn off during sliding or excessive e-brake use. Some rear-wheel drive drifters will also use the e-brake in conjunction with popping the clutch, and those with automatic transmissions may rely on it even more. Manual transmissions are preferred by most serious drifters. Several aftermarket manufacturers make e-brake knobs. These eliminate the need to depress the stock button that allows the e-brake to return to the start position once it is pulled. To determine if the e-brake has been modified for drifting, pull the e-brake up and let go. If it stays engaged, it has not been modified; if it snaps back to the start position most likely, it has been modified to be used in the drifting scene.

Those drivers who first get into illegal drifting practice in parking lots and on mountain roads. There are drifting schools and tracks that allow drifters to get off the streets and practice safely. Drifting in the mountains is very popular in some areas due to multiple S turns that test the drifter's abilities. Mountain running or racing through mountain passes is traditionally referred to as Touge (pronounced Toe-Gay) and roughly translated is Japanese for "pass" as used in "mountain pass." Popularized in Japan, cars will race up or down a mountain pass to see who can do the run the fastest. Touge is not drifting, but it is commonly confused with drifting. Many car clubs head to the mountains on a weekly basis to drive cars to their limits on mountain roads. Most do not intentionally try to break the rear end free as in drifting, but many frequently lose traction and slide off the road on the turns due to excessive speed. Generally, you can tell from the skid marks if a vehicle was drifting or participating in a Touge run.

Popular Drift Cars

Several cars are favored among drifters. Historically, the Toyota Corolla has been very popular because of its front engine, rear-wheel drive setup (FR). As with most vehicle references, including engine types, there are Japan versions, International versions, and United States versions. A Toyota Corolla may have a different engine depending on which country it is manufactured for.

Many enthusiasts refer to their vehicle based on a portion of the Vehicle Identification Number (VIN). All vehicles manufactured since 1981 have a 17 digit VIN in which the vehicle's description is contained in the fourth through eighth positions. The first three positions are the country of origin and manufacturer; the fourth through eighth position describes the vehicle; the ninth is a check digit; the tenth is the year; the eleventh is the plant it was manufactured at; and the remaining six are the production number.

The Toyota Corolla (**Levin** and Sprinter **Trueno** outside the U.S.) have been popular cars for drifters. They are also known by their chassis code of AE86, with the AE86 found in the 4th through 7th VIN positions such as JT2**AE86**xxxxxxxxxx. The AE86 is also referred to as a Hachi-Roku, which is Japanese for 86. The main difference between the Levin and Trueno is that the Trueno has pop-up headlights. The popular United States Corollas come with a 4A-GE engine, and many owners refer to their Corollas as a 4A-GE instead of, or in addition to, the AE86 chassis reference. The Toyota Soarer with the JZZ30 engine has also been popular; the Soarer is similar to the Lexus SC 300, 400, and 430 in America.

The Nissan Silvia has been an extremely popular drifting vehicle, particularly in Japan and Australia. There are several models, but the Nissan Silvia S13 and S14 are talked about the most in drifting circles. The Silvia S13 debuted late in 1988 followed by the S14 in 1994. Japan stopped producing the Silvia in August of 2002.

The Nissan 240SX in America is the closest model to the Silvia; however, it comes with the less popular KA24DE engine commonly found in some Nissan Xterras, Frontiers, and Altimas. This 155 hp engine is not as powerful, and being made of iron, is heavier. The Silvia has a turbo SR20DET made from aluminum, providing more power at a lighter weight (205 to 250 hp depending on the model). Because the SR20DET bolts right into the 240SX without heavy modifications being necessary, 240SX owners will often swap out the engines.

Commonly, the S13 SR20 engine is referred to as a "red top" due to the color of the rocker cover. Since engine swaps are very common in drift vehicles, use the engine swap table in Appendix B to determine if the vehicle you are inspecting has original equipment in Honda/Acura vehicles. The CA18DET engine found in early 180 and 200sx Nissans is also commonly swapped out for a SR20DET.

Knowing the difference between a desired Japanese vehicle and its American counterpart can assist in evaluating claims. The Silvia front clip in 1988 had fixed headlights and the 240SX had popup headlights. Because many Americans want the JDM look (Japanese Domestic Market), the Japanese front clip of a Silvia is frequently placed on a 240SX and the owner may start to refer to the vehicle as a Nissan Silvia.

The same can be true about the transmissions in these vehicles. Launching off the start line causes havoc on stock transmissions in particular. It would be common to find a 300ZX transmission in a 240SX, in which case you would also see a modified drive shaft.

The Nissan 180SX has also been popular, and it is related mechanically to the Silvia. Because of the high crash ratio of drifters, Silvia body panels were frequently used on 180SX's for repair, thus the term Nissan Sil-Eighty was created.

Another favorite Nissan drifting car is the Skyline. As with the Silvia, the Skyline GT-R has several models: the R32 (1989-1994), the R33 (1995-1998), and the R34 (1999-2002), which is considered by many as the holy grail of import cars. The engine number for these vehicles can be RB25DET or RB26DETT. The 2009 GT-R R35 was the first Skyline to come to the United States. Nissan changed from the RB engine to a V-6 VR38DETT in the R35 with a chassis code of CBA-R35.

Engine numbers by themselves tell a story. Many will give you year, make, model, country of origin, and displacement. The RB in this case stands for an inline six-cylinder engine; the 25 or 26 stands for a 2.5 or 2.6 liter engine; the D is for Dual Over Head Cam (DOCH); the E is for electronic fuel injection; the first T is for Turbo and the extra T makes it a Twin Turbo. The RB20DET is also found in the Skyline R31, GTS4, GTST, and Fairlady Z31 (also known as the American 350Z). The SR found in the Silvia can be decoded similarly, but the SR represents an inline four cylinder.

Although Japan never exported the Skyline to the United States, there are many here, most of which are still right-hand drive and were illegally imported. Skyline importation into the U.S. has been increasing steadily for the past few years. (See Gray-Market Vehicles in Chapter 7 for more information on the proper importation of vehicles into the U.S). The closet match to a Skyline in the U.S. prior to 2008 was the Infinity G35, which is similar to Australia's R-35. The G35 shares the same engine as the Nissan 350Z, the VQ35DE. Early in 2000, enthusiasts were swapping the VQ35DE with an SR20DET, and in 2006, they were swapping the SR20DET with the newer VQ35DE. Typically, Skyline GT-Rs are all-wheel drive AWD and the regular Skylines are rear-wheel drive (RWD).

With rising prices for the Nissan S13 and S14 as well as the Toyota AE86, alternative cars have been increasingly attending drift events. Other cars featured at drift events have been the Toyota Supra, Pontiac Solstice, Honda S2000, Nissan 350z, Mitsubishi Lancer Evolution (EVO), Ford Mustang, Dodge Viper, Chevrolet Corvette, Mazda Miata, Lexus SC430, IS300, Subaru WRX STI, and several other rear-wheel drive vehicles. The Mazda RX series have also been popular, particularly the RX-7, also known by its chassis code of FC3S, with the FC found in the fourth and fifth VIN positions such as JM1**FC**xxxxxxxxxxxx. An entire new group of drifting cars may surface with manufacturers adding more rear- and all-wheel drive cars to their lineups to meet the demand, such as the 2009 the Lexus IS-F, the Nissan 370z (new VQ37VHR engine), Hyundai Genesis, and the Subaru Impreza WRX.

Since drifting has taken many by surprise in the U.S., manufacturers as well as aftermarket parts companies have been fabricating drift-specific parts with the hope of changing drifters from the older above-mentioned cars to the new lines they offer.

The demand for drifting has already led to resurgence in small, rear-wheel drive vehicles. Manufacturers have already started moving the brake and gas pedals closer together to allow heal-toe driving. Some enthusiasts prefer shorter cars, saying that they are better than longer cars for drifting through tighter corners. Others may say longer cars are more stable and are necessary for maximum impact drifting. In professional U.S. drifting, there seems to be an increase in vehicles with larger engines producing more power. This is also fueled by the deep pockets of some manufacturers and aftermarket parts companies.

Today's weekend drifters will drift whatever car they own. Engine power can be compensated for with driving style; lower power means greater technique is needed. A low-power car like a Toyota AE86 requires as much throttle as possible while still being very light with the brakes. The driver must know the limits of himself and the car; to know the limits generally means a driver will be exceeding them frequently, causing damage consistent with such aggressive driving. Instead of Show and Go, the term Show and Dough should be used because of the high cost of maintenance.

Drift Setups

Knowing the common modifications to a drift vehicle can assist you in examining claims and collisions. Typical items that drifters (and many other types of driving enthusiasts) like to improve on are the engine, motor supports, coilovers, sway bar, limited slip differential (LSD) transmission, clutch, radiator, short shifter, big-brake upgrade, electrical fans, instruments, tires, wheels, and seats. Some companies have designed a clutch for drifting that they market as being able to take the abuse of a weekend drift event and then take them to work during the week.

Depending on budget, one of the first components a drifter will want to change is the suspension and LSD. An LSD transmission is crucial in helping the car sustain the drift all the way through the corner. Suspension setup is critical, as a stock suspension may allow for too much body roll. Rubber bushings may be replaced with a bearing.

Tires are important and need good grip or traction for control despite the fact that they are constantly spinning and breaking traction to slide the car. Street wheels and tires may be replaced with those marketed as drift set-ups (Search the Internet for "drift tires" and "drift wheels" to learn more about what is popular at this time). Beginning drifters will often have a set of good, sticky tires for the front and cheap tires for the rear until they get comfortable with sliding around corners. While inspecting a vehicle make note of the types of tires on the front and rear, then research those brands to determine what they were designed for. Falken Tires were an early-on leader in drifting tires. In 2006, they had a drift safety program in conjunction with law enforcement called D.O.T (Drift on Track). In 2008, their Azenis RT-615 was advertised as a Street – Time Attack – Drift tire, promising drivers they could race on Sunday and drive to work on Monday. One major tire manufacturer advertised their tires as "The official tire of getting sideways."

Since the 4-lug wheel pattern of the 240SX is a popular drift car and 5-lug rims are popular tires to use, it's common for 240 owners to convert the front tires. There are 4-to 5-lug adapters, but they may not be as safe for this type of driving as replacing the 4-lug hubs with 5-lug hubs. Lug conversion kits are used on a variety of vehicles; look for evidence that a conversion kit was used if that is important to your investigation.

Big brake upgrades are common among drifters; this would include rotors, pads, calipers, brake lines, and mounting brackets. However, bigger is not always better. Some big brake kits can actually lengthen the stopping distance when used in typical street driving versus track racing. To prevent frequent boil over from a driver who is hard on the brakes, the DOT 4 brake fluid may be replaced with DOT 5 (silicone based). If a vehicle was not designed for this change, other problems may surface down the road, such as caliper pistons sticking and leaking if they are not properly maintained.

To know what works and what is popular, many enthusiasts study what is working for those actively involved. Attending drift events and car shows and talking to car owners gives great understanding on what to look for and why. Read some of the many drifting specific websites to learn more about what is popular (see Internet Websites in Chapter 6 for sites).

Fraudulent Drift Claims

Drifting puts an enormous strain on the tires, engine, transmission, driveshaft, and differential. The need for replacement parts is expensive and continuous. Enthusiasts may take a $1,500 car and put $5,000 worth of drifting parts into it. Many beginning drifters can easily put $200 to $2,000 a month into their cars and can go through several sets of tires in a single event. Prices can double and then skyrocket for those who want to compete in a series.

Since collisions and broken parts are inevitable in drifting, it is imperative to evaluate claims from a drifting perspective depending on the location of collision and the type of car involved. In one claim, when an insured reported that his vehicle was damaged by a large rock in the roadway, the insurance investigator looked to see if the damages were consistent with the story. This investigator noted some inconsistencies in the insured's story and the damage she was seeing. The insured was a man in his 50s whose Mitsubishi Eclipse appeared to have been driven by a younger person. The contents of the vehicle as well as seat position did not fit the insured. The investigator noted that the insured did have a teenage son at home, but the son was specifically excluded from the policy. The investigator also noticed that the Eclipse had different tire set ups on the front and rear and that these tires were commonly used in the street race and drift scenes. Additionally, the area of the reported collision was on a mountain road known as a favorite among local drifters and enthusiasts.

She inspected the vehicle and noticed that there was no damage to the undercarriage of the vehicle consistent with running over a large rock. There was significant damage, however, to the entire bottom right side of the vehicle along the rocker panel and the right rear tire area. It is common (just watch several drift videos) for drivers attempting to drift around corners at intersections to lose control and hit the curb with the right side of the vehicle. Many of these collisions occur with such force that cars flip over. The damage that occurs in these collisions is consistent with the damage that occurred to this Eclipse.

Armed with the above stated investigative results, the insurance investigator confronted the insured with the inconsistencies regarding the collision damage and his statement. The insured admitted that he did not run over a rock in the mountains but did collide with a curb on the city streets. He still did not admit that it was his son driving; most likely, he knew his vehicle would not be covered due to the exclusion of his son from the policy. Nonetheless, this claim was denied due to his false statement that the damage occurred from hitting a rock on a mountain road. Additionally the insured could have been charged with felony insurance fraud for committing a "material misrepresentation" of the facts.

Drifting vehicles collide frequently. Hitting curbs and guardrails is common. In mountain roads, drifters commonly overshoot a turn and go off road. Damage can occur to the front, side, or rear of the vehicle as well as the undercarriage. When berms are present, significant damage can occur to the wheels or the vehicle can be sent airborne or even rollover. There is a real danger of going down a steep embankment if they are drifting along cliffs. If they race in tandem, sideswipe paint transfers may be evident. At many sanctioned events, we see cars colliding with the walls, causing either front or rear damage. Fixed object collisions involving a vehicle set up for drifting should be evaluated closely as to whether the damage matches the object claimed in the collision.

Gymkhana, Pronounced Jim-Ka-Nuh, has several definitions that relate to sporting events requiring driving skill. The sport is similar to autocross, and it has become more popular because of drifting. Gymkhana primarily occurs in large areas involving obstacles that the drivers maneuver around. Unlike drifting, Gymkhana is a timed event, but contestants are judged on their style.

One insurance company received a claim regarding damage to a vehicle that was reported as being caused by the car leaving the paved roadway and veering onto the dirt shoulder. The driver stated to the insurance company that he was on a mountainous road and swerved to miss a deer that ran out in front of him. During the investigative process, the insurance investigator visited the scene. He noted that there were skid marks preceding the point of collision at several turns that were consistent with drift skids. The investigator contacted the tow truck driver that was at the scene the night of the collision. He stated that the driver had a racing helmet and gloves and mentioned that he took the turn too fast while drifting. Once again, false statements to an insurance company can be cause for claim denial and criminal prosecution.

The damage may not always be significant, but it can be telling nonetheless. If a front-wheel drive car has unevenly worn rear tires, is that because they just rotated their tires or do they use their e-brake to throw the car into a sideways pitch going around a turn? Look closely at all vehicles involved in claims to determine if the story fits the car and damage.

Illegal Street Racing

Street racing has been occurring since the invention of the automobile. Illegal street racing has been around since there were rules, laws, or regulations prohibiting excessive speed on city streets. Street racing today is multicultural, involves both sexes, and includes all types of vehicles from stock to the heavily modified. For the past two decades, modified sport compact cars have been favored and have been gathering on any given night in parking lots, industrial areas, gas stations, and burger joints in cities around the globe. From 2005 to 2008, we have seen a resurgence of muscle cars joining this mix. SEMA conducted a survey in 2007 and found nearly 20% of the readers they polled of ages 16-24 were interested in muscle cars.

The racers may come alone, in pairs, or large caravans. Many races occur spontaneously when two or more willing motorists come upon each other in traffic. Others are highly organized and can involve from a few cars to hundreds. Age 30 and under seems to be the norm for these illegal street race gatherings, but in 2008 Maryland experienced a street race in which 8 spectators died from one incident; the ages of the victims of this tragedy ranged from 20-61.

There are always favorite areas for street racers to race, which usually depends upon the presence of law enforcement in the area. Mimicking legal drag races, these participants will set up eighth-mile to one-quarter-mile sections on our roads to race each other. Sometimes the participants refer to the quarter-mile as the 1320 referring to the number of feet in a quarter-mile.

Street racers use a number of methods to announce a race: word-of-mouth, texting, cell phones, honking their horn (3-honk), flashing their emergency lights, or posting on the Internet. There are many popular websites used by street racers that are portals for many things related to street racing; sites are used for listing meeting places, organizing races (legal and illegal), communicating through forums, and even sharing the location of police radar. A search in Google as of the date of this writing showed over 8,000,000 entries for "Street racing." Even though some of these races seemed to be spontaneous at the time, many were organized surreptitiously and involved co-conspirators willing to aid and abet in illegal activity via text messaging or other forms of electronic communication (using radio transmissions to commit crimes may be unlawful).

Tracking illegal nighttime racing involving sport compact cars has been monitored heavily in the United States since the mid 90s. In Orange and Santa Clara Counties, there were many nights when law enforcement would see hundreds to thousands of street racers show up at one location. San Diego Police Department discovered one illegal gathering of over 1,200 vehicles, both spectators and racers. The scene is unreal for those that have never seen it and quite a thrill for those who participate.

Once the stretch of highway is located, spectators line up on either side of the street, leaving enough room for two cars to line up side by side. A "flagger" stands between the front bumpers of the two cars to make sure that the cars are lined up evenly and no one has an unfair advantage. The drivers of the cars focus their attention on the flagger. He raises his hands up in the air, points to each driver one at a time to make sure he is seen, then drops his hands down to his sides letting the drivers know the race is on. The cars lunge forward and speed past the flagger, somehow missing him, and race toward the finish line.

The racing vehicles continue with several to hundreds of spectators on both sides. Frequently the spectators are too close to the road and are definitely in danger. Other times participants and spectators are still arriving when they suddenly realize that two high-speed cars are racing toward them. We have seen near-collisions with these new arrivals driving against the flow of traffic. We have seen racers lose control and drive right into, and over, spectators and their cars. *A Charlotte man was recently sentenced to eight years in prison when the car he was racing lost control, injuring several and permanently disabling two. In February 2008, eight spectators died while watching a street race in Maryland. While these spectators were focused on watching the street race in front of them, a secondary and unrelated street race drove through the crowd killing eight and injuring several more.*

When the racers reach the end of the run, the winner may flash his emergency lights to let the spectators know who won. The racers make a u-turn to head back at the same time the next set of racers are given the signal by the flagger to go. Racers continue, car after car, and if viewed from the air it looks like a circle of cars on one small street. They will run for hours – or until the police are notified and respond to the scene.

At some races, there are enthusiasts who act as lookouts. These lookouts are stationed at ingress and egress routes, ready to phone, radio, or text message a warning to others that the police are on their way. They will monitor the police frequencies, listening for any officers who may have been dispatched.

In one fact-collecting mission, we had been standing among the racers, video taping the action, when someone will yell five-O five-O or PO-PO (indicating that the police are coming). Everyone fled the area in a mad dash to avoid arrest and vehicle impoundment. This scene can be very dangerous.

I have seen video footage from law enforcement helicopters that shot infrared video of the scene as the police were breaking up the illegal activity and the spectators were running from the police. With the infrared cameras rolling from 2,000 feet high in a police helicopter, you can see the hundreds of hoods glowing from the heat of the engine, as well as the body heat of spectators running away. This is a great perspective of the invasiveness and danger involved.

I realize that street racing has been a part of American history and may never go away. At the age of 17, kids feel invincible and in total control, believing nothing can go wrong and that they can control every situation. I wish this were true.

Searching Internet video-sharing sites can really open the eyes of those who have not seen illegal street racing and the dangers involved. Internet sites such as YouTube (www.youtube.com) and MySpace (www.myspace.com) have been an outlet for street racers and drifters to post their crazy and unsafe driving antics on the Internet for all to see. Unfortunately, this type of video posting leads to others trying to outdo the previous post, perpetuating the danger. Several police agencies around the world have begun to prosecute these video participants whenever the information warrants it. A search on YouTube for "Street Racing" at the time of this publication lists over 29,400 videos with the number one video being viewed 2,748,435 times.

The amount of activity varies from city to city and year to year. In 1997, the scene was wild in California and then it died down (due primarily to law enforcement operations). Some thought it went away, but much of it went underground, some tactics were changed, or many went to unincorporated neighboring cities and ran somewhat undetected. Sometimes the law enforcement focus changed to other priorities or due to personnel shortages, and it just seemed like the problem went away.

In 2005-2007, those cities that thought the problem had gone away awoke one day to learn that racers in the hundreds were once again racing. What is going on with this scene during these times of apparent hibernation? In the cities where enforcement was strict and the penalties for racing were stiff, many studied police tactics and evolved. The waters were tested. Smaller groups gathered in parking lots and burger joints. Spotters were miles out, monitoring police activity and radio traffic. The groups would send out just a couple of cars to go run without witnesses. If they came back, without getting caught, then the group would assume that the area was safe and many more runs would happen. This isn't quite as thrilling and does diminish the amount of cars at any one site.

Where does the theft and fraud come into play during the illegal street races? Collisions, broken parts, accidents, and injuries all spur the theft and fraud aspect of this scene. It costs a lot of money to be competitive. Often these races are not just for the thrill of going fast; the goal is to be named king of the hill, or king of the vehicle class. In some scenes, there is a lot of money being bet on the sidelines as to who is going to win or loose. When someone does lose, he or she may not have cash. In such cases, the winner may choose to take car parts in trade. If the loser has a nice set of tires and wheels or an expensive after-market turbo, the winner may ask for those items as payment. Without hesitation, the loser gives up his tires and wheels, as he knows he can just make a false police report and file an insurance claim seeking payment for a phony loss. Many of these players are shocked when they find out that they are under arrest for felony insurance fraud.

Collisions frequently occur while involved in many of the various forms of street racing. Many of these collisions are falsely reported as innocent. We investigated an accident that appeared to be a typical rear end collision involving three vehicles. However, the three vehicles had been chasing each other in a street race at unsafe speeds while following each other too closely. When driver one got into trouble and had to hit the brakes, the other two cars were involved in rear-end collisions. The drivers knew they might be in trouble if they told the truth, so they claimed not to know each other and said it was just one of those things. One of the parties decided to enhance the damage to get his car tricked out with new accessories. Enhancing damage or claiming soft tissue damage can easily be proven by good traffic accident reconstructionists. Their lies led to fraud investigations showing that all parties involved were street racers and that fraudulent statements were made. In most states, any material misrepresentation can lead to a felony insurance fraud charge.

Racers are desperately trying to be number one and pushing their vehicles beyond their limits. Engines get blown and parts get broken. Do they bite the bullet and buy a new engine or parts, do they report a false theft to obtain insurance reimbursement, or do they go steal from another racer? The old adage that there is no honor among thieves is definitely true in this scene. Some racers come to watch or run, but they are also there to see who has a fast set up or expensive parts they desire. They then follow the owner home or scam his address in order to steal his car later for the parts.

Large sums of money, stereos, wheels, and titles to vehicles have been bet and lost in illegal street races. Cars have crashed, burst into flames, and people have died. Numerous fines from tickets, impound fees, jail time, and attorney's fees continue rack up. What happens at an illegal street race that is busted often dictates how many false auto theft reports are made. During many street race busts, invariably when the dust settles, there will be an "abandoned" vehicle or two. Law enforcement will run the plates to these abandoned vehicles to learn that there are no wants or warrants on the vehicle. A close inspection reveals no signs consistent with an auto theft.

However, several hours later the owner of the vehicle will call a police department to report his vehicle stolen. Such was the case during a Dragnet operation when a Ford Mustang was left behind. Several hours after the bust, the owner of the Mustang called to report his vehicle stolen. When the owner was asked if he had any teenage children at home, he indicated his son still lived at home but did not take the vehicle nor did he have permission to drive it. The investigating officers had the owner come down to the police station with his son for further questioning. It just so happened that video existed that showed the various vehicles racing that night just prior to the bust. When the father and son were shown the video, it included his "stolen" mustang racing and behind the wheel was the owner's son.

I can't tell you how many times I have heard or read street racers saying, "If you would provide us a track to race on, we wouldn't have to turn to the streets. That may be true for a few, but the follow-up statements they make regarding "street racing is in their blood," "the thrill of illegal racing can't be beat," and "it won't go away," holds more truth. I agree with the statements that street racing will always be here, but it can be minimized and not allowed to get out of hand as has happened in many cities.

Another reason an "available track" would not make a difference in the types of individuals we are discussing in this book is that many are after the thrill of doing something under the cover of darkness that is illegal (but in their mind not necessarily dangerous or harmful to others). Several of the professional sport compact racers I have dealt with over the years got their start by illegally racing on the streets.

Law enforcement and fraud investigators are trying to get the word out to keep it off the streets, reminding the participants that racetracks provide a much safer forum for their need for speed – no bumps, potholes, or spectators on the line, no vehicles driving towards them while they are racing and driving under the influence of drugs or alcohol. Racetracks have medical teams standing by in case there is an accident. I have worked in many cities enforcing illegal street racing with available racetracks within miles of the illegal site. While working in some states with available tracks, the complaint there was that the track was not open enough or that it was not a large enough to accommodate everyone. (Legal alternatives are discussed in Chapter 8).

As an auto theft investigator, I have found myself starting my training presentations by letting the audience know that by enforcing the auto theft and fraud laws involving street racers, they can and will save lives. In order to win a street race, you have to have a fast car. In order to have a fast enough four-cylinder powered car, the engine needs to be heavily modified. If auto theft investigators arrest these thieves and recover the thousands of stolen engines and transmissions from these street racers, they are taking away their power plants and keeping them off the streets. More times than not, when law enforcement action takes place at an illegal race, vehicles involved in the scene are discovered to have stolen engines, transmissions, and component parts. I know aggressive and consistent enforcement works. I have interviewed numerous ex-racers, and read a lot of chat on the Internet, and they indicate that they have had enough of the police enforcement and are getting involved in safer and less costly hobbies.

Our favorite saying is, "If it is predictable it is preventable." Knowing when and where these kids race makes it easy to crack down on it. As hard as anyone tries to keep a secret, word is going to leak out about what is going on. Law enforcement actions, or lack thereof, can dictate the extent of the problem any city will face. In February 2007, the Honolulu Adviser reported that roving packs of 300 street racers were cruising the highways after midnight and the police were "monitoring" the group. This is the biggest mistake I see across the country: cities that "monitor" this activity instead of taking preemptive action.

Allowing this activity to go unchecked has proven fatal across the globe. Everyone knows what the outcome will be from these large gatherings (street races or drift runs, drinking, drugs, gambling, theft, shots fired and people hit), so why wait? As the saying goes, "Nothing good ever happens after midnight." In the Maryland street race collision in which eight were killed, the neighbors that lived in that area stated they knew someone could get hurt and that they complained repeatedly to police about the dangers of the illegal street races. Law enforcement can't be expected to respond immediately to every call regarding street racing or related gatherings, but through consistent and strict enforcement, events such as the Maryland tragedy can be thwarted at "known" street race sites. With today's technology, neighborhood watches, and the Internet, steps can be taken to prevent areas from becoming acceptable illegal race sites (Chapter 7 has additional information).

Law enforcement receives calls frequently from property owners seeking advice on how to stop these large gatherings on their property. More times than not, any sales generated from these gatherings do not compensate for the large number of cars and enthusiasts that are present versus the much smaller normal paying customer activity. Adding insult to injury is the cost involved with the trash clean up and vandalism repair the following day.

"Show and Go" is a term often used to describe cars that both look good and go fast; this street scene is full of cars that fit this category. Enthusiasts gather to show off their latest modification and to see what others have done to their cars. Meetings typically take place at a local hamburger joint, parking lot, speed shop, or aftermarket parts store. Some of these gatherings look more like a street party, with music blasting, dancing, and drinking. These types of gatherings are also great venues for our Fast and Fraudulent crowd to discuss the latest insurance fraud scams and how to fix up a car with little or no money out of pocket.

To prevent accidents and save lives, the affected law enforcement agencies should conduct vehicle safety checks as groups of cars leave one gathering area to drive to the next. Agencies such as San Diego Police Department's Dragnet team have done this type of enforcement and have been very successful in curtailing illegal activity and recovering stolen vehicles and parts. In one enforcement operation they conducted in December 2005, they observed approximately 200 vehicles gathering. They inspected approximately 100 cars; 50 received citations for various violations (50%) and 18 were impounded for additional violations. Eight of the eighteen impounded vehicles had stolen engines and transmissions. Had San Diego allowed the gathering to go unchecked, illegal street races would have occurred, lives and property would have been endangered, and stolen property would still be on the streets. Additionally this type of proactive intervention has a long-lasting ripple effect on those who would have continued to race on another day. Riverside, Ontario, and other California Dragnet-trained police departments have had similar positive results.

Ontario California, July 2006, the Dragnet Regional Task Force was patrolling the city streets. A group of approximately 150 vehicles and an estimated 300 people were detained at fifty-three minutes past midnight for being involved in illegal street racing activity. Seven adults and one juvenile were arrested for racing, and their cars were impounded with a 30-day hold; 26 cars were impounded because the drivers had no license or had a suspended license; 60 juveniles were arrested for curfew violations. A hundred citations were issued and about 50 of those were referred to the Bureau of Automotive Repair for illegal emission modifications. (As discussed in Chapter 2 under Owner Give-ups, emissions violations can frequently turn to fraud acts by the vehicle owner).

In September 2008, Ontario again stopped a group of racers that had gathered to race. During that bust, 184 people were arrested (cited and released for being spectators), to which 47 were also charged with curfew violations. Additionally, three were arrested for racing, one was arrested for aiding the racing (flagger), and 74 vehicles were impounded. With a total of 193 arrests and 74 impounded vehicles at one location, the deterrent factor for future gatherings in Ontario drop dramatically. It is the surrounding cities that need to be ready for any increase as the racers look for a new meeting spot where law enforcement won't bother them.

Late-night Car Meets typically lead to street or freeway races as well as other illegal activities. The groups we deal with find it nearly impossible not to show off; the recipe of youth, testosterone, and horsepower generally makes showing off inevitable, whether in the parking lot or on the streets. Zero-tolerance to these types of late-night gatherings is imperative to save lives and protect property.

Many successful operations have occurred throughout the world. Street racers, like many humans, are all creatures of habit. The street racers find streets or highways that are particularly good for street racing and they will frequent that area.

Many progressive states have passed some excellent laws to help curb the problem of illegal racing. Unfortunately, most of these laws came about due to an increase in deaths and injuries, along with theft and fraud. Part of the thrill of illegal street racing is to have people witness your prowess on the streets. If there is no one there to see you, you may be less likely to race. These types of laws have made dramatic impact in diminishing the street races. In addition to anti-spectator laws, some states have enhancements for curfew violations and the second curfew violation results in the suspension of their driver's license. Other states have laws making it a misdemeanor to be a flagger. If one flagger starts 50-100 races, he can be arrested for 50-100 counts of flagging. Some cities that have known areas of racing and gathering have designated the streets as "no parking, stopping, or standing" between 10:00 p.m. and 4:00 a.m., avoiding the trouble that inevitably precedes an illegal street race.

If they gather on private property, ask the property owners to post "No Trespassing" or "No Loitering" signs between 10:00 p.m. and 4:00 a.m. Have them sign a victim's complaint form and keep it on file so when the racers gather illegally, the police can take immediate action through arrest and vehicle impounds. I know this sounds a little harsh, but the purpose is to STOP illegal street racing and related activities, which can save lives. (More solutions are offered in Chapter 7).

Highway Racing

Illegal street racing is not always about seeing who is the fastest in the quarter-mile; sometimes it is about who the fastest is on any given section of highway or freeway at any given time. Some prefer to do their racing during rush-hour traffic to make the challenge of getting from point A to point B more intense (and exponentially more dangerous).

Cannonball runs and Gumball Rallies, popularized by several movies in the 1970s, are still alive around the world in a variety of forms. One of the most famous is the Gumball 3000, www.Gumball3000.com. In 2008, the entry fee for one car was $120,000 which included the cost of shipping vehicles around the world. For 2009, the entry fee is $44,000 per car for two people; this contest is not for those on a budget. In 2002, the route went from New York to Los Angeles and had 175 cars entered. Video from that event included a Porsche going 206 mph while a uniformed police officer, who had originally stopped a Gumball driver, is seen sitting in the passenger seat. In 2003, the route was from San Francisco to Miami and was featured in a Gumball 3000 DVD. In 2007, the run started in London on April 29. The cars were then flown to Istanbul for the run and back to London. In 2008, it started in San Francisco, through San Diego and into Las Vegas, China, and North Korea, ending in Beijing, China for the Olympics. The United States will again be featured May 1- 8 2009, with the route going from Los Angeles to Miami.

I have interviewed officers that were on-duty during this run, and they mentioned how overwhelmed they were from an enforcement standpoint. Participants gladly accepted the $200 ticket and asked to have their picture taken with the officer. Other participants would stop during traffic enforcement and plaster the officer's car with Gumball 3000 decals when the officer wasn't looking. Searching car forums on a frequent basis turns up a variety of smaller Cannonball-type runs occurring throughout many cities on a regular basis. Most of the sites mention lawful gatherings driving from point A to B, but when you get several hundred sport-compact car enthusiasts together it is hard to control that much testosterone, and unsafe speed and maneuvering is almost a guarantee. Some of the routes announced to law enforcement are intentionally misleading. In the last one we monitored the organizer told law enforcement that the route would be heading north through their city when in fact they knew they were going south.

Cannonball-type racing is infrequent compared to the daily runs occurring on our highways, but similar problems involving high rates of speed on public highways can occur. In 2005, an editor of a large sport compact car magazine wrote about an afternoon test drive of a new car. He took his car northbound on the 57 Freeway in Los Angeles at speeds of 110 mph. He talked about taking this car into the San Gabriel Mountains on a twisting and turning two-lane road and pushing the car to its limits. Sport compact magazines too frequently mention their own experiences of driving illegally and dangerously. Headlines such as "Street Racing in Los Angeles" are perhaps not the best way to communicate to our youth the safety and responsibility required while driving on public roads. Similarly, billboard ads such as Subaru's 2009 Impreza WRX "Buy stock in rubber" and the Lexus IS-F "What the F!?" showing vehicles burning rubber on asphalt; along with Lexus "SO WORTH TRAFFIC SCHOOL", do not promote safe and legal driving in my opinion.

There are too many nicknames and trends change too often to list all of the slang used for racing illegally on our streets and highways. Two-cut, Cutting the Gap, Cutting Up, Hat, 3 Honk, Banzai, Midnight Runs, Chance, Loop, and Cell Racing are some terms that have been used to talk about various forms of racing on the streets and highways. Some of these types of racing involve going from one point in a city to another, while others occur at the moment one driver's eyes meet another's.

This unsafe highway racing, cutting in and out of multiple traffic lanes, frequently victimizes innocent motorists. In June 2007, one such race led to the death of a motorist in Ontario Canada when his truck was clipped by one of the racers, forcing his vehicle into a fatal rollover. *This racer once nicknamed himself "the cut king."*

Many states have very strict laws and fines when it comes to illegal racing on our highways. Racing and excessive speeds frequently lead to an impounded vehicle, serious fines, and instant jail time for the participants. This type of serious enforcement has been successful in stopping illegal racing for many. Unfortunately, violators blame their cars or law enforcement and try to get out of their wrongdoings by committing false auto thefts and fraud. Additionally, in states such as California, if the vehicle is illegally modified, the owner is required to put the car back together as stock, or at least within compliance (see chapter 2, Owners Give-Ups, for more on BAR repercussions).

In 2004, an insured reported his 2003 Honda S2000 stolen. He advised the police department and his insurance company that the vehicle was extensively modified when it was stolen. He was seeking reimbursement for the vehicle and aftermarket parts. He stated he paid $38,000 for the car and he had listed over $15,000 in modifications.

The insurance company received information that this insured was selling parts from this vehicle on the Internet. I started researching the Internet and found a post from someone in the same city as the insured selling parts from a 2003 S2000. The posting was under an Internet User Name and not a real name. The seller stated that he was selling everything off of his car because he had gotten caught racing on the freeway going over 140 mph. Photo 9 is a screen shot of the actual post.

> Home :: Forums :: Marketplace Forums :: For Sale and Wanted ::
Selling Everything Of My Car. Got Caught Racing Going 140mph+ On The Freeway
Pages: « ‹ **1** 2 3 › »

Photo 9

Parts listed for sale on the Internet included an exhaust system, tires and wheels, Individual Throttle Body (ITB), engine management system, ECU, suspension parts, sway and strut bars, and coilovers. Photographs of the vehicle were the same as those provided to the insurance company for the "stolen" vehicle. In comparing the insurance claim involved in this case with the items listed on the Internet, it appeared that we located the insured, and that he had parted out his vehicle for sale five days prior to reporting it stolen.

Since he still had items listed for sale on the Internet, he was contacted via a Private Message (PM) from the website and asked about the exhaust system. He wrote back and stated that he still had the custom exhaust for sale. He said there were a lot of people interested and that whoever came up with $2,900 first could have it. *This was the same brand exhaust that the insured said was on his S2000 when it was "stolen" some 24 days earlier.*

He used his cell phone number as a point of contact to arrange the purchase of the exhaust. This was the same phone number the insured in this case gave the insurance company further confirming that they had the right subject and posting. At this point, the case was turned over to California's Department of Insurance Fraud Division, who subsequently served a search warrant on the insured and recovered some of the "stolen" property at his residence. The exhaust system was under his bed at the time of service. The insured was arrested for Felony insurance fraud even though the vehicle was never recovered. (When writing search warrants it is imperative to include the suspect's computer for evidence that may be on his hard drive).

You may think that spontaneous races such as these are impossible to control, but they occur with such frequency in some cities that law enforcement can learn to work these with great success. Just as with illegal street drags, highway runners may meet at a local shop or gas station prior to heading out on a particular highway to run their cars. Working these gatherings is one way to nip the inevitable in the bud. Other enforcement techniques include the use of radar alerts, surveillance or speed cameras, air support, and public relations campaigns that get the community involved in reporting this dangerous behavior. As mentioned in Chapter 1 under Movies, successful highway racing enforcement can stop the dangerous activity, locate additional racing locations, and lead to many other crimes such as hit, run, insurance fraud, and false theft reports.

Spontaneous Simultaneous Rapid Acceleration, or the belief that freeway onramps are legalized drag strips due to the rapid acceleration needed to merge at the speed of traffic flow, are not justifications to exceed safe speeds. Highway Racing Enforcement is discussed in Chapter 7.

Time Attack

Popular for many years in Japan and Europe, Time Attacks gained tremendous popularity in the United States in the mid-2000s. These are circuit events where participants are racing against the clock; the fastest times win. Drivers compete alone on the track; they are allowed three laps – a warm-up lap, a timed lap, and a cool-down lap. At Time Attacks, you can find a variety of cars from exotic imports to daily-driven stock sedans, allowing anyone and any car to compete. In Button Willow, California, you will find a three-mile Time Attack course that can have seven classes with such categories as Unlimited AWD (All Wheel Driver), Limited AWD, Unlimited FR/MR (Front/Mid engine Rear drive), Limited FR/MR, Unlimited FF (Front engine Front drive), Limited FF, and Drift. At the 2009 Tokyo Auto Salon, drifting and time attack vehicles had a continuing influence on street performance trends. Japanese tuner shops and manufacturers are still focusing on the United States for their next big expansion.

Time attacks are a great opportunity for enthusiasts to test their car and abilities in a controlled and safe environment. Investigators that suspect fraudulent claims involving time attack vehicles should apply the same investigative techniques as previously mentioned in sanctioned drag and drift events. At the time of this writing www.timeattackforums.com was a good source of information on time attack events.

Ghost Riding

"Ghost Riding the Whip" generally refers to putting your car in gear then jumping out of it and hoping on top of the hood to ride the car while it rolls down a street with no one behind the wheel. "Ghost riding" because no one is in the car, and "Whip" which is slang for car. If there are passengers, everyone may get out of the car and dance around it while it is moving. As you could imagine, collisions do occur. Search a local video website for the term "ghost riding the whip" to view a variety of techniques and collisions. If you need to investigate one of these stunts gone wrong, a clue as to what transpired may be unique vehicle damage, foot prints on top of the vehicle, and injuries that are inconsistent with the accident. One famous video has been played by local news networks and can be seen on the various video sharing sites. The Ghost Rider climbs out of his truck and onto the hood while it is rolling down the street. The truck jumps a curb heading straight for a fire hydrant and phone pole. Just prior to the impending collision the Ghost Rider jumps to the asphalt street and rolls on the ground. I don't know how he initially reported this collision, but if he were to falsely report that he was driving the vehicle when it collided, the inconsistent injuries might be a giveaway. Ghost riding in Sweden generally involved motorcyclists driving at high rates of speed during times of peak traffic on streets and highways. Ghost riding has also been referred to as Hood, Car, and Urban Surfing.

Sideshows

Sideshows have been reported for years in Oakland, California. In the early 2000s, they spread across the country and have been seen as far East as Maryland. Generally, sideshows start out as late-night impromptu car shows or a get-together at a local parking lot when most businesses are closed. Sometimes they occur after a concert lets out and the attendees have a ton of energy they need to release. Drinking, music, and partying are a common precursor to the wild show that soon follows. Some participants will dart out into the streets with their tires spinning and then take over intersections, performing doughnuts or figure-eight stunts and maneuvers with their cars. One car after another takes over the intersection, disregarding all lawful traffic and frequently preventing legal motorists from driving through even if they have a green light. Not even halfway through 2006, Stockton, California police had cited 1,500 people and impounded approximately 400 cars for sideshow related activities.

Senate Bill 67, by Senator Don Perata of Oakland, California, allowed law enforcement to impound cars for up to 30 days if they are used in sideshows. The reinstated law would again be named the U'Kendra K. Johnson Memorial Act, after a 22-year-old Oakland woman who was killed in 2002 when a suspected sideshow participant being pursued by police crashed into the car in which Johnson was riding. SB 67 became section 23109.2 of the California Vehicle Code for those engaged in speed contest, reckless driving, and exhibition of speed. The city of Oakland also created an ordinance that made merely watching a sideshow a crime carrying punishment of 90 days in jail and fines of $1000.

A search in Google for ["sideshows" and "cars"] will lead to many interesting articles. In 2005, Dateline NBC produced a segment featuring sideshows, and DVDs have been produced showing this crazy scene.

It is too bad that many of our youth do not understand the dangers of their actions until something bad happens and it is too late. Many street racers know of someone who has lost a life to illegal street racing. It is not until they are personally affected that they see the light. Until then, it is a law enforcement and parental duty to enforce the laws that are already on our books to protect our youth. After a few enforcement sessions, many enthusiasts will not be so excited about midnight runs any more and lives will be saved.

Car Shows

There are hundreds of car shows every month throughout the world where enthusiasts gather to show off their passion and love affair with their vehicles. The shows can be make or model specific such as "Fun Ford Weekend", "Supras Invade Vegas", "Bimmerfest", or they can be something like "Hot Import Nights" where one can see hundreds of different makes and models. The vast majority of vehicles at these shows are legitimate, but very rarely do we attend a show without recovering stolen vehicle components.

For many years, NOPI (Number One Parts Inc.) held the NOPI Nationals in Atlanta, Georgia every September. This has been the largest car show of its kind in the world, comprised of nearly every automobile imaginable. In 2006, NOPI reported that 7162 cars were entered and 110,000 spectators attended. In 2004, they reported higher numbers despite the fact that Hurricane Ivan was in the area preventing many (including myself) from attending. In conjunction with the NOPI Nationals, Superstreet and Eurotuner magazines hosted the "Tour," an organized drive to the NOPI event across multiple states with a North, South, and West leg. Several hundred cars can participate in each leg. NOPI is one of the largest importers and distributors of original replacement parts in the country. In 2008, the NHRA stopped its Sport Compact drag racing series and sanctioned the NOPI Drag Racing Series instead.

We like to attend several shows each year to look for new trends and locate stolen property. Generally, within 20 minutes of walking through the doors of a show, we can find a show vehicle with a stolen engine and transmission; it's too easy. It is certainly not the promoters' fault, as they are providing a great arena for enthusiasts to show off their work. In fact, when we go to these shows and find stolen property in the show cars, we try not to take any action until the show is over and the awards have been given out. There are awards for a variety of modifications and classes. One year, the car that won the award for best overall show car had a stolen engine from one city and a stolen transmission from another. In this case, the owner not only won best show car but he got a free tow to the police impound where the stolen engine and transmission were removed and the investigation began.

Often law enforcement officers take heat for attending events such as these. The Internet conversations on forums and in blogs that occurs afterwards can be very intense. It is refreshing when true enthusiasts speak up and put these Internet flamers in their place, reminding them that the stolen parts frequently come from fellow racers and that it is not "fair" to the hundreds of entrants whose cars are winning awards, taking trophies away from those who work hard and pay a lot of money to try and win legally through pride and dedication. Suspects whom we have interviewed believe as we do that many of the vehicles at some of these shows have been built with stolen components or via insurance fraud money.

When attending these sport compact shows, we take samplings of the VINs and license plate numbers to compare them with insurance databases. Some shows indicate that as many as 25% of the show cars have a multiple claims history consistent with theft and fraud associated with this scene.

What happens to these cars when they are towed away due to possession of stolen property depends on several factors. Generally, by the time the stolen items are discovered and identified, we find that they have been missing for over a year; insurance companies frequently settle claims within 30 days and then become the legal owner of the vehicle and its parts. For example, if a Honda Civic was stolen and recovered missing the engine, transmission, airbags, and seats, this vehicle would most likely be considered a total loss, as it would cost too much to rebuild and give back to the insured. The insurance company instead pays off the insured and now owns the car. When we inspect a show car that has a stolen engine and transmission from a previous theft, we notify the insurance company that we have found some of their stolen property. The show car with the stolen engine and transmission is towed to a facility and inspected to determine if any other items on the car are stolen. Components that are determined to be stolen items can be removed (at the vehicle owner's expense) and returned to the previous owner, who, in this case, is the insurance company.

Many of the component parts to a vehicle are identifiable. It is important for vehicle manufacturers to be able to identify parts for safety and recall considerations as well as making the assembly process of the vehicle more efficient and cost effective. Those who believe they can remove identifiable numbers to avoid theft detection are in for a shock when they learn that it is a crime to possess items with the identifiable markings removed and, if discovered, the part can be taken never to be returned. In fact, many times parts that have had the numbers removed are crushed, and if it can be proven that the owner of the car containing the stolen items was involved in the original theft or knew the items were stolen, the entire car can be crushed. (For more on car crushing see Car Seizures and Dispositions in Chapter 7).

When we locate stolen component parts such as engines and transmissions on these cars, the investigation frequently leads to a chop shop (see Chapter 4 for more on Chop Shops). In the Fast and Fraudulent world of car clubs, teams, and crews, we frequently find the groups sharing theft and fraud tactics. It has been our experience that if we find one stolen engine in a team member's car we will most likely find more stolen engines if we look at the other members' cars. We have also found that if those same teams frequent particular performance repair shops, and we subsequently conduct a business inspection at those facilities, we will discover more stolen components and perhaps a chop shop or two.

At one car show we attended, a team had seven cars lined up against a wall. Three of those show cars in a row had stolen engines in them. Each of the owners stated that a particular performance shop in another county had installed the engines. We paid a visit to that shop and discovered several other stolen component parts as well as two stolen vehicles in the process of being dismantled, and several of the employees also had arrest warrants.

It is imperative that follow-up be conducted when information is received regarding a suspicious shop. Not following through with such information allows chop shops to continue operation, further victimizing many.

In addition to the stolen parts and fraud involved in some show cars, the street scene to and from the show is wild. Some car shows will attract 20,000 enthusiasts to view 500 cars. I have attended many shows where the line to get tickets to enter the event stretches for blocks and it takes over an hour to get in. For shows like these, the doors open at 5:00 p.m. and close at midnight; at 9:00 p.m., people are still lined up trying to get in. Think about ten or twenty thousand sport compact enthusiasts driving to an event, driving past a quarter-mile long line of fellow enthusiasts all staring at them. Do you know how hard it is for them not to show off by revving their engines or burning some rubber? Now think about all of these people spending hours looking at hot cars with hot accessories and loud music and wild videos. These ten or twenty thousand enthusiasts get in their cars to leave and they are pumped up ready to rumble. Law enforcement tries to be ready to keep them under control but the enthusiasts outnumber law enforcement ten-to-one, so the surrounding streets may not be safe to drive on for hours to come.

Many events also become a shopping day for thieves – not to buy some of the nice toys or parts, but to see what expensive parts they will want to steal later. The thieves may look for identifying information on the car in order to find it later, or they may follow the show car home. Even though some of these cars have $30,000 in accessories on their show cars, they are still daily driven and insured vehicles. There are also crews of thieves that patrol the parking lots looking for target vehicles.

When most people go shopping, they make a list of what they want before they go shopping. When these thieves go shopping, they may not have a list yet. As they walk the show floors or drive the adjacent parking lots, they are creating their lists. Driving by a RX-8 with nice tires and wheels, they may write down the license or tag number to identify the home address later. Their shopping list looks something like "Apartment complex, 405 and Sepulveda, gated, access code 5479, Black 2000 Si, 17-inch racing rims." What do they do with this list? When an order comes in from dirty speed shops or fellow friends for 17-inch racing rims, they pull out their shopping list and go steal them to fill the order.

This type of activity is frequently used with body shops looking for body parts and interior pieces such as matching airbags. Dirty performance shops frequently are also involved in buying and selling stolen property.

In the mid 2000s, another Japanese tuning trend started appearing more in the United States; high-end car shows commonly referred to as VIP Style (pronounced "bippu, vippu, veep, or VIP (as in whip). VIP style is not too different from the DUB scene, which features primarily American cars with 20 inch or larger wheels (see DUB magazine). VIP Style generally involves pricier cars such as Mercedes, Lexus, Infinity, BMW, and other luxury cars to which the term "Lux or Luxury style" has also been used. These custom-painted luxury cars with classy body kits are lowered (slammed), with oversized wheels and thin tires that can make it difficult to use them as daily drivers. The 2008 Tokyo Auto Salon showed the VIP lifestyle was not slowing down, expanding to the 30-something tuner crowd who were trading in their sport compacts for style instead. As with many trends, VIP style has manufacturers making items to fill the specific requirements of the trend, such as the extremely low profiles, wheel fitment, and camber angles. With any aftermarket part, make sure you do some research to determine the part's primary design to determine if it has bearing on your case or claim. *VIP Style reportedly got its roots from gangsters in Japan switching vehicle styles to avoid harassment by the police based on vehicle type and modifications.*

Teams and Clubs

The need to belong to a group of peers is very strong, particularly for the under-30 crowd. Car and motorcycle enthusiasts of all types are typically affiliated with car clubs. In the sport compact scene, sometimes these clubs will also call themselves teams, crews, and even gangs. Asian gangs have been the most prevalent in the sport compact scene over any other type of gangs.

Clubs that are into this scene are a very tight knit group. If your suspect/insured has a loss, you may be surprised to find out that several other team members have had a very similar loss. As previously mentioned throughout this book, when we find stolen components in one team member's car, we are likely to find more of the same from other team members.

While attending a car show in Texas we found four vehicles from the same club with stolen engines and transmissions in show cars. A team member of a VW racing group in Maryland was arrested and 15 stolen vehicles were recovered. When interviewed, one of the team members indicated that almost 100% of the stolen vehicles claims within his group were actually insurance fraud.

Whenever I observe team decals on a questionable car, I conduct a Google search of that team name. During one street race investigation, I found an interesting entry in Google from years prior: an auto theft victim had his car stolen and recovered stripped. The victim learned of the location of recovery and drove to the area. His assumption, which was true, was that the suspects who stole and stripped his car most likely lived in the general area. While driving around, he saw his tires and wheels on another street racer's car. This car had a team decal on the windshield that was the same team name as the case I was investigating. This indicated to us that this team had been involved in sport compact theft for many years. A probation search was later conducted on this team member and additional stolen vehicle parts were discovered, indicating the team was also operating as a chop shop and had most likely been doing so for many years.

The good side of teams and clubs are that the honest ones are as tired of the theft and fraud as we are. Speaking with these teams has been a great resource to understand the scene in general and to identify the thieves and chop shops. Don't be uncomfortable speaking with any team, group, or club, as you will learn much valuable information. Even the crooked teams will talk to you, as they may want to try and get inside your head as much as you do theirs. We have had dirty teams give information regarding other dirty teams because they don't want the competition. As long as we are stopping the theft and fraud, we don't care who gives us the information.

As part of normal questioning in sport compact car claims, the investigator should inquire about clubs, teams, or groups with whom the insured may associate and events he has been to. Learn as much as you can about the club; review their web site and online forums. To keep them from being defensive or protective of their club affiliation or website interest, I frequently mention that service shops or car club members of various cities target cars. I also ask for any photos of the vehicle, particularly in cases such as this, where the vehicle has been modified. A series of photos over a time frame of at least one year can provide much useful information. These types of questions can lead to additional investigative leads.

Motorcycles

One of the fastest growing trends in theft, fraud, and the street scene are Sport bikes (performance driven versus highway cruising). Motorcycles have always been high-theft vehicles with a low recovery rate, but sport bikes have many more losses. Customization of sport bikes today is where choppers were in the 60s and 70s. Cars may have a 65% recovery rate while motorcycles only have a 25% recovery rate. According to FBI statistics, one bike is stolen every 7.5 minutes in this country, while vehicles in general are stolen every 26.4 seconds. In 2000, there were only 30,000 motorcycle thefts compared with more than 71,000 in 2006, rising more than 135% and costing nearly half a billion dollars. North Carolina experienced a 200% increase in motorcycle fatalities in 2007, eclipsing the national average. There were 6.2 million registered motorcycles in the United States in 2005 with 1.1 million more bikes sold in 2006 and 2007 (there were over 240 million cars and trucks registered in 2006). More information can be found at the Federal Highway Administrations web site www.fhwa.dot.gov and www.bts.gov). Based on registration versus theft rates, motorcycles are stolen twice as often as other vehicles and have a nearly 40% lower chance of recovery. Sport bikes are also seven times more likely to be stolen than the other bike types.

Progressive insurance conducted a study in 2005 in which the top five stolen motorcycles were all sport bikes and four of the top five crashed motorcycles were of the same make and model as the most stolen bikes; Suzuki, Yamaha, Honda, and Kawasaki.

Commonly stolen sport bikes are the Suzuki GSX-R, the Yamaha YZF-R, the Suzuki Hayabusa, the Honda CBR, and the Kawasaki ZX-R. The top five stolen sport bikes for 2005 were:

1.   Suzuki GSX-R
2.   Yamaha YZF-R
3.   Honda CBR
4.   Suzuki Hayabusa
5.   Kawasaki ZX-R

The street, race, show, and drag scenes have made things worse. If you have not seen what the sport bike scene is all about, you are in for a shock. Traveling at over 100 miles per hour on a crowded freeway while riding a wheelie (on the rear tire only) and splitting lanes is just a warm up. There are too many dangerous stunts to describe (Search Google or YouTube "Motorcycle Stunts" or Freestyle for some insights). According to the National Highway Traffic Safety Administration's Annual Assessment Final Report for 2006, motorcycle deaths rose by over 5% while traffic fatalities overall declined. This was the ninth year in a row that NHTSA had seen an increase in motorcycle deaths. The 4,810 motorcycle fatalities made up 11% of all traffic deaths nationwide in 2006, compared with 5% in 1997. From 1997 through 2006, the number of motorcycle fatalities had increased 127%, an increase that far exceeded that of any other form of transportation, with 27 years of age being the average for sport bike fatalities.

The California Highway Patrol investigated 15 motorcycle fatalities in northern San Diego County for part of 2007. Of those 15 fatalities, 11 were the operator's fault, with speed being a primary factor in many of the deaths (there were nine additional fatalities in the same area investigated by other agencies). The death rate for sport bikes is four times higher than other motorcycles, and they have the worst overall insurance losses among all types of motorcycles based on registrations according to the Insurance Institute for Highway Safety and Highway Loss Data Institute's analysis in September 2007. Sport bikes made up less than 10% of the registered motorcycles in 2005 but accounted for 25% of the fatalities.

In 2005, there were 4,553 motorcycle rider fatalities, of which 44% were from single-vehicle crashes and 56% were from multivehicle motorcycle crashes. Although some motorcycle riders assume a primary collision factor in a multi-vehicle collision was because someone had turned in front of them causing the collision, many fail to understand how their speed influences people's ability to judge a motorcycle's distance before turning. Speed was cited in 57% of the sport bike collisions.

During 2004, 300 young motorcycle operators (15 to 20 years old) were killed, and an additional 8,000 were injured. According to NHTSAs Traffic Safety Facts, during 2004, 38% of motorcycle drivers between the ages of 15 and 20 who were fatally injured in crashes were not wearing helmets. Of the young motorcycle drivers involved in fatal crashes in 2004, more than one-third (39%) were either unlicensed or driving with an invalid license. Information on young drivers is available from the National Center for Statistics and Analysis, http://www.nhtsa.dot.gov/people/ncsa.

In the 21st century, our youth continue to push the limits beyond anything previous generations can comprehend. This is great for science and human rights but insane and dangerous when it comes to the X-games factor on our streets. Since I live in a target rich environment (Southern California), I can't drive on our freeways for more than a week without seeing a dangerous stunt on a motorcycle or modified vehicle. Crashing is guaranteed due to the insane nature of the stunts these riders perform. You can classify motorcycle riders into two groups: those who have gone down (crashed) and those who are going to go down. With these sport bike riders, the two groups become those who have gone down and those who will go down again.

According to HLDI, sport bikes had the highest overall collision coverage losses among 2002-06 model bikes, almost four times higher than losses for touring motorcycles and more than six times higher than cruisers. Nine of the ten motorcycles with the highest losses were sport bikes. The Kawasaki Ninja ZX-10R topped the worst list with collision losses more than nine times the average. Five of the ten motorcycles with the highest overall losses had engine displacements of 1,000 cc or larger. For a detailed analysis, see the Insurance Institutes news release at www.iihs.org/news/rss/pr091107.html.

When the sport bike scene first took hold, we saw a lot of fraud and false theft reports due to the increase in collisions from stunts and the overall desire and demand for this sport activity. However, only so many crashes could be reported to the insurance company before the insured would be flagged or the insurance rates became too high. Those sport bike enthusiasts who have gone down too many times may turn to theft and fraud to stay in the game.

Sport bikes have a metal frame covered with expensive plastic, giving them their shape. Going down on the bike can ruin most of the plastic as well as damage the frame and other components, costing thousands of dollars to replace. Since many of these owners have worn out their welcome with their insurance companies, they turned to theft to rebuild the bike. Frequently all that is recovered after a reported theft are pieces of a frame. The engine and plastic are on a thief's bike or for sale on the Internet (if they are not on the insured's next bike with an aftermarket frame).

When "bike night" was in full swing in large cities across the nation, we would see thousands of sport bikes gathering and cruising on the highways. "Bike Week" events can draw hundreds of thousands of enthusiasts. To see what is happening in your area, do an Internet search for "bike night" or "bike week" and add your city to narrow down the search. Just from this type of simple Internet search, you will come across various motorcycle forums and can locate one near you. There you will find meeting places and times as well as routes they will be taking for their ride.

Many enthusiasts use communication systems such as Chatter Box™ that they can attach to their helmets and can talk to each other while riding in groups. These systems may have several channels and sub-channels. Frequently when searching motorcycle forums discussing an upcoming ride they will list what channel they will be on, such as 15-38. Knowing which frequency they will be using allows anyone to listen in regarding the routes and plans. There may even be chatter from the front to rear driver giving warnings about when police are or are not present, inciting various forms of exhibition of speed (check your state laws to determine if using radio transmissions to commit crimes is even lawful). Several police agencies that work these types of groups monitor these communications to prevent dangerous activity.

Just like sport compact enthusiasts, sport bike enthusiasts cannot resist showing off and doing unsafe acts on public highways during these gatherings. Keeping both tires on the ground seems to be impossible for many of them. Attend one of these gatherings as a spectator if you want to learn a lot about this type of scene.

Enforcement operations regarding sport bikes is generally the same as sport compacts but the escape routes, coupled by extreme speed and nimbleness of the bikes, do make pursuit more difficult (the Suzuki GSX1300R Hayabusa and the Kawasaki Ninja ZX-14 can push 200 mph).

As with sport compacts, more success (and safer streets) can be gained by working the gatherings *before* the bikes hit the street. Myrtle Beach, Florida is a common destination for "bike week" type gatherings. At one bike week gathering in 2006, several auto theft officers assisted Myrtle Beach

Police in recovering 32 stolen motorcycles, four vehicles, and four trailers with a total value of over $400,000.

Stolen, unrecovered, motorcycle engines also make their way into other vehicles such as sand rails, Mini-Pro Funny Cars, Dwarf Cars, Mini Sprints, and Legends. If you have tracks or contests in your area that draw vehicles such as these, they can be fun events to watch while also recovering a stolen engine or two.

When investigating claims involving motorcycles, use the same techniques described for any modified vehicle. Additionally, if you suspect that the insured is into stunt riding, check for stunt-related crash bars and cages, sliders, flat-topped gas tanks, and stunt bars. Additional signs of involvement may include a deflated rear tire, levers that may be cut to avoid them braking off when the bike goes down, and, although not recommended, some may disable the tip-over sensor (fall detection switch). They may also bypass the kickstand safety switch or install a hand mounted rear brake and some sort of bar for protection when doing wheelies such as a 12 o'clock bar or round bar located at the rear of the seat.

One reason motorcycle recoveries are so low is the lack of identifiable parts. Typically, there is a number on the engine and a VIN number on the headstock or near the headstock, as well as a VIN on the certification label in the same area (some manufacturers are much more attentive to parts markings). If the suspects do not swap engines and frames, they may grind and re-stamp the true numbers replacing them with salvaged or cold numbers. Paying close attention to all of the numbers and labels can lead to stolen motorcycle recoveries. The same mistakes are made in motorcycle VIN switching as are in cars.

Several great chop shop cases involving motorcycles have been discovered because the stolen parts were being sold on eBay. The Arizona Auto Theft Task Force (RATTLER), busted one ring in which they discovered over 1,000 eBay entries under six different (but connected) user accounts. Checking online ads can also be a good source for suspect data. Several motorcycle rings will advertise a bike for sale online and when an interested party responds, they will then steal a matching bike to sell them.

Understanding what is involved in each of the eight previously described events in this chapter will allow you to have a better understanding of suspicious reports and what may have caused the damage the insured is claiming. If you know an event occurred before, during, or after the claimed damage, focus some of your attention on those resources to assist you in providing clues to the facts of your investigation. Our website, www.ProtectOurStreets.org, maintains a list of events occurring throughout North America, which may assist you in your investigation.

See Appendices for field guides and sample questions to ask during a sport compact investigation.

Chapter 4: Auto Theft, Methods of Operation

Determining Methods of Entry and Defeat; Was it Stolen?

After examining thousands of thefts, one becomes accustomed to the usual methods used by suspects to steal a vehicle. Each vehicle make and model has preferred methods used by thieves to enter the vehicle and start the car; this is their MO, or Method of Operation. MO changes from city to city, thief to thief, car to car, and year to year.

Every thief has their own method of entry they prefer, which is based on how they were taught or which methods they were exposed to. If they have a background as a locksmith, they may employ lock pick tools. If they spent time in a particular prison, there may be a favorite method of entry (in addition to car jacking). Of course, there are still many old-school thieves out there using slim-jim type devices and dent pullers.

We can become too accustomed to what we generally see regarding theft MO. This comfort level can get in the way of seeing the entire picture being presented. After your first initial inspection of a recovered stolen vehicle, step back and look at everything. Important items can be overlooked if we just focus on what we expect to see. Take an interest in how this theft could have occurred, and ask questions if there is something that is unfamiliar to you.

When a local agency arrested an auto thief, they discovered some electrical connectors that had been taped together. The suspect would not talk regarding how or what this device was used for. The agency sent the photographs out through the Western States Auto Theft Investigators Association (WSATI) for assistance in identification. One of the responses was that the connectors were similar to a stereo connection used in some Hondas and Acuras. I took the photos to a stereo installation shop and from there was able to determine that these connectors were also part of an integrated anti-theft device. Had the vehicle and connector been recovered without an arrest, this information could assist investigators in their search for an auto thief that had been, or is currently, a stereo/alarm installer. In conducting a background check on this suspect, it was learned that he had been a stereo and alarm installer.

You should have a pretty good idea on what methods for theft are used in your area. In California, a typical entry method for a locked Acura Integra was to pull the glass out away from the doorframe, reach in with your arm, and unlock the door. Our suspects would only do this with door glass that did not have a frame around the entire window. They knew they could not pull the glass out if the frame was around it. This type of entry was referred to as "Folding." I had the opportunity to travel to Baltimore and work with the Baltimore County Police Department's Regional Auto Theft Team (RATT). While they were showing me how their suspects stole cars, they referred to window entry as "Flexing." Their suspects wouldn't care if the window was surrounded by a frame; they would pull the entire window frame away from the car, reach in, and unlock it.

Our suspects thought this was impossible because they never tried it. Using this MO difference between states can be useful in identifying suspects. If all of the sudden there is a spike in folding when your state usually sees flexing, the investigator should consider the suspect recently moved into his area (see Chapter 1, Contributing Factors in Theft and Fraud, Florida Saturn thief who moved to Vegas).

Gaining Entry

During a recovered auto theft investigation, one of the first steps to take is to determine the method of theft and to identify how was entry gained. Was a Jiggle key used? Was the column compromised? Does the vehicle have a smart key or a transponder/immobilizer? What are the unique characteristics to this particular make and model? Even determining how the vehicle got to the recovery location can be useful in determining if the vehicle is an owner give-up.

Many Japanese vehicles built up until the mid to late 90s, had door and ignition locks that were easily defeated. The standard method was to use an old worn key to unlock the doors and ignitions of these vehicles. These old keys were so worn that they looked more like the end of a small scissor. In fact, the Toyota Camry was listed as the most stolen vehicle in the United States for at least a decade because it was so easy to steal using small arts and crafts scissors or similar pointed items. One of the favorite tools used to steal a Saturn was a fingernail file or cuticle scissors.

Some suspects would make their own worn key by filing down a good key to make a point. These types of keys were commonly referred to as shaved keys, as they were shaved down. When the shaved or worn key is placed into the door or ignition lock the suspect would jiggle or wiggle the key up and down while turning the lock. Thus, these keys are also referred to as Jiggle or Wiggle keys. The terms Shaved, Jiggle, Wiggle, Worn, and who knows what else, refer to a key (other than the one made for a vehicle) that is used to enter a car. These shaved keys can also be used to start many Japanese vehicles prior to 1995 and some into the early 2000s (non-transpondered). Photo 10 is a jiggle key made from a butter knife.

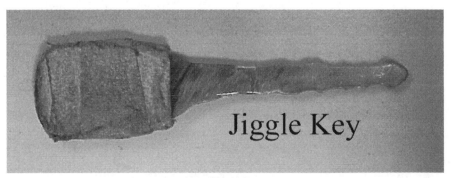

Photo 10

Frequently when auto theft suspects are arrested, they have several worn or shaved keys in their possession (along with a variety of other tools). Many states allow an additional charge to be filed against these thieves for possession of burglar tools.

Almost every method of entry used to steal a vehicle will leave some sort of clue or evidence. Look for these clues to determine if a vehicle was entered unlawfully, which can help to distinguish between a real theft and a fraudulent one.

Many locks consist of a series of spring-loaded wafers that the key slides over. Once completely inserted, the wafers (also known as tumblers) rest against the key in each of the key cuts, which allow the car to be opened or started. As the original key slides in and out of the lock it creates a wear pattern on the wafers particular to that key. When a different key is used, such as a jiggle key, new scrape marks are made on the wafers. A new and distinguishable mark appears where the foreign key or object slides across the wafers. Forensic locksmiths or others who are trained can view the wafer with a light such as an illuminated scope and see the new scrape marks.

Knowing how a vehicle was entered should be part of every vehicle investigation to determine if fraud is part of the claim or to identify MO to help in determining who is responsible for the theft of the vehicle. If the insured states unknown suspects took his locked vehicle and he has all sets of keys, there should be some evidence to support his statement. When this vehicle is recovered and an examination of the locks and glass show no signs of entry, the question of was this car really stolen needs to be addressed.

Photo 11

If the window was folded, there should be a pry mark where the suspect first pulled the window out to get a hold of it. To pull the window out generally leaves some sort of prints on the inside of the window from fingers or gloves. Examine the entire window frame looking for the pry mark. Sometimes high-theft vehicles have been broken into so many times that the paint cracks and chips away at the stress point where the window frame meets the door. This type of damage can be seen while driving by and viewing the open door as depicted in photo 11.

Some suspects prefer not to use keys at all to unlock the door. These suspects frequently use a favorite straight edge screwdriver, ice pick, or knife. Many door handle mechanisms are made of plastic and inserted into the metal door. A door is only as strong as its weakest point; thieves take advantage of this principle and breach the area between the plastic door handle insert and the metal door.

Sliding their screwdriver or knife between the plastic and door allows them to get the blade under the locking mechanism and unlock the door. This type of entry is generally visible as the screwdriver or knife makes marks in the doors metal as it is sliding, pushing or pulling as depicted in photo 12. Marks may also be visible on the internal workings of the lock mechanism.

Photo 12

Some suspects will still break a window to gain entry. This is generally not the preferred method, as it is more obvious to law enforcement, and they don't want to be sitting on glass while they are driving a stolen vehicle. The quietest method to break a car window is to attack a side window. The front windshields generally have a safety glazing material that makes them difficult to shatter, whereas the side glass is tempered and shatters into tiny pieces.

The easiest way to break a car side window without personally touching it is with ceramic or porcelain chips from a spark plug. Auto thieves will break the ceramic material around a spark plug into small pieces. Throwing one of these chips with moderate force will cause the window to shatter very quietly to allow entry. Some suspects refer to these ceramic chips as ninja rocks or magic rocks. It is generally difficult to determine if the porcelain chips were used, as the pieces are small and difficult (not impossible) to find after throwing (these chips have been added to some states definitions of "burglar tools").

Another popular method is to use a spring-loaded center punch. The safe way suspects use this tool is to place it in the corner of a side window and push. Pressing in the corner helps them to keep their hand from going through the glass and getting cut. Evidence of this type of entry can sometimes be seen from the part of glass the punch first hits. Both of the above methods are frequently used to enter a car if an alarm is suspected and they just want to burglarize the vehicle and not steal it. Shattering the window may not cause a vehicle alarm to go off. If the window has tinting on it, then using the spring-loaded center punch will keep the entire window intact and allow the suspect to pry it out as one piece. Some suspects will tape the window with duct tape to prevent the pieces from falling into the car. There are a host of other methods of entry depending on the sophistication of the vehicle's electronics and security systems.

The majority of all new cars today are supplied with a remote keyless entry system to unlock the doors and turn off the alarm. Most use a radio frequency to send the signal and a few use infrared. There have been verified reports of other frequencies causing interference, creating vulnerabilities in the system. Personally, I have pressed my key fob for my car and activated the alarms of nearby vehicles. We have all heard stories of suspects using jamming signals that intentionally prevent an owner from locking his car when he pushes his key fob. For vehicles than do not use a rolling code key fob system, it is possible for a nearby thief to capture the code when the key fob is pressed (most new cars have rolling codes). Once captured, he can then send the signal back to the vehicle telling it to unlock the doors.

Inside the Car

Once the vehicle is entered, the thief works on defeating the ignition and steering mechanism. One of the first things I do on every recovered stolen vehicle I inspect is to grab the steering wheel and see if it is in the locked position. If the steering wheel is locked and does not turn, then you must determine how the suspect steered the car once it was stolen. The locking steering wheel must be defeated (there are, however, more cars each year that are manufactured without locking steering wheels). Many Japanese vehicles have a metal pin that rests inside the steering wheel shaft to lock it in place. This locking device may be part of the ignition assembly.

Photo 13

79

A plastic steering wheel assembly cover covers most of these ignition lock assemblies. Suspects can generally pry the lower plastic piece away exposing the ignition assembly and steering wheel lock. The inside of this plastic cover can be a good source of fingerprints as demonstrated in photo 13.

Ignition assemblies are frequently made of a metal that can be easily broken with a hammer or pry tool. Breaking this metal causes the steering wheel locking pin to drop with the assembly and allow easy access to the ignition. Many of the Japanese ignition assemblies contain a plastic insert (relay) on the opposite side of the ignition that is held in with one or two screws. Unscrewing this plastic relay exposes an area where a screwdriver can be inserted and the car can be started and driven away (on cars without transponders).

After freeing the steering wheel and accessing the ignition one must make sure the transmission does not have any type of mechanical or electronic lock. If the transmission is locked, you must determine how the car was driven away.

Ignition bypasses such as these are generally obvious because of the broken parts hanging down or resting on the floorboard. However, don't be fooled by a fraudster. Some insureds who are staging their own vehicle theft know what a good theft looks like. We have seen cases where everything at first glance appeared to look like a real theft, but upon closer inspection, we noticed that nothing was broken, such as the plastic steering shroud or steering wheel locking pin – everything had been carefully unbolted. Thieves don't care if a piece of plastic gets broken, but someone staging their own theft might.

Of course, as mentioned early in this chapter, an older Japanese vehicles ignition system can be defeated with the use of a jiggle key and there may be no obvious signs of defeat. In these cases, you should examine the lock wafers to see if a jiggle key was used.

We have seen countless methods of entry and bypass. As previously mentioned, some methods of theft are area or city specific. Others are suspect or gang specific. We were investigating a group of thieves that were stealing older, unprofitable, and undesirable types of vehicles. When asked why they wasted their time on such vehicles they indicated those makes and models were what they were taught how to steal and they were comfortable in stealing them. Knowing why a vehicle is stolen will aide in your investigation substantially. Vans are frequently stolen to assist in other crimes such as burglaries, or they may be stolen to have a vehicle large enough to transport a group of friends to the beach. Oldsmobile Cutlass, Buick Regal, Chevrolet Monte Carlos, and older Cadillac's may be preferred by gang members due to their status and size. Neons have been popular among those who are addicted to drugs for both transportation and trade. Honda Accords may be popular with crooked body shops who want their stolen parts to fix their customers' cars.

If your state is close to the border and there is a demand for the vehicle in the border country, chances are you will not see the vehicle again. Each bordering state may experience different vehicle losses and MO. Arizona may recover more four-wheel drive U.S. stolens after they have been gutted and modified to use for smuggling in undocumented citizens. This would let their investigators know they are working with thieves referred to as Coyotes. If a Dodge Caravan was recovered with the rear interior missing and a smell of gas and oil, the first thought for some investigators on who stole this van might be motorcycle thieves (vans are frequently used to transport stolen motorcycles).

Know your area, know your players, know your makes and models, and you will know your suspects, whether it is a real thief or an owner give-up.

Transponder Keys and Theft

There are many types and variations of anti-theft transponder/immobilizer systems on the market. The word transponder comes from the words transmitter and responder. Without going into detail on each type, we will generalize about how they work and what to look for. There can be two to four components. The majority of cars sold today have a key with a transponder in it, (radio frequency identification chip, RFID); an induction coil (antenna of sorts) around the ignition that communicates with the key; and a computer in the vehicle that receives communication from the antenna telling it the code from the key. These Magnetic Coupled Transponder systems are passive, thus do not have their own power, and the key must be in close proximity to the antenna to communicate at the 125 kHz frequency range.

If the computer recognizes the code from the key, it will send a signal allowing the car to start. Without the correct transponder (chip in the key), the car will be immobilized. Some keys manufactured today no longer have the mechanical key cut, they instead rely only on the transponder to activate the system and allow the vehicle to start. Most systems will immobilize the fuel, starter, or both, if the incorrect key or transponder is used.

Older keys use the same code continually, which made it possible for suspects to use code grabbers to electronically capture the code and bypass or clone it. Many of today's vehicles utilize what is referred to as a rolling code, which means that the code changes with each use of the key, making conventional code grabbing devices useless. Without the correct code, the car will not start. Rolling codes are also used with keyless entry devices on most models today.

If you want to test the transponder system on your personal vehicle, you can wrap a heavy piece of foil completely around the plastic head of your car key. This foil prohibits the transponder chip embedded in the key from transmitting to the antenna. In most cases, you will be able to crank the engine but the car will not start as the fuel has been disabled. You can also do this if you are testing the effectiveness of a transponder on a recovered car to ensure the system was working at the time of theft. You must make sure the foil is thick enough and covers the entire key head, or to be safe you could use a non-programmed key or a cut key that has no chip in it. *Bypassing the transponder system is explained in more detail in the Immobilizers & Transponders Bypass section following this section.*

Since transponders can make it impossible to steal the car with a jiggle key alone, suspects have devised ways to obtain their own working transponder key. When vehicles are assembled, only a set number of keys are programmed to operate the vehicle. Several vehicle types store that data in a vehicle's computer. In most cases, if a vehicle owner wants to add or replace a key to their car, they will need to have a dealership or locksmith use electronic devices that will allow the new key to be recognized by the vehicle. Author Michael Hyde of National Auto Lock has written several books detailing which vehicles have transponders and what is necessary to make keys for them, for more information go to www.vintrack.com/transponders.htm.

Many manufacturers have to allow for the reprogramming of the immobilizer's system to add keys to the vehicle or in case keys are lost or parts are damaged. Manufacturers are stuck in the middle many times between creating a secure system and keeping costs down for consumers. Some manufacturers created such secure systems that vehicle owners and locksmiths complained about how much it costs to have replacement keys made on vehicles equipped with immobilizers.

Because some vehicle manufacturers required the registered owners to bring the vehicle to a dealership to have a key added or made, California signed into law Senate Bill 1542, requiring automobile manufacturers to allow registered locksmiths, on behalf of the registered owner, to obtain the necessary information to make a working key or start the car without dealership involvement. This process was to be implemented for 2008 model year vehicles. Manufacturers such as Mercedes, that previously never allowed locksmith access to their key systems, were given until 2013 to comply. In addition, manufacturers that sell less than 2,500 cars were exempt. Other states have been working on similar laws. The National Automotive Service Task Force (NASTF, www.nastf.org) became involved in working with the implementation of this process under the program Secure Data Release Model (SDRM).

There will always be a need to be able to add or subtract keys from a system. It is inevitable that some vehicle owners will lose their keys and need new ones made, or the electronics that go into creating immobilizer systems can go bad and need replacing. Because of this, manufacturers have protocols that allow them to modify, change, or bypass immobilizers. Some manufacturers have built-in software backdoors in case they need to get around a key issue. This information can be accessed by anyone who knows where to look. In addition to published data, hackers are continually looking at ways to defeat immobilizers and reverse engineer software.

Thieves will exploit this need for replacement keys and employ scams to get keys to someone else's vehicle. Personally, I have written down a VIN, ordered a key for that VIN, then unlocked the car and programmed the key to work with the immobilizer and drive the car away without any special tools. I have seen numerous television news shows and newspaper articles explaining how to get a key made to someone else's vehicle. Because of the ease of this process, some states have made it a felony for a dealership to make a copy of a key without proper identification.

During the investigation of an auto theft, the victim should be asked to provide the insurance company with all sets of keys they own. When examining the keys submitted, the investigator should ensure they are original issue and not replacement keys. Sometimes replacement keys are marked with special identifiers to assist in this determination. Comparing the insured's key with an OEM key may provide clues. The investigator should know how many keys were originally issued to the owner from the dealership and if they are transponder based.

For example, if a Volvo dealership issued two sets of keys with one valet key when the car was purchased, then that is what the owner should turn in. The owner should also be asked if they have had any additional keys "ever" made for the vehicle. Once the vehicle is recovered, the vehicle computers should be checked to determine how many sets of keys are programmed to work the vehicle. (Not all vehicles store this data, but dealership records may show if extra keys have been added). If it is determined four sets of keys have been programmed to a three-key vehicle, then the investigator needs to determine when the fourth key was added and by whom. If keys have been added or deleted, check to see if all of the insured's keys work with the vehicle. Some systems delete original working keys when they are modified to add new keys. There has been increasing security regarding replacement keys and some states require vehicle dealerships to maintain copies of records for many years when a vehicle owner requests a duplicate key.

Vehicle owners who leave their valet key in the vehicle glove compartment are frequently victimized by auto theft. Suspects frequently check the glove box for such a key, which gives them a working transponder key to steal the car. One vehicle manufacturer had a snap in the vehicle owner's manual in which to attach the valet key. Most of these owners kept this manual in the glove compartment. These cars soon became the target of theft by a group of car thieves that learned of this irresponsible practice. When the thieves were identified and search warrants served, it was discovered that the suspects had access to several hundred different car keys and their group was responsible for hundreds of car thefts.

We have seen many cases in which the suspects are operating out of car dealerships, lube stations, repair facilities, and other businesses in which the keys are surrendered for a short period of time. Auto theft suspects employed by such places have gone through the glove boxes of customer's cars to look for valet keys. Also included in glove boxes for these suspects is the home address, which is generally located on the vehicle registration. Armed with the home address and key, they then steal the car later. Patterns develop and are traceable when several cars are stolen and it is determined that they were serviced at the same shop.

There are a variety of tools that can be used to determine if the systems have been hacked, changed, bypassed, or if different keys were used. The computers and electronics involved are emerging technologies that we are studying and using to identify theft and fraud.

Immobilizers, Transponders and Bypasses

Most of the newer systems cannot be defeated with a jiggle key or by cracking the steering column, due to the transponder systems we just discussed. Other methods and techniques have to be utilized. As with the bypassing of mechanical systems such as key door locks and ignitions, bypassing a transponder system frequently leaves some clues behind. Visualize each method described below and think about what clues would be left behind for you to discover the method of entry and defeat.

Immobilizers have, and will continue to be, instrumental in deterring auto theft. When GM introduced their first immobilizer type system in the 1980s, the theft rate on Chevy Camaros dropped dramatically. Ford experienced a 75% drop in thefts of its Mustangs when their immobilizers were first added. Most anti-theft devices such as immobilizers have an immediate effect on deterring auto theft. However, once the anti-theft system has been on the market long enough, word gets out on how to bypass the system.

When the Lexus was still fairly new, investigators were told, and believed, that the ignition could not be bypassed. The "experts" told us that if someone tried to bypass the door locks or ignition, the system would shut down to prevent theft. Even though these Lexus vehicles did not have a transponder, this was touted as a secure system. In the mid-90s, when I was investigating a Lexus theft/recovery in San Jose California, the door lock was damaged and the ignition looked like it had been punched. The insurance company that was processing the claim suspected the insured because, like most everyone else at the time, they thought the system could not be bypassed. Asking questions about this Lexus recovery locally didn't get me the answers I needed. I talked to auto theft investigators in Florida and learned they had been experiencing these Lexus theft/recoveries for some time, and one of their suspects had recently moved to the area where I recovered this Lexus. After speaking with the investigator in Florida, I was surprised to find out how relatively easy it was to bypass this Lexus door and ignition system. Previously when we would recover one of these vehicles, and it was obvious that the system had been tampered with, we suspected the insured. Cases like these are great lessons for all investigators to continue sharing information with each other and to remain open minded as to defeating security systems.

In 2002, an auto theft task force in Southern California (CECATS) had a rash of Lexus thefts where, upon recovery, there were no apparent signs of forced entry. After arresting several suspects, they learned that a "milled" key was being used, yet another way to steal a car that "they" said could not be stolen.

I first learned how to bypass the immobilizer systems in Honda and Acura vehicles from suspects and those in the aftermarket industry. I heard subjects talking about reprogramming immobilizer keys by using the emergency brake on a vehicle. I thought to myself that I was hearing another urban legend and that it wasn't possible, but almost a year later I saw a technical service bulletin from a manufacturer explaining the procedure to reprogram a key using the emergency brake.

In 2005, I was speaking to a service technician of another manufacturer. He showed me the procedure to reprogram a key to a particular make of vehicle, which utilized opening certain doors and locking certain doors as part of the procedure. Another method involved the gas and brake pedals. Over the years, I have seen a variety of ways to bypass immobilizers, also known as backdoors. All investigators should keep this in mind when determining if the reported theft is real or an owner give-up. Even if they used a backdoor, there may be evidence left behind.

We make it a point to try to bypass new systems before the thieves learn how. Too frequently, we learn how systems are defeated and cars are stolen from suspects after they are arrested. Instead of waiting, we can be proactive and learn how systems work before hand. Knowing how a system is defeated can help an investigator get to the appropriate chop shop or ring sooner and prevent insurance companies from pursuing a case as "owner give-up" when in fact it was a real theft.

Many vehicles are made and distributed to other countries long before they come to America. Japan, Europe, and Australia may get their vehicles up to five years ahead of the United States.

Knowing this can help you in understanding how a "new" vehicle is stolen. When the Subaru WRX first came to the United States, we didn't know how someone could steal this immobilizer system. Speaking with fellow Australian IAATI members gave us great insight, as they had experienced theft recoveries on this vehicle for the previous five years. Now, when I see what I think is a "new" trend, I send out an email to my counterparts here and across the world asking if they have already seen this. The information you get back can save you hundreds of man-hours in investigations and point you to the right direction to the chop shop or organization.

Once you determine how a vehicle is being stolen, work with the vehicle manufacturer's research and development department on improving the systems. Honda of America has been extremely responsive to fixing potential weaknesses when provided with our findings.

For detailed information on immobilizers, contact your favorite locksmith, forensic locksmith, auto theft investigator, or our group. Be very careful when receiving information from anyone on how something can or can't be bypassed. The key, lock, and immobilizer industry can change quickly without warning.

A large police department in California was investigating a stolen vehicle that was used in a drive-by shooting in which someone was murdered. The vehicle in question was reported stolen by the owner. A question arose on whether it was equipped with an immobilizer. The inspector in charge of the auto theft investigation was told by several forensic locksmiths that the vehicle in question was so equipped. They based their information on the color of the key. Everyone in the industry at the time knew that the color of key for this vehicle meant that it did have an immobilizer. The inspector wasn't satisfied with this answer and kept asking questions throughout the industry. One day he got a call from a forensic locksmith who had spoken with the particular key manufacturer. It turns out that this key manufacturer had changed the color of the key and no one in the industry had been told.

One of the things I love about auto theft investigation is that the vehicle systems are constantly changing and suspects are reacting to those changes by learning how to defeat them. We are becoming more involved with manufacturers, assisting them to build systems that will not be so easily defeated. Once again, we look to the weakest link in the chain to determine how strong the system is.

We look at cars as evolving rolling computers, with some vehicles having over 100 microprocessors. As with any computer, it has vulnerabilities. Hacking a car's computer is becoming a necessity and a valuable asset. Most of the good transponder systems may have a rolling code that has trillions of possibilities. Investigators and manufacturers tend to focus on the trillions of possibilities and give up, instead of looking for the weak link as suspects do. Some of the most secure government computer systems in the world can be hacked; so too can a vehicles' computer or immobilizer.

Some 21st century auto thieves carry immobilizer components with them as part of their tool bag. This could consist of a Key, Antenna, and Computer (Engine Control Unit or ECU) for a particular make of vehicle that all match. Photo 14 is an ECU and key set from an Acura.

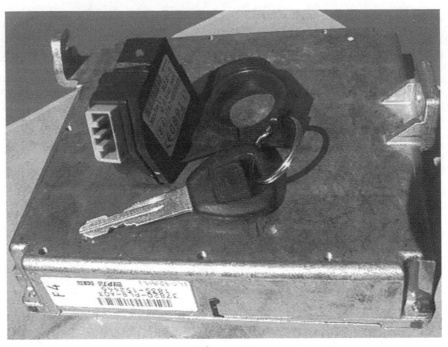

Photo 14

Other common acronyms for ECU are ECM, Engine Control Module; PCM, Powertrain Control Module; and BCM, Body Control Module. Typically, these are obtained from salvaged vehicles, but many are from stolen vehicles. We receive reports from enthusiasts across the country that their ECUs were stolen from their cars. Some enthusiasts with popular cars may be the victim of ECU thefts multiple times from the same car. Others have reported that their local car dealerships have had to carry extra inventory on ECUs due to the high demand.

If there are just three things keeping thieves from stealing a car (key, antenna, and ECU), they may bring their own and swap them into the intended target vehicle. If a suspect is found to be in possession of these items, he could be charged with possession of burglary tools depending on the circumstances.

When tuners change from an older engine to a newer engine, they frequently need to bypass the immobilizer system that the newer engine works with. In cases where the immobilizer system needs to be bypassed, some tuners, as well as thieves, will use a similar ECU that has had the immobilizer removed. In these cases, it doesn't matter if the wrong transponder key is used, as the ECU is no longer looking for the correct code.

Older ECU systems (OBD-I, prior to 1996) typically did not use immobilizers. Some tuners (and thieves) may remove the newer stock ECU (OBD-II) and use an older one with a "Jumper" wire harness that would allow the older ECU to connect to the newer electrical connections. Photo 15 depicts a jumper wire harness that allows an OBD-I ECU to plug into the existing OBD-II plugs.

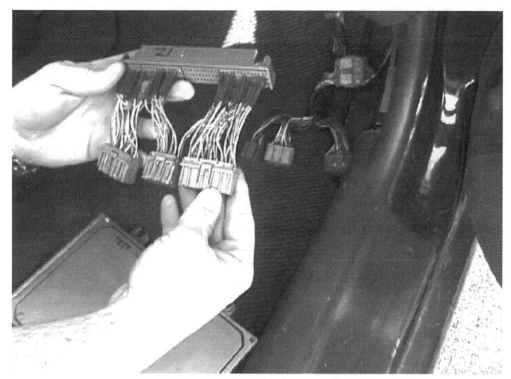

Photo 15

Jumpers or wiring harnesses may also be used when model year changes require different connectors; a 2002-2004 RSX ECU would need a jumper to work with 2005-2006 RSX connectors. Using an older ECU that doesn't have an immobilizer in it can allow the vehicle to drive without a transponder key. Some auto thieves use a jumper and ECU to bypass systems and steal cars. In this type of scenario, the thieves would unplug the OBD-II ECU and plug in the OBD-I ECU or an OBD-II ECU that has had the immobilizer chip removed. This type of ECU swap only disables the immobilizer. The thieves would still need to bring their own key or peel the steering column, break the steering lock and turn the ignition relay.

On Board Emissions Diagnostics Systems II, OBD-II, is a federal standard for the United States and several other countries. It began in the 1990s but by 1996, all vehicles in the U.S. had to have it. OBD-II changed the way a vehicle operates by putting limits and controls on several areas of the engine. Most tuners do not want these controls thus ECUs are frequently modified by them to increase power and performance. Adding a new exhaust system may only bring a couple of extra horsepower. However, if you adjust the ECU to work with the new exhaust system the power gains become much higher. Typically, when a vehicle starts to slide and lose control, the vehicle's computers will take over and correct the problem. This type of safety intervention frustrates drifters, racers, and those who want to have a great burnout. Modifying an ECU can not only give someone more power but it can also contribute to engine damage if done incorrectly.

Gone are the days of listening to the engine and turning a screw to tune the car. To have a finely tuned modified vehicle requires someone who knows cars, personal computers, and great knowledge on the vehicles' computer. Personal computers at a racetrack are just as common as wrenches these days. Armed with a laptop and data logging program, one can best adjust the timing, rev-limit, boost, and make many other performance-enhancing modifications.

One well-respected aftermarket ECU company is Hondata. They specialize in Honda/Acura ECUs. Through their research, they have learned how to get the most out of an ECU without the limits imposed by the government via OBD and emissions. There are many aftermarket companies that piggyback ECUs, and some that replace them entirely. Hondata modifies existing Honda ECUs to enable them to work with a tuners' changes. Since ECUs are frequently tweaked to make a vehicle run better, they are frequently damaged.

The tuner market has created a high demand for ECUs and thus they have become the target of thefts throughout the country. Some ECU modification companies require that the owner send in their ECU for modifications. To avoid this downtime, some dishonest tuners steal ECUs and send them in to be modified. If you are working a case in which numerous ECUs are recovered, there may be ways to determine who the victim is. Several auto theft suspects that have been arrested were using these modified ECUs to steal cars as the immobilizers had been removed. Contact us for additional information regarding these types of cases.

When investigating a possible transponder bypass, make sure you question many different sources about how the system could have been bypassed. With heavy engine modifications occurring, some aftermarket ECUs bypass the factory immobilizer system. Always ask the victim of a car theft about any modifications that they may have had done. This includes asking about remote start systems that have been installed, as many of them bypass the immobilizer permanently.

Almost every method discussed regarding bypassing an immobilizer system will leave some sort of clue. Look at the immobilizer controls such as the key, antenna, and ECU or theft module. Also, look at each area that the immobilizer system is disabling, such as fuel or ignition/spark. Many systems just disable the fuel, so some suspects make sure the car is getting fuel by jumping the fuel cut-off relay in the fuse box area of some vehicles.

On many improper bypasses, the "Check Engine, Security, Theft, or Immobilizer" instrument light will come on. Always check to ensure that the electronic systems are functioning properly. There have also been instances when the immobilizer system itself becomes faulty, thus making the vehicle vulnerable to theft. Check for any stored diagnostic trouble codes (DTC) within the vehicle's computer system, as they provide clues to the vehicles vulnerability to theft. We have seen cases in which the stored DTC indicated a faulty immobilizer. Check with the National Highway Traffic Safety Agency (NHTSA) to see if there are any recalls or known issues with the particular vehicle you are inspecting. Technical Service Bulletins (TSB) are also a good source of information regarding vehicle issues that could compromise systems.

There are many aftermarket engine diagnostic readers available. As of this writing, we have not found one aftermarket product that can read all of the data useful to an investigation. The only way to get that data is take the vehicle to a dealership, find the right technician, and have them use their vehicle-specific computers to read everything. Periodic checks at www.VINtrack.com may reveal some useful theft detection tools.

Today's vehicles are becoming more computerized. In 2003, California Air Resources Board (CARB) allowed Controller Area Networks (CAN) systems added to vehicles and wanted to see all vehicles implement CAN by 2008. CAN systems make the vehicle more like a computer network than ever before. Depending on a vehicle make, there may be forty CAN modules throughout a vehicle connected by network wires. These modules have their own tasks but all should work together like any other computer network. CAN systems can be more difficult to bypass and may require different tools and software.

Alarms

Although there are many varieties of alarms on the market, many of them follow the same general principal for protecting a vehicle. A myriad of techniques are used by suspects to quickly defeat alarms. Most of the methods they use will leave a clue behind so an investigator can confirm if the alarm was active when stolen. Society, for the most part, has become immune to many audible alarms. They go off with such frequency that people tend to ignore them, giving a legitimate thief the extra time he needs to defeat the siren/alarm portion if he does activate it. Alarmed vehicles parked at residences are frequently set off by the thieves until the owner gets so frustrated he turns the alarm off. Once he does this, the thieves go to work and steal the car. Some victims state their alarm was active when in fact it was not.

One ring of auto thieves we were working explained their primary method of attacking the alarm: One suspect would stand with his hands on the hood in a ready position (good source of prints). Another suspect would silently gain entry into the car to access the hood release (some vehicles design make it possible for suspects to access the hood release from outside the vehicle). Once the hood release was activated, the suspect quickly cut the power to the alarm's siren or horn. Several other methods are also used, but a good investigation will include checking the integrity of the alarm when the vehicle is recovered to see if still functions. This includes checking for blown fuses.

When investigating such claims, contact the manufacturer of the alarm and run your particular auto theft scenario by them to assist in looking for clues. Most manufacturers will tell you their systems cannot be defeated, particularly after-market dealerships. However, some of the best suspects used to be alarm installers and know exactly how to defeat them. A good investigator should keep track of what types of alarms are being compromised and who may have originally installed the system. There have been cases where dishonest alarm installers have programmed their own remote to a customer's car so they could enter the car later. It may not be advantageous to advertise the type of alarm you have installed, as an experienced thief will then know what it takes to defeat it. Some experts recommend putting a different alarm manufacturers sticker on your car to confuse potential thieves.

Transportation Alternatives reported that in 1997, the non-profit Highway Loss Data Institute (HLDI) surveyed insurance claims data from 73 million vehicles, to see which devices could prevent theft. Looking at cars from many different model years, across the country, the study concluded that cars with alarms "show no overall reduction in theft losses" compared to cars without alarms. See Chapter 8 for additional information on theft prevention.

Chop Shops

Throughout this book, there are examples of how chop shops have been identified during street racing operations. "Chop shop" is a term typically used when a person is responsible for taking possession of two or more stolen vehicles to change their identity or to dismantle and sell the individual parts of the car. Chop Shops are not always "shops"; they can be located at someone's home, in a parking lot, at a business, or overseas. We have seen cars taken to a chop shop and completely dismantled in less than 45 minutes. Some insurance companies conduct demonstrations in which, without any power tools, they dismantle a vehicle of its interior, doors, hood, trunk, tires, and wheels in less than 10 minutes.

There are many chop shops operating within residential areas. Frequently, we see a young suspect operating a chop shop out of his parent's home without their knowledge or consent. While working as an auto theft detective, I received information that there was a Porsche chop shop operating in a nice residential neighborhood. This information came from an outside source and the neighborhood was completely unaware of his activity. We received information that the resident had a team of thieves who would steal the Porsches and drive them to his house late at night.

After several weeks of staking out the suspect's residence, I saw his garage door open and around the corner came a nice 911 Porsche. The car entered the garage with the door closing quickly behind him. The door opened again later that day and a truck exited the garage with items in the bed covered by a tarp. While the garage opened and closed, I was able to see various pieces of porsches throughout the garage.

I immediately notified my partner, who started working on a search warrant, while I followed the truck. The truck went to a remote area in the mountains and the driver started disposing of Porsche pieces into the field. When back up arrived, the pieces were identified as belonging to stolen porsches from the Los Angeles area.

With a search warrant in hand, we went back to the house and entered the garage, discovering numerous Porsche parts belonging to more than 20 stolen Porsches. The suspect would take an electric saw to a $130,000 Porsche, and cut off the flared fenders and dismantle the rest of the car, truly fitting the term chop shop. This case typified the speed and anonymity to which a chop shop can operate within a residential area without raising suspicion.

Chop shops are not difficult to find. One way to find them is the old-fashioned pin map approach. Every time a vehicle is recovered, put a pin in a map at the location of recovery. After a while, you will see a pattern where stolen vehicles are being dumped. Typically, the suspect chop shop is somewhere within a one-mile radius.

One such pin map revealed cars being recovered stripped in an area close to a performance shop. One of the recoveries was of a rare Type-R Integra that had been stripped of some unique identifiable parts. Those parts were later seen for sale at the performance shop located near the site of recovery. Further investigation revealed that the shop was placing orders for stolen parts to cut their operating costs.

There are a couple of exceptions to take into consideration. If there is gang activity in one of these areas, it may be a rival gang dumping cars near the others turf to trick law enforcement into thinking that it is the other gang operating as the chop shop. Another exception is in certain canyon areas where people start seeing cars at the bottom of a ravine and they get the same idea to dump their cars there.

Sometimes the statistics are not the only indicators you should be looking at to determine problem areas when it comes to theft and fraud. If you want to get an idea of what additional theft and fraud problems you are facing, go to your local auction or salvage yard. Look around to see what the majority of cars are that are being salvaged. When I first started working auto theft and fraud in Arizona, there was only one sport compact car listed on the top ten stolen list, so it appeared that there was not a problem in that state. However, while visiting an auction yard, I noticed a high percentage of sport compact cars in varying degrees of damage; most of them were theft recoveries. I asked the yard manager if he remembered any sport compact salvage buyers who stood out. He stated that there was one young buyer who was buying a lot of the totally stripped sport compact cars. Frequently, visits to individual buyers like these will reveal a chop shop.

Some chop shop suspects will steal a car, strip the parts off it, and dump the frame in an area where it will be discovered quickly. Once the recovered car is taken to the salvage yard, the same thieve will bid on the shell to buy, as he already has the parts to it that he stripped off. In doing this he, gets a clean title, as the car has been recovered and taken out of the system. He buys the car for a small amount of money, because it is stripped of all its parts, but gets to sell it at a considerable profit because he is using the parts he stole off it to make it complete again. Some thieves report making $12,000 per car doing this. One of the first clues to this emerging problem is the number of speed or performance shops opening up in your area. As the shops grow, so may the theft and fraud. Good questions lead to great chop shops.

If a surgical strip is recovered and sent to an auction for sale, that vehicle should be flagged for latter follow up. The insurance company or law enforcement should track the vehicle to where it was sold and re-inspect it to make sure the vehicle was not put back together with the original stolen parts. Frequently, this type of follow up leads to a chop shop. On any vehicle inspection, ensure that all parts are examined and belong to the vehicle. Don't just stop your investigation because you have identified a stolen engine or transmission; look at all the parts including the airbags, seats, doors, and any other item needed to rebuild or fix a vehicle.

For example, several traffic enforcement officers who had been to our training had stopped a vehicle due to a modified exhaust system. Instead of just issuing a citation for the modified exhaust, they determined the engine and transmission were also stolen. Once at the tow yard, they inspected all of the components and discovered that the airbags, airbag sensors, seats, fenders, and trunk lid were also stolen from other vehicles. One traffic citation turned into a recovery of several stolen components and the identification of a chop shop. Instead of one traffic citation for modified exhaust, they were able to get a potential street racer off the streets and locate a chop shop.

Hundreds of chop shops have been indentified and busted because of diligent follow up stemming from street racing enforcement operations. This occurs with the most success when traffic enforcement officers include auto theft investigators during the operations or when they allow them to inspect any impounded vehicles. During the Riverside operation discussed in Chapter 7, auto theft task force detectives identified several stolen engines and transmissions at the scene. Over the following few weeks, they visited some of the suspects' homes, as well as the homes of their friends, and located three chop shops and recovered additional stolen property.

Keeping the Car, Changing the Numbers

VIN-switch, Re-Plate, Re-Tag, Re-Birth, Re-Number, Clone, Switch…These are just some of the terms used to describe a vehicle that has had its Vehicle Identification Numbers changed. Most of the VIN-switched sport compact cars we have seen involve enthusiasts that crashed their vehicles and needed a new body. They steal a like car, swap out their engine and transmission (if it is better than the stolen car's) and put the identifying numbers from their crashed car onto the stolen car.

Frequently, they just change the main numbers such as the Federal Safety Certification Label located on the door or doorpost, the public VIN located on the dash (photo 16), and the body VIN located in the engine compartment (there are many more identifying points that will not be discussed in this book). VINtrack™ software assists law enforcement in determining if VIN numbers have been changed or counterfeited; for additional information, visit www.vintrack.com.

Photo 16

Many times these VIN switches are not as meticulous as those we see from professional auto thieves. They may section in a new firewall number or just cover it with Bondo. The public VIN plates on many of these are easy to change, as many of them are attached to the dash and the suspect just changes the dash and doesn't touch the rivets or VIN plate itself. Matching the interior colors is one way to detect this type of switch.

Investigate every part of a sport compact car to ensure it is safe, legal, and not stolen. Contact your local auto theft detective or us if you have concerns or questions in proper VIN switch investigations.

Chapter 5: Modifications, Personalization, and Fraud

The *Fast and the Fraudulent* world of vehicle modifications not only leads to voided warranties, fraud, and theft; they may also lead to serious injury and death. Many modifications make a vehicle handle better and safer but we are talking about some that are obsession-fed and not necessarily done to make the car safer. The *Fast and the Fraudulent* crowd may want to modify their cars for drag, drift, street, or show. Their desire to create a unique or fast vehicle can be quite costly. This enormous cost has been frequently funded by fraud. When investigating these types of claims, determine for what reason the design and purpose of each modification was made.

The reasons for modifying a car are as unique and as varied as the individual owners of the vehicles. Customization, Personalization, and Individualization are used interchangeably to describe this scene – and the peer pressure involved to stand out. Our young society is caught up in a current-day version of "keeping up with the Joneses." Only the Joneses are MTV, VH1, Reality shows, celebrities, car shows, drag strips, and the dozens of car magazines. Many times, it is more about looking good than going good. The automotive scene is constantly changing, forcing many to constantly modify their cars to stay on top of the game. The "fast and the fraudulent" becomes the "fast and the glamorous" with the amount of money some of these enthusiasts are putting into their vehicles. Many enthusiasts will completely restyle their vehicle for aesthetics even though the modifications may have a functional reason.

As a general rule of thumb, the more expensive the car, the more expensive it will be to modify it. Other factors to consider are the popularity of the vehicle. Civics have been plentiful and much desired, thus aftermarket parts have been plentiful and less costly. The availability of parts frequently dictates the degree to which a model is modified. The majority of the fraud that we see typically occurs with the popular and many times less expensive vehicles. Some tuners start out on a project and then realize there was more to it and they need to spend much more money then they had planned. This type of situation may be a precursor to fraud.

As previously discussed in Chapter 1, the aftermarket parts business is a $38 billion dollar industry. Automobile manufacturers recognized the impact and monetary gain personalization was having on their market and began making cars to fill the need for speed, performance, and style to get some of that $38 billion. In the beginning, there was a battle between the consumer and automakers regarding whether or not aftermarket parts bought and installed by a third party should void a vehicle's warranty. Some thought it was just a way for the automakers to gain control over some of the modifications by providing their own. However, there are many cases when automakers should not honor the warranty for customers who put turbos, nitrous oxide, or complete engine swaps into their vehicles due to the excessive vehicle modifications and shoddy installations.

Depending on the modification, there are times when the vehicle's warranty is voided. When a warranty repair is denied by the automaker for a modification the owner chose to do, we have seen false theft and fraud claims made by the owner hoping to get the insurance company to pay for their mistake. A good investigator will attempt to find a local dealership or service facility to determine if the owner had been turned away for a repair due to modifications.

Trying to pass off racing damage as normal wear and tear or as a defective part is fraud. Many manufacturers offer warranties to cover any repairs to correct defects in material or workmanship. Most exclude repairs that are caused by abuse of the vehicle or damage to any component that is the result of any competition or racing events. Question everything you do not understand. For example, if you notice that the rear license plate or tag is bent, or shows signs of previous bending, ask yourself why. Illegal street racers have purposely bent their license plates down so law enforcement, or other potential witness, cannot read their plates. Some hardcore racers have installed remote switches that lower their plates from within the car to avoid detection. Others frequently put false or paper plates on their vehicles.

Many manufacturers today offer popular accessories and improvements so the consumer does not have to turn to aftermarket parts and risk warranty issues. When installed by the manufacturer, the parts are generally covered under the manufacturer's warranty. However, some manufacturers will sell aftermarket parts that are not intended for the street. Scion offered performance parts from Toyota Racing Development (TRD) and some items, such as the cold-air intake, were marked "off-highway use only" and were not covered by warranty.

The 2008 Scion tC had dozens of TRD accessories available to boost performance and handling that didn't void the warranty. Nissan had its Nismo parts that were divided into categories. The S-tune category included normal upgrades, which were covered under warranty and the R-tune category included drivetrain components that would not be covered. Toyota also coined the term BPU, Basic Performance Upgrades, which included a better exhaust system with enhanced boost.

The aftermarket parts industry rallied with some automobile dealerships and launched an aftermarket parts warranty referred to as ProPledge. If a consumer buys a car from a ProPledge dealership, they can add the performance and accessory upgrades into the price of the car and have it covered under warranty. Determining if the parts in question were covered under warranty can assist in determining MO in many investigations.

After the first *The Fast and the Furious* movie came out in 2001, a variety of agencies reported a measurable increase in theft and fraud involving sport compact vehicles throughout the country. The neon light kits featured in the movie reportedly caused a 1300% increase in their sale after the movie was released. *2 Fast 2 Furious* came out in June of 2003 and graphics were heavily featured. Guess what? Shortly thereafter we saw an increase in graphics similar to those featured in the movie. The third in this series of movies was *The Fast and the Furious, Tokyo Drift*, which came out in June of 2006 and generated the same type of activity related to drifting setups and related accidents. See Chapter 1, "Movies Blamed for Street Racing Deaths" for more information. The fourth installment in this series is reportedly simply titled "Fast and Furious," featuring the tried and true sport compacts, muscle cars, SUVs, and audio-visually modified vehicles, along with new trends that are sure to follow and will be worth monitoring.

Cars are many times modified in stages. We will break down the modifications into three areas: the exterior, the interior, and the engine, as well as explain some of the warranty pitfalls associated with each modification. When examining or inspecting a vehicle that appears modified, do not be shy about asking the owner/driver what has been modified and the modifications purpose. Take an interest in the car from their perspective and you may learn a lot by having them open up about their passion and describe what it is all about.

Some modifications may appear to make the car safer when in fact they create additional dangers. As explained later in this chapter, larger brakes can actually decrease stopping distances. Some enthusiasts install racing seats with 5-point racing harnesses instead of stock seat belts. Many of these harnesses are not installed correctly and increase the risk of injury, particularly harness straps that are mounted at more than a 45-degree angle, as they can cause the shoulder straps to compress the spine.

In 2006, SEMA surveyed close to 5,000 enthusiasts regarding their buying habits and which item they would buy for the vehicle first. They listed air Intake as number one, followed by exhaust kits, custom wheels, window tinting, engine swaps, stereos, suspension, plus size tires, alarms, headers, ECU chip enhancements, floor mats, performance tires, and body kits. The majority of their purchases came from the Internet, followed by custom shops. Sixty-four percent of the enthusiasts listed race vehicles as the type of vehicle they were most interested in; for more information go to www.sema.org.

Whether an item is original equipment manufacture (OEM), a knock-off, copycat, or counterfeit, it can have a substantial impact in your investigation of the circumstances. Price and quality are the main concerns. If an insured were claiming reimbursement for parts, you would not want to pay the value of an OEM part instead of the knock-off price. This happens frequently with wheels, but it applies to anything made, including headers. Counterfeit parts have been growing on the street and can be extremely difficult to distinguish from the real ones and it is best to have the manufacturer view the parts or photos if you have any doubts.

Exterior Modifications

Most research indicates that teens choose a car based on its exterior styling. Exterior changes are frequently the first modifications that are made to a car. Exterior modifications generally comprise the largest expenditure of retail sales in the aftermarket arena. These modifications would include performance tires, wheels, suspension, custom lights, ground effects/body kits, graphics/vinyl/decals, custom exhaust tip, neon lighting, front-end conversions, and custom paint.

Body Kits

Body kits or ground effects come in many materials, shapes, and styles. They can consist of a front and rear bumper, side skirts, wing or spoiler, carbon fiber hood, trunk lid, fenders, door caps, lip kits, and even vertical doors kits. You can buy them in sections or as a complete kit. Some can transform a car to such a degree that it is difficult to determine what make or model the car originally was. The main purpose of the body kits we see is looks, as few truly improve aerodynamics. However, some pieces such as wings, splitters, canards, diffusers or undertrays can have a real impact for some, such as those involved in Time Attacks. Prices vary greatly depending on the quality. You can buy a full kit, which consists of side skirts and front and rear bumpers for as little as $350 to several thousand dollars.

Unfortunately, many of the kits, when installed, are so low to the ground that they make it almost impossible to drive the car without bottoming out. I have seen many cracked kits from the car scraping the ground when trying to enter or exit a driveway. A full body kit can cost several thousand dollars, where as some enthusiasts will add sections at a time, such as side skirts, front or rear fascias, wide body panels, or a carbon fiber hood. As mentioned in Chapter 2 in "Keying," if someone wants to change the look of their car, they may vandalize the car themselves in order to get insurance money to pay for a new kit. Some insureds already have a kit, but it is not a wide body kit, so they will report their current kit "stolen" looking again towards having the insurance company pay for it.

Many body kits are bolted on while others are molded to the body of the car. When claims come in for damage to a body kit and the insurance company covers such aftermarket modifications, the investigator should make sure that the insured is not trying to get more then they deserve. I have seen insureds report body kits stolen when there was no evidence on the car that the particular kit had ever been on it. I investigated another insured that wanted to get reimbursed for the cost of having the kit molded to his car when that type of addition was not covered on the policy.

Although manufacturers of body kits generally take a great deal of time and attention to cooling issues, one should ensure that any front modification did not interfere with the vehicle's cooling by restricting air to the radiator. In some cases, these kits have been proven to increase airflow to the radiator; however, some manufacturers could present issues over warranty coverage claiming that the aftermarket grill was responsible for engine-related damage. In any modified vehicle investigation in which the vehicle is still covered under warranty, pursue the possibility that the owner was turned away from a dealership because he voided the warranty. Too many times, we discovered that the owner has made a false claim for repairs because of warranty coverage issues.

Suspension

Lowering the vehicle can improve handling by lowering the center of gravity, but many times the owner lowers the car for looks. Enthusiasts can spend several thousand dollars by adding full threaded-body coilovers or less than five-hundred dollars for springs and shocks. Some who choose to lower their car may not have or want to spend the money, so they cut their springs, which lower the car. Springs are developed to support a certain amount of weight. When a coil or two are cut, it weakens the spring's ability to hold up the car. People who use lowering springs without changing their shocks will experience premature shock wear. Some people who continue to use their stock shocks with lowering springs may cut their bump-stops (bump-stops are the pad of rubber at the end of the shock to prevent it from bottoming out; *Google "bump-stop" and "coilovers" for photos and more information*).

Lowering a vehicle too much can adversely affect performance and handling. Some coilovers may come with warnings that warn of warranty issues. Some manufacturers have recommended against the fitting of aftermarket shocks and springs to their vehicles if they are still under warranty. Some have invalidated warranties on suspension-related breakages if the modification had occurred.

Brake Upgrades

Big brake upgrades became very popular in 2005 for looks as well as functionality. Proper brakes are important for slowing down from high speeds, but many of the high-end big brakes can actually take longer to bring a daily driven car to a stop. These big breaks become most functional when they are hot, and daily driven cars may not get them to the optimum temperature. With all of the rear end collisions occurring on our streets everyday, the last thing we need are a bunch of cars that take even longer to stop in a panic situation. You should always want to know what every modification is designed for by the manufacturer and what the owner/driver's intention was in installing it. This information can distinguish casual enthusiasts from a hard-core street, drift, or drag racer. If you insure illegal or unsafely modified cars, your exposure to risk increases dramatically.

Be cautious in jumping to conclusions regarding a single modified item, as some just buy the big brakes because of the bright colored calipers and the status and are not involved in racing. Other brake upgrades may include stainless steel brake lines and special brake fluid. Some enthusiasts who cannot afford the brakes may just buy some upgraded pads and rotors, while others just paint their existing calipers to make it look like they have an upgrade. For the Do-It-Yourselfer, this type of installation may create some warranty issues. Big breaks are a major upgrade for the serious performance nut.

Clutches

A good strong clutch is important if you want responsive power and control. Choosing the correct clutch system is imperative to prevent damage down the road. The clutch system includes the pressure plate, flywheel, and clutch disc. Remembering that something is only as strong as the weakest link, too much clutch can cause damage to the axles, differential, or transmission. Investigate further if your insured is using a racing clutch and is making related damage claims.

Engine Modifications

For many, the engine is the heart and soul of the vehicle and can be quite costly and addictive to modify and upgrade. Some of the modifications include engine dress-up kits, cams, throttle bodies, spark, cold air intake, headers, exhaust, turbocharger, supercharger, and nitrous oxide. For many the goal is increased horsepower with the hope of increased speed. Many have taken a vehicle producing 160 horsepower stock and modified it to produce well over 500 horsepower. Unfortunately, in the group we deal with on our streets, this additional power, converted to speed, has led to an increase in deaths and injuries. Insurance companies base their rates on the type of vehicle being insured. A turbocharged, horsepower-producing sports car will most likely cost more to insure than a stock Honda Civic. However, by the time a hard core enthusiast is finished with his vehicle, it far exceeds what the manufacturer intended for that vehicles size and weight as well as what the insurance company originally agreed to insure and on which the premiums were based.

Several studies have shown that more horsepower generally equates to a vehicle being driven faster, which increases the probability of a collision, particularly with sport compact cars (due to the driver's lack of ability and the lightness of the vehicle). The real problem with horsepower increases in these vehicles can be attributed to the young age of these fast and fraudulent drivers and their inability to keep the car within safe speeds.

In 2005 Progressive Insurance conducted a study of horsepower and collisions regarding their insureds over a three year period and found that vehicles with over 200 horsepower were involved in 17% fewer claims (however, when those cars were involved in a collision the resulting payment to the parties involved was 22% higher). In the group that we deal with, more horsepower does equate to more collisions, injuries, and deaths. The majority of cases my colleagues and I have investigated involve cars modified to increase their horsepower. We are not seeing the *stock* 200-plus horsepower vehicles involved in collisions as often as we do vehicles that have been *modified* from their original sub-200 horsepower rating.

According to the U.S. Government's energy statistics in 1980, the average new car had 100 horsepower. In 2004, the average new car had 181 horsepower (an 81% increase). Projections are for continued increases. Google "500 horsepower" and you will find many modified vehicles that are well beyond what any manufacturer intended. There continues to be a horsepower war with many manufacturers. At the 2005 North American International Automotive Show, 18 production cars had more than 500 horsepower, and there are vehicles like the 2008 Dodge Viper at 600 horsepower and the 2009 Chevrolet Corvette ZR-1 at 620 horsepower. Since the Environmental Protection Agency (EPA) recently received the go-ahead from Congress to regulate greenhouse-gas emissions from vehicles, it's too bad that we can't create a green war instead of a horsepower war.

In states such as California, if you are going to modify your vehicle, the parts must be legal and conform to emission laws. Frequently aftermarket items will be labeled "50 state legal" or "C.A.R.B. approved" (California Air Resources Board). If the part does not increase emissions, it is granted an exemption and issued an Executive Order number (EO) which allows the part to be installed on the vehicle. These numbers are generally on the part itself and supporting paperwork is supplied. A list of approved items by category can be found at the Air Resources Board web site at http://www.arb.ca.gov/msprog/aftermkt/devices/amquery.php.

For Japanese vehicles such as Honda or Toyota, American sport compact enthusiasts may want the Japanese version of the engine, which is not allowed in several parts of the United States without some modification. Changing the original engine to a different type than was originally manufactured and installed is often referred to as *swapping, transplant,* or *hybrid.* Modifying parts of the engine such as swapping heads and blocks may be referred to as a *Frankenstein.* The need for more speed or the need to fix a blown engine makes this a common vehicle modification.

In states like California, swapped engines must come from the same year or newer vehicle. It must have the correct emissions components with it, including the ECU. Frequently, vehicles that have had engine swaps, particularly JDM engines, will be referred to a smog referee to ensure that it complies to that states emission laws. For those who live in California, the restrictions are even greater. Even if your vehicle was certified clean in 49 other states, it still has to be certified by California as clean.

The EPA generally allows engine switching as long as the resulting vehicle matches exactly to any certified configuration of the same or newer model year as the chassis. For example, a federal EPA certified (federal or 49-state) engine could not be used in a vehicle that was originally certified for California. The emissions laws generally apply to the latest year; if the vehicle is a 2005 and the engine is a 2007, the 2007 emissions standards apply; if the engine were a 2003, the 2005 standard would apply.

Engine and vehicle classifications may not be degraded either. For example, if you had a Ford F150 truck with a 300 6-cylinder motor, you cannot install a Ford 460 V-8 because this motor was never available for the 1/2 ton Ford truck chassis. It is legal, however, to install a Chevrolet 454 V-8 since this motor was found in the 1/2 ton chassis. Another example would be if a diesel motor was available for the vehicle in the same model year, you could not install it within a chassis that originally had a gasoline motor. Non-Air Resources Board-approved or EPA-certified internal parts could not be used either, nor is voiding the vehicle manufacturer's emission warranty allowed.

The Clean Air Act also prohibits any person from removing or rendering inoperative any emission control device, and fines range from $2,500-$25,000.00. For more information, visit the EPA's website at www.epa.gov/otaq/imports, and click on the engine-switching link on the left side of the web page. In addition to the EPA regulations, many states have their own requirements when it comes to engine switching.

With muscle cars, we would talk about our engines with such terms as big or small block and engine displacement. In high school, I had a 1956 Chevy wagon with a small block V8 bored out to a 409. In speaking with most Japanese vehicle enthusiasts, they refer to their engine by its manufacturer's model number, such as B18C1 for an Acura Integra, K20Z3 for a 2006 Honda Civic, SR20DET for a Nissan Silvia, RB25DET for a Nissan Skyline, 4A-GE for a Toyota Corolla, FC3S for a Mazda RX-7 and 4G63 for a Mitsubishi Lancer.

Common Tuner Modifications

Increased horsepower gains from vehicle modifications vary greatly depending on the type of vehicle and restrictions it has from the factory, as well as the type and quality of the aftermarket components and how they are installed. We will primarily discuss modifications that you can see versus internal modifications such as camshafts (cams). If there are claims in which the engine is ruined, then it may be important to know the internal workings of the engine, for example, if the insured was running a stage three racing cam and the constant high revs were part of the claim, not because someone had "stolen" their car and over revved it.

Take an interest in each vehicle you look at and ask questions. Each modification may have a performance-enhancing purpose, but some may be just because the modification is trendy or for looks. Many of the modifications are to increase the horsepower of the vehicle by changing and adding such things as an air intake systems, header, fuel systems, engine management system, pulley system, and exhaust.

Air Intake

Photo 17

One of the first affordable power upgrades that the tuner can do is to replace the stock air intake. The engine needs to draw in air to be mixed with the fuel for the appropriate combustion. Stock systems consist of a tube and an air box that has a paper air filter. The paper filter is necessary to ensure particles from the air do not reach the internal workings of the engine. All vehicles need air, and with the right tuning, more air equals a faster car. Stock systems may have a tube with several bends and a small air box, and they are designed to be quiet - another reason some tuners do not like them. Some stock systems such as the Subaru WRX are designed for power and efficiency and may be better left alone.

Various enthusiasts just replace the paper air filter with a high flowing filter, which can add up to three horsepower. Some aftermarket filters come with the possibility that the increase in airflow comes with an increase in unwanted particles reaching the engine, providing potential for engine damage. If a vehicle is an Ultra Low Emissions Vehicle (ULEV), using an aftermarket filter may affect the emissions and can be illegal in many states. More commonly, I see what is referred to as a "short ram" style intake, which replaces the stock tube and air box with a short tube and a

102

cone shaped filter at the end (photo 17). For the serious tuner, the length of the tube can make a difference in speed and power, the longer tubes producing more bottom end power and a shorter tube for the top end.

The air box is located within the engine compartment and the filtered air can get quite warm. For this reason, some tuners like to use what is referred to as Cold Air Intake. The intake tube gets direct access to outside, unheated air, which in turns allows for more oxygen and increased horsepower. Tuners with cold air intakes could be considered more into speed.

The intake tube may be routed to the front grill area or use an air ram that sends the air from a hood scoop or similar device into the air box located in the engine compartment. Some cold air intakes end at the bottom of the grill facing the ground as depicted in photo 18.

Photo 18

These types of systems can be quite dangerous in a rainstorm as they can act as a vacuum and suck water directly into the engine. In some cases when this occurs, the owner may make a false theft claim and indicate the "thief" must have damaged the car when he stole it. Some tuners will remove the intake system prior to an inspection by law enforcement or an insurance company because they don't want to draw suspicion to themselves. In these cases there should be clues left behind from the previous modification. Some cold air systems have a bypass valve that helps to prevent this and allows the user to reroute the tube during wet conditions.

As mentioned in Chapter 3 under Sanctioned Drag Events, we have seen cars with one headlight removed to assist with the cold air intake. Numerous daily driven cars have blown their engines while racing at a track. Either unable or unwilling to pay for the damages, the owners roll the cars onto the streets and falsely report them as stolen. When we see these "recovered stolen" vehicles with the single headlight still missing and the intake system removed, you can assume the vehicle may have been modified for racing.

Although there are many factors relating to horsepower increases, one may expect a five to ten horsepower increase with the right air intake system. These systems can also increase gas mileage by one or two miles per gallon, but that is usually negated by the increased horsepower leading to a heavy foot off the line. Add an aftermarket intake manifold, and one may see an additional increase of six to twenty horsepower.

Exhaust Modifications

The exhaust is frequently modified after intake modifications. Stock exhaust manifolds are frequently shaped like a log. This conserves space compared to an aftermarket tubular manifold with its long pipes (or runners) for each exhaust port (also referred to as Headers and depicted in photo 17). This portion of the exhaust modification ends at the catalytic converter. Enthusiasts may continue beyond the catalytic converter, which they refer to as cat-back exhaust. Some racing exhaust systems claim to add five to twenty horsepower.

Headers are a somewhat easy bolt-on modification. The majority of stolen engines I have recovered from these sport compact cars had the stock exhaust replaced with headers. These modifications are easy to determine, as the individual tubes stand out over the log setup that may be concealed with a heat shield. To keep excessive heat from building up in the engine compartment, some tuners wrap the pipes with a silica-based fabric called heat or header wraps.

At some point during this modification project, the tuner may want to add an aftermarket engine-management system. This may piggyback their existing ECU, or they could replace their ECU, which allows direct engine management. Several software packages exist for engine management and allow for a plug-and-play experience that can give control over most tuning changes they make. Some of these changes can invalidate a manufacturer's warranty and could be cause for concern during an investigation. Since many of these systems are PC based, there may be data on an insured's computer hard drive that can assist in determining the cause of an incident. Sometimes these systems are confused with the vehicle's ECU, but they may just be an addition, piggybacking on the ECU.

Turbochargers and Superchargers

Turbochargers (turbos) are the next step from the cold air intake. Many cars come from the factory with turbos. They compress the air going into the engine, allowing more air to flow. More air can equate to more fuel for more power. Exhaust air spins a turbine, which spins an air pump and produces the compressed air or "boost" as it is commonly referred to. That compressed air is then cooled down with an Intercooler. Intercoolers look similar to radiators and they can frequently be seen through the front grill (some are top or side mounted). Superchargers are not as common on the sport compacts we typically deal with, however some models such as the Saturn Ion Redline do come with superchargers. The main difference between a supercharger and a turbocharger is that the supercharger is powered by the engine via a pulley/belt whereas the turbocharger spins from the exhaust air. Superchargers are frequently referred to as Blowers. Forced air induction systems may be used when speaking about turbos or superchargers.

Bolt-on turbochargers have been popular for many years for vehicles that do not come with them. However, problems can arise if the modification is not done correctly. Just providing more boost may not be the answer. Air, fuel, and spark should also be addressed, not boost alone. If the air/fuel mixture is wrong, it can also mean more problems to the pistons or other internal components. To avoid this, some enthusiasts will install aftermarket pistons, rods, fuel pumps, and injectors to avoid the air/fuel mixture from going lean and causing internal engine problems. Some manufacturers promise there will be a 30-60% increase in power with their turbo kits while others can go higher.

Turbo failure is not uncommon, and many enthusiasts only use synthetic oil and have it changed frequently to avoid the issues the additional heat brings. Failing to allow turbos to cool down after a run can cause problems. Some people install turbo timers to monitor when it is safe to shut down the turbo, allowing sufficient cooling.

Frequently when listening to these sport compact vehicles driving around our cities, there is a strange noise heard with the release of the vehicles throttle, generally followed by a shift in gears. This hissing noise comes from a blast of muffled air being released from under the hood through a blow-off valve. Blow-off valves are frequently installed when a turbo is added to the vehicle. The blow-off valve's job is to release the unused boost between shifts. This release goes into the air and may violate emissions laws.

Some turbo-charged vehicles have added water/methanol injection systems to increase boost and help keep the temperatures down. These kits can be identified by a water/methanol plastic reservoir, pump, boost switch, and nozzle to spray the mist into the throttle butterfly.

Nitrous Oxide is used frequently among street and drag racers. The term NOS is commonly used when talking about nitrous oxide. NOS is the brand Nitrous Oxide Systems and does not apply to all systems. In states like California, the use of nitrous is illegal in all but a handful of American cars. Depending on which state the vehicle is registered in, it may be legal to have installed but illegal to have it hooked up while on public highways; in some states, it is illegal for minors to possess. Nitrous Oxide gas used in vehicles is similar to what a dentist may use; however, it contains an odor that is nauseating to prevent huffing and other misuse. Check your local statutes to see what limitations apply in your state (as of this writing the Center for Cognitive Liberty & Ethics published a list of state statutes regarding minors in possession of nitrous oxide at http://www.cognitiveliberty.org/dll/N20_state_laws.htm).

A variety of problems can be associated with the use of nitrous oxide. Typically, the nitrous bottle is mounted in the trunk area and a steel hose carries the gas to the intake of the vehicle. Exceeding bottle pressure of 1100 psi can cause the engine to become excessively lean, resulting in costly engine damage. Stock fuel systems may not be sufficient and may cause the mixture to be too lean and damage the engine. Running lean fuel can cause a variety of internal problems. Some may add high-flow fuel pumps to avoid problems.

In addition to internal engine problems when using nitrous incorrectly, there are other concerns one should be aware of. Nitrous bottles are frequently heated to obtain optimum pressure. Heating may be done with a propane torch or a heating element. If they are overheated or heated too quickly, a catastrophic explosion could occur. Activating the nitrous system without having the engine running may cause an explosion.

The amount of horsepower gained from the previously mentioned modifications varies considerably depending on the vehicle make and the manufacturer's part or modification. Additional factors include how those changes are managed via aftermarket control units or software, other modifications, and even the type of fuel used. High-octane fuel (100+) is desired by many hard-core racers but costs considerably more. It generally has no downside but can be a clue as to how seriously into racing someone is.

Racing fuel is not uncommon and many enthusiasts will display the octane rating as a decal on their car; 100 octane and higher may be bragged about. Several Union 76 gas stations and some independents sell 100-octane race fuel to their customers. As with regular fuel prices, racing fuel prices went up 50% from 2005 to August of 2008 with some paying as much as $8.25 per gallon. This price jump has affected the amount of racing that we saw at the tracks in 2008.

Some racers will purchase 100-octane aviation fuel from airports, which is less expensive but may contain lead. The use of aviation fuel in today's vehicles may damage oxygen sensors and the catalytic convertor. In 1996, the EPA made it illegal to introduce leaded gasoline into a licensed street vehicle. Use of such fuel in the United States was banned by the EPA but there was a moratorium placed on the ban until 2010 (see 40 CFR Part 80 for prohibitions).

To determine the total effect modifications have had on a particular vehicle you are inspecting, you must take all of the above factors into consideration. Many of the changes a tuner makes to the engine are generally designed to provide increases in horsepower. This horsepower increase is frequently measured at the wheels (also referred to as wheel horsepower, or WHP). Dynamometers, generally referred to as "dynos," are used to determine the effect of horsepower increases to the wheels; some refer to them as a chassis dyno. To determine the wheel horsepower, the drive wheels of vehicles are driven onto a set of rollers that measure the power of the wheels as they turn the rollers. A tuner may increase the horsepower of his vehicle 100% but by the time that increase reaches the wheels there could be a loss of 15-20%. Brake, flywheel, or crank horsepower is the measurement of power at the engine, before it goes through the transmission and driveshaft, where it would then be measured at the wheels (WHP).

Put all of the previously mentioned modifications together and a vehicle can produce several hundred additional horsepower. Significant increases in power can drastically change the classification at which insurance carriers initially insure a vehicle, exposing themselves to more liability without the protection of increased premiums.

Black Boxes and Event Data Recorders

Many times a vehicle can tell a story as to what happened to it and why through its electronic components. Today's vehicles contain thousands of bits of information running through internal networks that are being processed, and in some cases stored or even sent electronically to remote locations. Vehicles may be equipped with collision detection hardware or software, such as those used by On Star. Such vehicle data has been used to verify customers' insurance claims regarding vehicle issues. With warranty claims on the rise, manufacturers are scrutinizing the claims to determine the true cause. When a car is brought in for service due to engine problems, a technician may be able to determine if the damage was due to that weekend drag race or other over-revving activity. About 25 million vehicles currently contain such devices and most cars manufactured after 2004 have them installed.

Much has been written lately regarding event recorders that are in vehicles (black boxes). These are also known as Event Data Recorders, Crash Data Recorders, or sensing and diagnostic modules (EDR/CDR/SDM), and they have been around for a long time. Unlike airplane black boxes, these devices do not gather voice recordings. They are the 'brain" of the restraint and air bag system, and come to life generally when the air bags are activated in a frontal crash or near collision based on the g-force (they are usually silver boxes, not black). The data captured from these devices has been able to help safety engineers build safer vehicles. With our lawsuit-happy, finger-pointing society, supporting data is a must to determine product liability versus operator error.

Data recorders are necessary in today's vehicles due to the massive electronics and software used. Recently EDRs have been getting a lot of attention in the media because people are worried about "Big Brother." These devices have evolved to assist vehicle manufacturers in designing safer vehicles. They constantly record everything from speed, seat belt use, and air bag deployment to throttle positions and braking action. Typically the last five seconds prior to a crash or significant g-force (1-2 g's) is recorded. Once data is saved, it is typically retrievable for as long as 250 ignition cycles, or about 40-60 days of driving. (For a list of vehicles and more information on EDR, go to www.boschdiagnostics.com and search for crash data retrieval).

California became the first state to pass a law protecting the privacy of drivers whose vehicles come with "black boxes." The law, signed by Gov. Gray Davis, took effect on July 1, 2004. It stipulated that car owners must be told their cars carry the recorders and says the information can only be downloaded with consent from the driver, a court order, or anonymously for medical or safety research. Section 9951 of the California Vehicle Code requires manufacturers to disclose to customers whether event data recorders or "black boxes" are installed in vehicles. At least 16 other states have enacted similar legislation. Other states have made rulings that the data contained in an EDR belongs to the vehicle's owner and permission must be granted prior to accessing it.

Typically, if the data concerns the vehicle, there are no issues. If the data contains information on the driver, i.e., where the driver was and when, then privacy becomes a concern. Insurance companies typically have a right to ask for the data concerning a claim.

Several cases over the years have resulted in information used to help determine the facts of an accident. On Christmas Eve, 2002, a head-on collision killed the second driver and critically injured the passenger. The offending driver had crossed over the divided highway into oncoming traffic and then fled the scene. EDR data showed the offending driver was traveling at 71 mph in a 40 mph zone and the victim was traveling the speed limit. The suspect was convicted of vehicular manslaughter and sentenced to eight years.

In June 2003, Edwin Matos was sentenced by a Florida judge to 30 years in prison for double vehicular manslaughter. Evidence from a data recorder in his 2002 Pontiac Trans Am helped convict him. Data showed that Matos was going more than 100 mph in a 30-mph zone before his car struck another vehicle and killed two teenagers.

On August 16, 2003, South Dakota authorities used data recorder information from a 1995 Cadillac to make a case against the Governor of the state, William Janklow, who was accused of speeding through a stop sign and killing a motorcyclist. The investigation showed Janklow was traveling at 71-mph in a 55-mph zone and that he had run a stop sign. He was charged with second-degree manslaughter on August 29, 2003. It was reported that permission to access EDR data declined from 75% in 2002 to 38% in 2003, particularly after all of the press involved in this high-profile case mentioned that the EDR helped convict him.

In addition to some state laws, the National Highway Transportation Safety Administration (NHTSA) advised automobile manufacturers to notify owners if their vehicle contains event data recorders. Vehicle manufacturers have begun to add this information to the owner's manual. Insurance companies should also add similar information in the policy to avoid future concerns on how the data will be used.

Some racers use their own aftermarket versions of event data recorders. Much more sophisticated, these devices track their vehicles performance during a race or run. Some companies offer devices that track a variety of information and may refer to them as data loggers (more on data loggers are mentioned in the interior modifications section).

Engine Identification and Swaps

A swapped engine can be a significant factor in evaluating claims involving the Fast and Fraudulent crowd. As mentioned throughout this book, engines are frequently damaged due to illegal racing and modifications. The need for replacement engines is great and brings with it an increased potential for theft and fraud. Honda and Acura have been popular for many years, resulting in an incredible number of used and stolen engines out in the market.

The stock engines in many of these cars are frequently replaced with bigger, newer, faster engines. Sometimes these engines are from vehicles that were never destined for a particular country. This is frequently the case in the United States, where smog laws are strict and out-of-country engines are illegal without following strict guidelines (particularly in California). Many car enthusiasts refer to their vehicles by a portion of the VIN (Vehicle Identification Number). A Civic owner may tell someone that he just performed a swap into his EG Civic. In layman's terms, this means that he put a different engine in his 1992-1995 Honda Civic.

Every vehicle manufactured has a VIN. In countries such as the United States, Mexico and Canada it is a 17 digit VIN; A sample being 2HGEG2257SH123456. If an owner refers to his EG Civic, you can see in this sample that the 4th and 5th digits of this VIN contain the vehicle descriptors of EG. Owners may also refer to this as the chassis code. The fourth through eighth positions of the VIN are referred to as the Vehicle Description Section or VDS (The engine swap table in appendix

B has additional information on VINs). When a vehicle is assembled, the manufacturer records the engine data as it relates to the VIN. This industry standard allows enthusiasts to know if the engine is stock or if it has been swapped; investigators can use the same published information.

VTEC engines were very popular with several Honda and Acura vehicles (VTEC stands for **V**ariable **V**alve **T**iming and Lift **E**lectronic **C**ontrol; starting with the K20A series engines, VTEC added variable timing control and became i-VTEC). Many VTECs have been stolen and have yet to be recovered. VTEC engines typically run in size from 1.6 liters to 3.2 liters and like all Honda/Acura engines, the number designator indicates the engine size. For example, the engine prefix B18C1 indicates a 1.8-liter engine and a K20A3 engine prefix indicates a 2.0-liter engine. Even though the B16A engine is only 1.6 liters, it is still a very popular engine to swap among enthusiasts. Many tuners will refer to the first letter of the engine prefix when talking about their engines using such terms as B or K series. Swapping a D series engine with a B series engine makes for a cost effective modification since D series engines are plentiful.

Some engine swaps are very easy and bolt right in while others require significant vehicle modification. Swapping a dual overhead cam engine into a vehicle that had a single overhead cam can cause the valve cover to hit the hood when closed, creating a small ding that can be seen from the outside of the hood. This can be a clue to discovering an engine swap in a vehicle without having to open the hood.

A complete swap could include the engine, wiring harness, ECU, axels, and custom shift linkage. Immobilizers, Transponders and Bypasses in Chapter 4 discusses additional issues regarding engine swaps that affect the immobilizers and the fact that tuners may have to use jumpers to get the ECU to talk to the rest of the system.

With the introduction of the K-series engine, the B-series will slowly be replaced as a desirable swap. The K-series offered the improved VTEC system (iVTEC), larger ports, and a host of other improvements. Several different types of K-series engines found in the Civic Si, CRV, Accord, Element, RSX, TSX, and the RDX came with a K23A1 turbo engine. They come in 2.0, 2.3, and 2.4 displacements. The most popular has been the K20A2, which came out of the Acura RSX Type-S.

These engines generally do not just bolt right in to older model vehicles. The engine mounts and other components need to be changed. One leader in engine swapping is Hasport in Arizona. Hasport offers mounting kits and engine harnesses for many models. Common mounts are based on the chassis code, which is the forth and fifth digit of the VIN, including the EP (2002-05 Civic), EK (1996-00 Civic), EG (1992-95 Civic), EF (1998-91 Civic), CRX and DC (1994-00 Integra) chassis. A B17A engine is quite a bit larger then the original D-series engine, making a 1988-89 Integra a popular vehicle to own and tune. Hasport mount kits allow the easy installation of the 89-91 B16A, B17A and B18A engines into an 86-89 Integra. A quick clue to a swap might be the after market engine mounts such as Hasport, or obvious modifications surrounding the engine mounts (More on engines in Chapter 7, Stolen Engines, Transmissions and Component Parts).

Tuners frequently mix and match engine blocks and heads (Frankenstein's). Non-VTEC engines are plentiful, may be referred to as an LS engine, and can be found in an Integra LS with a B18A1 and B18B1. One way to improve these non-VTEC engines is to add a VTEC head to it from a B16A, B17A, or B18C engine, thus creating an LS VTEC. Similar swaps are done with a B20Z block from the CR-V and may be referred to as a CR VTEC. Observing VTEC heads on non-VTEC blocks can confirm whether the vehicle engine components have been swapped. The heads should be scrutinized as they can also provide detailed information as to what vehicle it came from. Common markings can lead to the year, make and model, as well as the VIN.

Photo 19 depicts an Integra B18C5 head. From the arrows starting point you should see four faint circles. The arrow is pointing to a blowup of that area. In this case, the 0\0 stands for the year 2000; the \9 stands for the 9th day; and the 0\9 stands for September. The last circle is generally the shift. Other numbers indicate that it belongs to an Integra Type R (ITR).

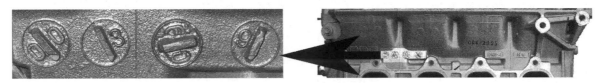

Photo 19

Appendix B is a Honda/Acura engine chart that can assist in identifying if an engine swap has occurred. If Internet access is available during your investigation, it is always fruitful to Google an engine prefix to assist in identifying the vehicle a particular engine came from.

Drift Setups in Chapter 3 mention several popular swaps not related to Honda and Acura. For example, the SR20DET is found in the Nissan Silvia in Japan and is a very popular swap for American drifters. It is seen in many Nissan 240SX's as the drivers prefer it to the stock KA24 engine. For Mitsubishi the 4G63 engine (in North American production from 1990-1999) is a very popular engine and should be monitored for theft.

Replacement engines (also known as crate engines) most likely will not have the same numbering systems as stock engines and investigators should be careful before taking action with these.

Swapped engine follow up can lead to chop shops and multiple stolen vehicle recoveries and arrests. While attending a sport compact car show in Tucson, Arizona I observed a 1997 Civic with a decal from one of the local shops. The first six characters of the VIN on this vehicle were 2HGEJ8. The engine in it was a B16A3. Using the engine swap table in Appendix B, I was able to determine from the VIN that the engine type should have been D16Y8, not B16A3. The engine was painted over and was difficult to read, and the transmission number had been removed and the remaining holes were filled in. The method of operation (MO) on filling the anti theft holes after removing the VIN plate was unique, and we had recovered several vehicles before in the area with the same MO. The shop identification decal was the first lead we had regarding this MO. Previously we had been given a name of a possible suspect that would fill in the holes after removing the numbers but we did not know which shop he worked at.

Instead of impounding the vehicle at the show for the missing/altered numbers, we decided to follow up later. This vehicle was listed for sale and arrangements were made to look at the vehicle the following week. During this meeting, the owner gave us the name of the shop and the subject that installed the engine. He also gave us some additional shop and installer names. Because of the vehicle owner's cooperation, we allowed him to maintain possession of the vehicle with the condition he would not sell or remove any of the items.

One of the names he gave us was an individual who had been featured in one of the sport compact car magazines. In that article, we confirmed his name, location, and the fact that he was driving an Accord with a Prelude engine in it. Through one swapped engine investigation, two chop shops were identified and one key suspect was arrested.

Interior Modifications

Studying the interior of a vehicle can answer many questions regarding how the vehicle is used (Stereo, Audio-Visual, and Electronic losses and other interior fraud schemes were covered in Chapter 2 as well as Chapter 3).

Interior modifications include custom pedals, gauges, gauge housings, custom shift knobs, shift meters, custom or racing seats, 5-point racing harness, harness bars, steering wheels, speed/rev meters, tinting, complete restyling of the interior fabric, and roll bars and cages.

When first inspecting a modified vehicle for clues, always ask yourself, "What is that item/accessory used for?" Starting with the Who, What, When, Where, Why, and How will shed new light on any investigation. Determine what every button, gauge, or piece of equipment is used for. Some street racers will have a brake kill switch within reach of the driver. The purpose of this switch is to disable the break lights in an effort to avoid law enforcement detection. Suspects may kill their lights when trying to get away from law enforcement; with a brake kill switch they can ensure they are not as easily seen.

Items that appear to be defective or missing are just as important to consider. Suspects that know they have a stolen or illegal engine under their hood have been known to disable the hood release and add an alternative way to access the engine compartment. When law enforcement asks them to open their hood, they falsely advise them it is broken. As mentioned in Chapter 3 in "How to Drift", the e-brake may appear to be broken when in fact it has been modified to drift.

If there are a variety of gauges in the vehicle, determine what each of them is used for. Some may be to control boost, report on the air/fuel mixture, or advise the driver when to shift. Many of these items were developed for racing, so you should ask yourself why these gauges are on a streetcar and what modifications do they support. Some of the devices have memory functions that may contain useful data, including information about how fast the vehicle was traveling and over what period of time. The gauges may be mounted on top of the dash, next to the windshield on the pillar post, in the dash, or replace the stock gauges.

Shift lights are easily seen from outside of a vehicle. Generally, they are mounted with an aftermarket tachometer (photo 4, Chapter 2). Some shift lights connect to the vehicle's electronics and are much smaller. Their purpose is to flash a light so the driver knows when to shift without worrying about redlining the car (To see this in action, type "Shift Light" in your favorite video site such as YouTube).

Data loggers and monitors can vary in size, shape, and function. They may be mounted permanently or used with portable handheld devices. Depending on the unit's memory capacity, a data logger may store many hours of data, capturing 10-20 pieces of information per second including speed, distances traveled, RPMs, temperatures, pressures, and even G forces.

Roll bars versus roll cages can be another indication that the vehicle you are inspecting is pushed beyond its intended limits. Some tracks require roll cages on cars running under 10 seconds – another clue that the vehicle is a serious contender and most likely should not be on our streets.

Racing seats with five-point racing harnesses (seat belts) are generally found in the more serious street racer's vehicle. However, there may be just as many installed for show as there are for go. Five-point seat belts may be good for a child's car seat, but we have seen too many installed as aftermarket belts in sport compacts that could actually cause damage due to improper installation from the weekend warrior.

Each accessory has a purpose and tells stories; if you don't know the purpose of an item, ask a question. If the vehicle being inspected was involved in a collision and the drivers' airbag did not deploy, perhaps the stock steering wheel was replaced with a racing steering wheel (which don't have airbags).

Missing Items

With every ounce or pound of weight removed, the vehicle can produce a better horsepower/ weight ratio and allow it to accelerate faster. For quarter-mile racing, that can equate to $1/10^{th}$ of a second improvement for every 100 lbs removed. Items removed vary by individuals, needs, and desires. Removed items can include the passenger seat with brackets, rear seats and cushion, rear seatbelt brackets, speakers, floor mats, spare tire, jack and trunk liner, power steering, headliner, air conditioning, door panels, seats, sound deadening material, roof support webbing, side impact door beams, and firewall layers. In addition to stripping the interior, an enthusiast may install a smaller/lighter fuel tank, battery, carbon fiber hood, alloy wheels, flywheels, air conditioner, and power steering pumps.

We have seen vehicles stripped down to the bare minimum, leaving only the driver's seat in the interior compartment. To reinstall all of these items back into a daily driver requires a lot of time. When one of these vehicles blows an engine or crashes during a race, the owner may not want to spend the time and energy to reinstall all of those parts. Instead, they may move the vehicle to a recovery area in a nearby city and falsely report the vehicle stolen. Upon recovery of a suspect stripped sport compact vehicle, the investigator needs to take a close look as to what may have actually been stolen versus the totality of missing items and their purpose or need in the black market.

Typical Costs Associated with Modifications

In California, progressive cities will issue citations for the illegally modified vehicle violations and make the ticket non-dismissible (cannot be "signed off" in the field). They require the driver to take the vehicle to the Bureau of Automotive Repair to correct the smog violations. This can cost the owner close to $5,000 once all the fines and corrections are calculated. Some states have websites, which list typical violations in reference to "street legal" vehicles. Check with your local traffic department or state patrol to determine what is allowed in your state.

The cost to modify a vehicle for street, show, drift, stunt, or drag can vary greatly. The quality of parts and material along with installation costs can run from just a few dollars to over $100,000 per vehicle. For many, the sport compact scene is more about looking good than going good and costs can be kept down.

In one sport compact magazine, an example was provided of the costs associated with fixing up a 1999 Civic while *not* spending a lot of money. These modifications are a good example of some of the items an enthusiast might want to add. The vehicle was purchased for $6,000. For looks, they added:

- $1,500 paint job, saving money by doing some of the prep work themselves
- $100 on shaved molding, antenna and miscellaneous body pieces
- $150 for a JDM Civic Type R (CTR) wing
- $100 for a JDM CTR rear hatch
- $300 for a carbon fiber hood
- $250 for carbon fiber mirrors
- $100 for JDM window visors

It cost less than $3,000 to make their car look good from the outside. Expanding on the interior, they added:

- $800 for a racing seat
- $700 racing harnesses
- $400 JDM EK9 navigation system
- $250 gauge cluster
- $100 door panel inserts
- $40 air vent pocket tray
- $40 armrest eliminator
- $25 shift boot
- $100 CTR carpeting
- $50 Mugen shift knob

These interior modifications cost an additional $2,505. For tuning, they added:

- $150 air intake
- $300 header
- $150 aftermarket radiator
- $100 radiator fans
- $500 carbon after-cat exhaust
- $100 MSD spark plug wires
- $40 Iridium spark plugs
- $40 short shifter
- $80 in-tank fuel pump
- $20 aftermarket radiator cap
- $80 radiator cooling plate
- $10 brake reservoir covers
- $30 LP dry cell battery

This added another $1,600 to the total investment. For braking and handling, they used:

- $2,000 4 piston caliper, slotted rotor, and brake line set
- $350 rear brake upgrade
- $1,200 coilovers
- $150 40mm front strut bar
- $700 racing bars
- $150 lower control arms
- $2,000 aftermarket wheels

The breaking and handling modifications added $6,500 to the price tag. The grand total to fix up this $6,000 1999 Civic – while keeping the cost down – was $13,605. Many enthusiasts have much more that that invested into their vehicles, such as complete engine swaps that can add several thousand dollars more.

When you compare the cost of the modifications to the income of the tuner, it would be very difficult to surmise that the vehicle was built without stolen parts or financed through insurance fraud (barring their parents paid for it).

Factory versus Aftermarket & Warranties

Common modifications include several different areas. In some cases, the type or combination of modifications can tell the investigator what the car is primarily used for. Other factors may be involved regarding who manufactured the part, who installed it, and what was it designed for.

Several manufacturers offer a variety of modification packages from body kits to complete engine and performance upgrades. Some of these are created by divisions within the manufacturer's control while other manufacturers partnered with aftermarket companies; Chrysler SkunkWerks, Ford's Special Vehicle Team (SVT), Lexus F Sport, Nissan Nismo, Subaru Performance Tuning

(SPT), and Toyota Racing Development (TRD) logos may be seen on several of their cars that have had such modifications.

Several different warranty issues were raised throughout this chapter. To protect consumers, the Magnuson-Moss Warranty Act came into being (US Code - Title 15, Chapter 50, Sections 2301-2312). This is the federal law that governs consumer product warranties. Legally, a vehicle manufacturer cannot void the warranty on a vehicle due to an aftermarket part, unless they can prove that the aftermarket part caused or contributed to the failure in the vehicle. If a vehicle manufacturer fails to honor emission or warranty claims, the affected party can contact the Environmental Protection Agency (EPA). If federal warranty protection is denied, they can contact the Federal Trade Commission (FTC).

JDM -- Japanese Domestic Manufacturer

In Chapter 1 and throughout this book, we have mentioned how desirable JDM parts and vehicles are in the North American market because they are different from USDM or because they add power. Part of the reason we see some many JDM parts in the United States is due to the Japanese compulsory inspection process known as "Shaken." The vehicle inspection process in Japan is a bi-annual process with very strict regulations. As a part of the inspection process, the condition of almost every component of the car is taken into consideration. The cost involved to pass the strict inspection process can be cost prohibitive for some. A vehicle in Japan may be practically worthless after just seven years of minimal use. These vehicles are often disassembled and the engines and transmissions are then exported for resale.

In Japan, people use public transportation more than they use their own vehicles and the vehicles therefore accumulate very few miles. Additionally, owning an automobile is more of a luxury, due to the high population to land ratio. On average, imported engines have 30,000 to 40,000 miles or less. In contrast, a 1991 vehicle driven in the U.S. would have an average of over 140,000 miles. This low mileage, coupled with lax emission requirements, adds to the popularity of JDM engines and other parts.

Since there is generally no warranty on JDM engines outside of Japan, and frequent problems occur, suspect claims may follow. Always check to determine if the engine or transmission is JDM. Many times these engines are not considered legal in several states. Honda and Acura change the engine number format on JDM versus USDM engines, making it easy to determine if the engine belongs in the vehicle. For example, in the United States the engine prefix could be B18C1 whereas in Japan the prefix would be B18C. Most of the Honda/Acura JDM engines we see in North America have two to four alphanumeric characters for the make and model stamped into the engine (see photo 20 under Stolen Engines, Transmissions and Component Parts in Chapter 7 and Appendix B for additional information).

Other manufacturers may have more subtle differences. In addition to the engine number differences and missing smog equipment, salt-water residue may be a clue to a JDM engine. This type of residue is common since the vehicles are imported by ship.

Many importers buy the entire front clip of the Japanese car, which gives them the engine, transmission, ECU, harnesses, relay boxes, lights, side markers, and molding options. Desirable front clips in the United States have been the Toyota Aristo, featuring their 2JZ-GTE engine; the Acura Integra with their rectangular headlights versus U.S. round ones; and the Nissan Silvia with fixed headlights versus U.S. popup lights.

SUVs, Trucks, and Other Trends

It does not really matter what type of vehicle they own; the owner's passion for the vehicle and individual tastes drive the modifications. Although we are focusing on Sport Compacts, the principals of theft and fraud we focus on here apply to all vehicles. Desire equals demand, which in our case equals theft and fraud. Light truck sales (including SUVs) represented more than half of all vehicle sales in the United States from 2001 to 2007. In 2008, the sales fell just below half but still represent a significant amount of vehicles on our streets.

Prior to the gas crunch of 2008, some SUV and truck owners were intent on having the biggest and most aggressive vehicle on the block. We have all seen trucks raised so high that drivers need a stepladder to get in. These types of modifications are costly and bring a completely new set of problems with them. Many times the height is not just illegal, it is also unsafe; these vehicles are prone to more accidents and rollovers. That off-road look is very popular on-road in many areas of the country. Although outfitted for it, many of these trucks will never go off-road. Use the sport compact investigative techniques discussed in this book for SUVs and trucks when investigating claims that may be suspicious. The same techniques and tactics are used with lowered vehicles and those equipped with hydraulics, as those that are modified to race.

Local enforcement statistics can be used to determine what types of trends are emerging in your area. In 2001, the California Highway Patrol had a 150% increase in tickets issued for vehicles raised above the legal height. Generally, there are laws on the books in every state controlling vehicle modifications. Many times these laws are under-enforced, which allows dangerous trends to get out of control. According to the Specialty Equipment Market Association, sales of suspension products, brakes, steering components, custom wheels, and tires totaled $6.5 billion in 2002. In 2006 the Wheels, Tires, & Suspension products market segment generated close to $9 billion in sales.

Popular Types of Cars

Throughout the past decade, several makes and model vehicles have been consistently popular with the Fast and Fraudulent crowd. This may change depending on what area of the country the owner is from. The Fast and the Furious sequels (2001-2009) have unfortunately had an influence on theft, fraud, and illegal street racing, deaths and injuries. With each release of similar movies, investigators should focus on claims that are submitted involving the featured cars or trends.

The following popular cars span the last decade and are not all inclusive, as there would be too many to list (FWD = Front-wheel Drive; RWD = Rear-wheel Drive; AWD = All Wheel Drive). "The Fast and the Furious" (F&F1); "2 Fast 2 Furious" (F&F2); "The Fast and the Furious, Tokyo Drift" (F&F3); and "Fast and Furious" (F&F4).

Acura Integra	FWD	F&F 1
Acura RSX	FWD	
BMW	RWD	
Chevrolet Cavalier	RWD	
Dodge Neon	FWD	
Dodge SRT-4		
Eagle Talon	AWD	
Ford Focus, Probe	FWD	
Honda Civic	FWD	F&F 1
Honda Fit	FWD	
Honda Prelude	FWD	
Honda S2000	RWD	F&F 1, 2, 4
Hyundai Tiburon GT	FWD	F&F 3
Hyundai Genesis	FWD	F&F 4
Infinity G35	RWD	
Lexus IS300	RWD	
Mazda Protégé, 6	Varies	
Mazda3 (protégé replacement 04)		
Mazda RX-7	RWD	F&F 1, 2, 3
Mazda RX-8	RWD	F&F 3
Mini Cooper		
Mitsubishi Lancer Evolution (EVO)	AWD	F&F 2, 3
Mitsubishi Eclipse, Spyder	FWD	F&F 1, 2
Nissan 350z (Fairlady Z in Japan)	RWD	F&F 3
Nissan 300zx (Fairlady Z in Japan)	RWD	
Nissan 240sx (Silvia)	RWD	F&F 1, 3, 4
Nissan Sentra SE-R	FWD	
Nissan Skyline	RWD	F&F 2, 4
Scion tC	FWD	
Subaru Impreza STI, WRX,	AWD	F&F 4
Suzuki Aerio SX	AWD	
Toyota Supra, Corolla,	RWD	F&F 1, 2
Toyota Matrix XRS	FWD	
Toyota MR2 Spyder	RWD	

| Volkswagen Jetta | FWD | F&F 1 |
| Volkswagen Touran | FWD | F&F 3 |

Muscle car representation has been increasing at most of the illegal street gatherings I have attended in the last few years. The owners are typically older than the sport compact crowd is and there have been less insurance claims involving these cars.

Dodge Challenger	F&F 2
Dodge Charger	F&F 1, 4
Dodge Viper	F&F 2, 3
Chevrolet Camaro	F&F 2
Chevrolet Corvette	F&F 2, 4
Ford Mustang	F&F 2, 3, 4

Chapter 6: Internet Investigations

Throughout this book, we have discussed the importance of the Internet, particularly as a communication tool for the Generation Y Fast and Fraudulent crowd. Knowing where to look and how to search on the Internet will assist in locating suspects, identifying trouble spots and trends, preventing deaths and injuries, locating stolen property, and effectively reaching our youth. Chapter 3 provides numerous examples of how suspects and questionable activity were identified by using the Internet.

The Internet has become the first stop for many modern theft and fraud investigators. Today's younger generation uses the Internet as an extension of friends and family. Instant and constant communication gives users an outlet to express ideas, seek answers, and profit. Sales involving stolen property have skyrocketed in proportion to the use of the Internet.

Investigators find stolen property as well as theft and fraud schemes daily (Internet auction fraud is the most reported Internet related crime to the FBI). Sometimes it is as easy as searching for an item or serial number via a search engine such as Google or directly from sites that sell property such as Craigslist.org and eBay.com. Some responsible sites require the seller to place a photo as well as the serial number of the item being sold. We have had several cases in which a stolen engine was recovered by observing the photo of the item and its numbers on the Internet.

One quick method to recover stolen property is to Google high theft items. For example, there are tremendous amounts of stolen B18C1 Integra engines that have never been recovered. If you type "for sale B18C1" in Google you would most likely see tens of thousands of hits. We typically click on the newest postings and look for identifying information. These searches can be narrowed down by adding city, zip code, phone prefix, or other local information into the search such as: "for sale B18C1" San Diego. Using quotes can help narrow your searches or restrict your searches depending on what you are trying to accomplish. If you just typed: for sale B18C1 instead of "for sale B18C1" in quotes, you could see 100 records versus 30,000 thousand records. Using Craigslist, you can search by cities quite easily for similar items of interest.

As mentioned in previous chapters, if a vehicle was involved in some sort of race that caused damage to the vehicles drivetrain, a quick check of the Internet may show probative results.

Saving the Data

Since websites and their data can disappear quickly, it is recommended that if you find information that is of interest, that you save the data while you look at it. Bookmarking the site is not enough. Several choices may exist for saving the data, depending on the type of browser you are using, (most likely, Microsoft Internet Explorer or Mozilla Firefox). You can save the page you are looking at by choosing File from the tool bar then choose Save, Save Page, or Save As. While saving from

Microsoft's Internet Explorer you may have choices such as Web Page Complete (html, htm) or Web Archive (mht). The complete method will save the page with an additional folder containing other components of the page and the archive will save it as a single file. Mozilla's Firefox uses HTML only for the single file method. Using either of these methods should save what you were looking at on screen at the time of the save. However, if you want any associated links, you will need third party software or you will need to click on that link and save that page as a separate file. (At the time of this writing Firefox had several free add-ons that would save the entire page and some of the links/pages behind it). If one method of saving the file does not work, try another. If all else fails, use your computers "print screen" function and paste the picture into a word document or graphics program.

Forums

Many of the websites listed at the end of this chapter have an area within them titled "Forums." Using forums can be a great starting point to locate questionable activity in your area or to learn what is popular. Most forums are broken up into areas of interest such as drifting, motorcycles, photos, classified, events, and cities or states. Google any term you are interested in to get started. If you work in the Houston area and want to know what is happening regarding street racing or drifting, type "street racing Houston" in the search engine and look for interesting chat from the various forums. Some forums will require you to register and have a login and password; it is worth signing up as a member (it's most likely free) in order to be able to use the forum for research. Forums generally have a variety of sections that allow you to narrow your focus with categories such as Events, Car Talk, Classifieds, Meeting and Social Calendars, Vehicle Categories, Photos, Crews, and Teams.

Trying to pass off racing damage as normal wear and tear, a collision, or as a defective part is fraud. Many manufacturers offer warranties to cover any repairs to correct defects in material or workmanship but exclude repairs that are caused by abuse of the vehicle or damage to any component that is the result of any competition or racing events. We have worked several cases in which a street racer was involved in a collision while at a track. Since these participants were known, photographs and video were taken of them during the collision. These photos and videos later made it to various automotive forums. Several of these participants had reported that the collisions occurred outside of the racetrack on public streets. One person reported that his motorcycle had been stolen when in fact it had gone down on a track during a race. Additionally, there was a lot of "talk" on various forum sites regarding the collisions and damage to the vehicles. Searching the various forums provided enough "evidence" to convict these participants of fraud.

Tools and Techniques

To stay current as to what is happening in your areas of interest, consider using Google Alerts or other similar services. With Google Alerts, you can be notified daily via email of multiple items of interest. We commonly have alerts on such words as "Auto Theft" and "Street Racing." For more information, search on Google for "Google Alerts."

Victims locate their own stolen property on a continuous basis. They can assist in running down Internet leads (if they are not suspects themselves), since they know the item that was stolen and can recognize it from a photo or description. The victims on web auction sites frequently find complete automobiles, watercraft, and parts of stolen vehicles. It is advantageous to have victims search for their stolen property online, and they should be advised to search for several weeks, if not months, for their property. In January 2009, a victim of a Honolulu sport bike theft recognized his bike for sale online in Craigslist. He notified Honolulu PD who responded and confiscated 32 sport bikes from a body shop; all with their identification numbers removed. *This chop shop was identified because a victim located his bike for sale on the Internet and the police department followed up on the lead.*

Local law enforcement agencies simply do not have the time to search eBay for several weeks, waiting for a particular item of stolen property to appear. Additionally, many times the stolen property has been taken outside their jurisdiction and they cannot follow up on it.

With sites such as eBay, searches can be saved and future like listings can generate an email notification so the investigator or victim can be automatically notified. Searches can also be narrowed down, for example, the Suzuki GSX-R is the most stolen motorcycle. I could log into eBay and click "Advanced Search" to narrow my area of concern and choose several categories from drop down lists to search terms such as: Motorcycles / Suzuki / GSX-R / 2005-2008 / Color / City or ZIP.

In Santa Clara, California a victim of an auto theft found the parts of his vehicle for sale by a seller in the neighboring city. It was easy to show that that the parts to this unique vehicle belonged to the victim. In Arizona, the victim of a street racer-type auto theft started searching the local sites for her tires and wheels. Knowing they were unique, she quickly found them for sale in the same city as the auto theft. By locating the suspect who was selling her items, investigators were led to a chop shop suspect who was responsible for many auto thefts.

A victim of mirror thefts from a BMW M3 searched eBay for similar mirrors. He found someone selling the same style and color mirrors in the city within hours of the theft. Investigators conducted a probation search of the seller and found that he had been responsible for numerous BMW M3 mirror thefts throughout several adjoining cities.

In 2003, the FBI took down a large, eBay-linked fencing operation based in Chicago. The suspects were accused of selling millions of dollars' worth of stolen goods. They would even auction off things they didn't have yet, then go out and steal them.

All buyers on Internet classifieds should be made aware that the item might be taken away by law enforcement if it is identified as stolen at a later date. Buyers in these cases are generally unable to collect the money they invested and they lose the item they purchased. The buyer should ask for photographs and serial numbers for items they purchase to help flush out the questionable items. Law enforcement routinely browses the Internet for illegal activity and has had many successful cases. However, the volume is so high it is impossible to monitor it all; eBay Motors alone has had over 20 million daily transactions.

Frequently, we look at pictures of vehicles and their components on the Internet and can determine that the item is stolen. One investigator was searching for a stolen engine when he came across a photo of a different engine that had the identifying numbers removed. After a short investigation, he was able to identify the seller and arrest him for possession of stolen property.

Finding Chop Shops

The saying "birds of a feather flock together" wasn't coined for idle reasons. We have attended hundreds of car shows throughout the country, located, and recovered many stolen vehicles or vehicles with stolen parts. Frequently, we have located stolen parts in a vehicle belonging to a particular car club or "team." We have inspected the remaining vehicles belonging to fellow team members and found stolen parts in several of the team member's vehicle. By searching the team's Internet site, investigators can be led to other car clubs or teams with whom they have associated. Inspecting those team members cars have resulted in additional stolen vehicles and parts. Occasionally the team may have obtained the stolen parts without knowledge that they were "hot." The common bond in cases such as these may be that the team frequents a particular speed or repair shop that is installing stolen components and charging the vehicle owner for the items as if they had purchased them legitimately.

Import parts swap meets can be a good source for education and stolen property. Trying to identify an engine block while it is in a vehicle can be difficult at times. Having tables full of identifiable parts out on display for easy viewing makes this task much easier. Searching the Internet or Internet forums is an easy way to locate part swap meets in your local area.

In Chapter 7 we will discuss the importance of searching the Internet before, during, and after any investigation involving the modified vehicle scene or similar group activities including law enforcement operations.

Suspects also conduct Google searches in an effort to determine more facts and to cover their tracks. During search warrants, investigators have followed the search terms used on the suspect's computer to determine knowledge or involvement of a crime. In one such case, investigators learned that the suspect involved in a fatal hit and run conducted searches on his computer for such terms as "hit and run" as well as terms to locate a repair facility.

Internet Websites

Even though there is misinformation on the Internet, it is still an invaluable resource in dealing with the Fast and the Fraudulent problem. Groups, suspects, trends, and dishonest shops can be identified, as well as stings can be conducted.

Websites come and go, as do associated magazines. There are too many to list and sometimes it is best just to use a search engine to locate sites that favor your particular interests. If you want to learn about what is happening in a particular city, use search terms such as "street racing" and then the city or location of your choice. Similar searches can be conducted within sites such as MySpace, Facebook, and YouTube. If you are interested in a particular make of vehicle, there are most likely websites specializing in just that such as Honda S2000 and s2ki.com or Nissan Silvia and www.nissansilvia.com.

Within many of the listed websites are forums, events, club listings, and other useful information that make it hard to categorize them. What follows are additional website addresses that at the time of this writing were sources of additional information:

Forums, Events, Information:
www.streetracing.org
www.clubsi.com
www.tunerzine.com
www.nopionline.com
www.battleoftheimports.com
www.importracing.com
www.superstreetonline.com
www.timeattackforums.com
www.hotimportnights.com
www.extremeautofest.com

Car Clubs:
www.streetsourcemag.com
www.tunerfriends.com

Drifting:
www.drifting.com
www.formulaD.com
www.usdrift.com
www.d1gp.com

Magazines:

Dsport	www.dragsport.com
Turbo	www.turbomagazine.com
Super Street	www.superstreetonline.com
Honda Tuning	www.hondatuningmagazine.com
Sport Compact Car	www.sportcompactcarweb.com
Import Tuner	www.importtuner.com
Euro Tuner	www.eurotuner.com

Motorcycles:
www.stuntlife.com
www.superstreetbike.com
www.stunterschool.com
www.bikenightusa.co

Dragtimes.com is a database of quarter-mile drag racing timeslips submitted by drag racing enthusiasts. This site is for participants to share information about their car or motorcycle and what modifications they made to achieve those times.

Whowon.com and NHRA.com are good resources to identify which tracks are in a particular state or city.

The Internet is fluid and constantly changing, with thousands of useful sites related to the sport compact scene. Great cases have been solved, stolen property recovered, and suspects arrested all based on Internet searches.

Chapter 7: Law Enforcement Operations, Enforcement, and Solutions

The most effective way to reduce theft and fraud in any given city or area is to find the one individual officer or investigator that shows an interest in the scene. Through training, education, support, and enforcement, most problems can be prevented or resolved. Be sure to include educating the District Attorneys and Judges that will be affected by the enforcement operations in order to have the most effective outcomes.

Once you let your investigator loose, you will not have to worry about the effectiveness of your efforts. Your biggest issue will be determining where to put all of the recovered stolen vehicles and component parts, along with how to manage all of the informants and information you will receive. To get a jump-start, you can go to a local race or show. At the majority of shows we have attended, we have identified stolen vehicles and components. Once you recover this stolen property from the individual in possession of it, they will be extremely cooperative in supplying you information to get their property or money back. This will lead to additional chop shops, stolen vehicles and components, and arrests.

Once an interested investigator gets involved, the recoveries and informants can become overwhelming for one person. The information presented in this book can be used as a guideline to assist investigators managing this scene. We are always available to assist agencies in handling the Fast and Fraudulent scene.

Car Seizures, Crushing, and Dispositions

Arresting perpetrators and seizing their vehicles has been the most effective deterrent against this illegal and dangerous activity. If you want to save lives, protect property, and make your city safer, you must have a "zero tolerance attitude." This type of enforcement must be ongoing and consistent for it to be long lasting and effective. Agencies that disassemble, shred, burn, crush, or otherwise destroy the vehicle (at the owner's expense) have seen impressive reductions in racing activities, injuries, and deaths. Agencies that have not taken such action have seen racers continue in their illegal activity causing additional injuries and fatalities.

As mentioned throughout this book, many vehicles involved in this scene are powered with stolen engines and transmissions. Owners of these vehicles try to disguise the theft by removing or altering identifying numbers. Most states have laws prohibiting the possession of vehicles and components when these identifying numbers have been removed. In California, section 10751 of the vehicle code is frequently used in such cases, but most states have similar statutes. In addition to vehicle code violations, there generally exists a penal code section making it a crime to remove identifying numbers on any piece of property.

Probable Cause to inspect a vehicle involved in this scene is generally not very difficult to come by. There are vehicle and penal code violations, curfew violations, and municipal ordinances that are usually in place to allow proper enforcement. Some vehicles, such as the Honda Civic, may come from the factory with their headlights at the lowest legal height. If the vehicle is lowered at all, you could assume it is in violation without having to measure it. For states with emissions laws, the sound and look of the vehicle may be enough for a stop. Many of the items presented in this book lead to probable cause for a closer look into probable violations. Emission regulations are a headache to most tuners but a powerful tool for law enforcement in those states that regulate them.

Since vehicles generally fall under the warrantless search rules, identifying stolen vehicles and their components should be carried out whenever inspecting vehicles. This has proven to be the easiest and most effective method to get these offending vehicles off our public streets. Numerous case law decisions have been rendered reaffirming law enforcements right to inspect vehicles for contraband. In our case, the contraband could be related to illegal street racing activities and stolen property, but primarily these are simple vehicle inspections enforcing the vehicle code.

In *Carroll v. United States*, The U.S. Supreme Court ruled that if an officer has probable cause to believe that evidence or contraband is located in a motor vehicle, he may search the area of the vehicle he reasonably believes contains that evidence without a search warrant to the same degree as if he had a warrant.

In *Chambers v. Maroney*, the police had the vehicle secured and clearly had an opportunity to obtain a search warrant. The U.S. Supreme Court ruled that it was lawful for the police to search the motor vehicle at the station house after the vehicle was seized. Even though the vehicle was in police custody and there was no risk that the vehicle or its contents would disappear, the U.S. Supreme Court ruled that it was not necessary to obtain a search warrant to search the vehicle.

In *Florida v. Myers*, the defendant was arrested and his automobile was inventoried, seized, and secured in a locked impound lot. Approximately eight hours later, a police officer who had probable cause that the vehicle contained evidence or contraband went to the impound lot and searched the car a second time without a warrant. The U.S. Supreme Court ruled that the second search by the officer was a valid search under the motor vehicle exception, even though the vehicle had already been subjected to an inventory search and was impounded.

In *United States v. Ludwig*, the Tenth Circuit Court of Appeals found that a search warrant was not required, even when there was little or no risk of the vehicle being driven off.

In *United States v. Johns*, the U.S. Supreme Court upheld a search of contraband that had been taken from a vehicle and was in police custody for three days prior to the search. Even though the courts have ruled in favor of warrantless searches, this exception should not be abused. Some state constitutions have additional limitations.

During street racing enforcement actions, many agencies discover stolen engines and transmissions within the suspect vehicle. Some agencies remove the stolen components from the vehicles, namely the engine and transmission, and the owner/suspect is then given what is left of his vehicle back.

Too frequently, the vehicle owner just installs another stolen engine and transmission, and the theft and street-racing cycle continues to endanger lives on the streets and to victimize other car owners by stealing their parts.

Throughout the world there have been many serious street racing-related accidents perpetrated by those who have previously been warned, cited, or arrested while involved in street racing. One-month impounds here in the states and three-month impounds in parts of Australia have not been a deterrent to the habitual racer. Seizing and crushing the cars has.

Police Departments such as Ontario, Los Angeles, and San Diego did not want to contribute to this theft cycle and have obtained court orders to crush cars containing stolen components like engines and transmissions, thus putting a stop to illegal street racing and related stolen vehicle activity. The value of crushing an illegal street race vehicle far outweighs the value of the metal the car represents.

On November 20, 2007, the Ontario Police Department in California crushed seven cars that were impounded during illegal street racing enforcement. 60 Minutes Australia made a trip to the United States to film this crushing, as well as to see how we are addressing the problem of illegal street racing. Most of the agencies involved in crushing illegal street racing vehicles have invited the press as well as the suspect/owner to watch the vehicle crushing. Crushing has been used in several cities around the globe. Canada has been plagued by deaths and injuries related to street racing, so when fines for street racing had risen ten times to $10,000 and still had little effect, Ontario, Canada Attorney General Michael Bryant gave police in the province the right to seize and crush any car modified for street racing. He insinuated that if it can be established that a car is being used for the unlawful purpose of street racing, the police will seize it and the owner/driver will never see it again. Bryant said cars adapted for street racing could be seized and destroyed even if charges have not been made and a race has not taken place. Bryant was quoted as saying cars built for street racing are as dangerous as explosives and can cause catastrophic damage.

In Victoria, Australia they have a law that allowed the seizure of a street racing vehicle for 48 hours on the first offense. The second offense allowed for a three-month seizure and the third offense could lead to a permanent seizure. From 2006-2008 approximately 5000 vehicles were seized for first offenses with only 137 on second offenses and 14 on a third offense. 53% of the vehicles were impounded between the hours of 4:00 p.m. and midnight; the majority (20%) occurred on Saturday; 48% were for improper use of a vehicle; 37% were 18-21 year-olds followed by 22-25 year-olds at 29%; 17% were clocked at speeds between 90-100 mph.

In 2007 New South Wales, Australia was to present drivers caught street racing with video footage of their impounded vehicles being crushed or crashed in an effort to curtail street racing, burnouts, and other showboating activity. The video footage of the car crushing would also be used in road safety campaigns and some of the vehicles would be crash-tested to determine the safety consequences of these modified vehicles. This video crushing was referred to as the "YouTube law."

However, like too many other legislative actions, it appeared that no cars had actually been crushed nearly 18 months after the legislation even though more than 300 were confiscated in 2007. Then in October 2008, a father of four was killed when a street race went wrong and one of the vehicles collided into the van he was driving.

Since new laws were introduced in July 2007 more than 52,000 provisional drivers had their drivers licenses taken away; 2,000 were charged for violating the 11:00pm curfew of having more than one person under 21 in the vehicle; and 2,500 were charged with driving banned V8 and turbocharged cars (see Chapter 8 for more legislative examples).

Many state statutes indicate that when the vehicle comes into police custody, and it can be proven that parts of it are stolen, "it shall be destroyed, sold, or otherwise disposed of under the conditions as provided in an order by the court having jurisdiction." The "Otherwise disposed of" section can be used to retain a vehicle for training or undercover stings, as long as when the vehicle is destroyed when it is no longer needed.

If you want to save lives and stop the dangerous activities, destroying the entire car is the best solution. It has been proven too many times that selling the car only contributes to the problem and puts the car back out on the street. Agencies that have removed the stolen engine and transmission from a seized vehicle, and allowed it to be sold at auction, have more times than not contributed to the problem reoccurring.

Some opponents of crushing do not understand this aspect and think that crushing the vehicle with its components is a terrible waste. In reality, the terrible waste is the lives and property that are lost when these vehicles resurface on our streets. Agencies that have initiated vehicle crushing have been extremely successful in curtailing street racing and in saving lives.

If the car is to be crushed, all parties that have a legal right to the car or its components get notified of the destruction hearing and have a right to bring forth relevant evidence prior to the vehicles being crushed. Insurance companies should insure their underwriting guidelines have protected them from governmental seizures or related criminal behavior to avoid a potential claim from the insured regarding the crushing of a vehicle. Without such protection, insurance companies may find themselves paying off a total loss claim due to the vehicle being crushed.

Depending on the circumstances, the choices for vehicle disposition vary. Generally, after 30 days of a vehicle theft, the insurance company will pay off the owner of the vehicle for a total loss, and the insurance company becomes the owner of the missing vehicle or parts. When the parts of the stolen vehicle are subsequently recovered, as is frequently the situation with street racer type cases, the insurance company is notified and advised that the parts were recovered in another vehicle.

In some cases, where it can be shown that the owner of the car did not have any knowledge that the vehicle contained stolen or questionable parts, the insurance company may agree to let the vehicle's owner keep the component parts for a fee. Other times the insurance company will ask for the parts back, at the owner's expense, to be sold at auction to recover some of their losses. In Riley v. Mid-Century Insurance, the courts ruled that where the insured had no knowledge that the vehicle itself was stolen, and the police seized the vehicle, the insured was allowed recovery from the insurance company under the same comprehensive coverage as if the vehicle was stolen from the insured even though the police had seized it.

In order to send a message to suspects and to avoid further victimization of the insurance industry, there have been cases where, instead of giving the insurance company back just some pieces of their vehicle, they are given back an entire vehicle that contains their stolen component parts. San Bernardino County has successfully argued such cases. *Sasia and Wallace v. Scarborough Implement Company* has been used as precedent case law in order to keep a vehicle as whole instead of parting it out. For example, a vehicle is impounded because it is determined that the engine, transmission, and other component parts are stolen; and it is shown that the owner of the vehicle had knowledge that the component parts were stolen.

In *Sasia*, San Bernardino County argued that the defendant put himself in the situation and was therefore liable for any costs associated with parts removal. They further argued that if these key components are removed from the vehicle then it no longer is a car. Additionally, with regard to restitution, the courts have ruled that restitution can include the amount that would deter future conduct. They argue that the vehicle should not have its components removed and the victim (insurance company) should be given the entire car. Even though the shell of the vehicle belonged to the suspect/defendant, he loses his rights to it based on his actions. From the case standpoint, "When things belonging to different owners have been united so as to form a single thing, and cannot be separated without injury, the whole belongs to the owner of the thing which forms the principal part; who must, however, reimburse the value of the residue to the other owner, or surrender the whole to him."

With the information presented in this section, it should be clear that crushing the vehicle so it cannot resurface on the street has been a very effective deterrent, aiding our ultimate goal of saving lives and protecting property. Merely seizing the car from the owner and selling it or parting it out and selling the shell contributes to the theft and street race problem.

Stolen Engines, Transmissions and Component Parts

By now, you should have a greater understanding as to the scope of the theft and fraud problem surrounding this scene. Many of the vehicles that law enforcement seizes are seized because they contain stolen engines and transmissions. As mentioned in Chapter 2 under Engine Scams, engine and transmission theft is very common with the Fast and the Fraudulent scene. These engines have also been heavily modified for increased speed on our streets. Experience has shown that although these seized vehicles may have not been involved in some form of exhibition of speed at the time of the impoundment, they have been previously – and most likely will be again in the future. This becomes obvious during the street race operations, as several of the vehicles we have impounded for stolen component parts have a previous history of exhibition of speed and prior thefts and frauds. We also come across vehicles that have been caught in these operations before and warned to stay away. These same vehicle owners were given information on local tracks that allow for legal racing, yet they continue to seek the thrill of illegal street racing.

One problem I see on a daily basis is the difficulty in identifying and recovering stolen property, particularly on the street during a late-night operation. To make this easier, law enforcement needs to be more thorough when taking an initial auto theft report, particularly involving a modified vehicle. When a vehicle is stolen, it is imperative for the investigating officer to find out what modifications were made to the vehicle prior to theft, including previous ownership. Even though many police reports have a check box to report if the engine or transmission is original, the questions should still be asked of the owner to ensure it does not contain an engine swap.

This information is extremely important for several reasons. If the vehicle is recovered missing any of these identifiable parts, their unique serial numbers should be obtained and they should be entered into the stolen vehicle or parts systems as still missing. Just checking the report box indicating that the engine or transmission is missing is not good enough. Obtain the engine and transmission records from the ISO database (https://claimsearch.iso.com), the manufacturer, or your local auto theft task force and have someone in records enter them into the state stolen vehicle system as well as NCIC (National Crime Information Center).

Why is this so important? Throughout the country, auto theft investigators are conducting business inspections and locating loose engines and transmissions. Traffic officers are conducting traffic stops for vehicle modifications and looking under the hoods. Wouldn't it be great to run the number in the system to be able to determine instantly if it is stolen? More often than not, stolen component numbers are not entered into the stolen vehicle systems and never make it into NCIC.

What has to take place when the numbers are not in the system is time consuming, and the questionable property may never be recovered, even if it is later determined to have been stolen. To confirm if a component part is stolen, the investigator generally runs the number through ISO or checks with the manufacturer to get the VIN of the vehicle to which the part belongs. They must then run the VIN through the stolen vehicle systems to determine if vehicle is a current stolen.

If no current theft record comes back, the investigator's work is not finished, as the vehicle may have been recovered missing that item. The investigator must then conduct an off-line search to locate previous theft records to this VIN. If he locates a previous theft report, he must contact the reporting agency from which the theft occurred. The recovering agency and the involved insurance company then try to determine if the item in question was ever recovered when the vehicle was recovered. This can take days or weeks depending on whether or not the files were archived.

Had the missing items been entered to begin with, all of these steps and man-hours could have been avoided. The process can be so lengthy and involved that if it is determined later to be stolen, it might be too late to do anything about it before the part has again disappeared. If you do invest a lot of time into identifying the part and can show that it was not stolen, give the owner a letter with your contact information stating the facts so they can show it to the next officer who stops them.

Photo 20

Non-JDM Honda/Acura engine numbers will be in two rows as depicted in photo 20. The first row of five characters describes the Make/Model/Type as discussed previously and in Appendix B. The second row is the engine serial number, which can also give us the year. Both rows should be present or it may be stolen. Non-American engines (JDM) will generally have 2-4 digits on the first row (B18C versus B18C1) and are not in American databases (some European spec engines have five characters on the top row). Pre-1999 Honda/Acura factory replacement engines may start with a 0 in the second row. Some 2000 replacement engine bosses are blank, so make sure you do not seize them thinking the numbers have been ground unless you see the grind marks or other alterations.

When a stolen vehicle is recovered, it is just as imperative to ensure that the components in the vehicle belong to that vehicle. Too often police officers recover stolen vehicles and report that the vehicle is intact when in fact it has been stripped of its components. They don't do this intentionally, as the recovered vehicle does have an engine, transmission, and body parts; the parts just don't belong to that vehicle and the officer doesn't check. Thieves frequently steal vehicles, strip the parts they want, and then replace those stripped parts with lesser-value salvaged parts to make it look like the vehicle was not stripped.

Several typical examples come to mind. During one of our field training sessions, we were inspecting vehicles that had been recovered and were in a salvage yard waiting to be sold at auction. The police report indicated that the vehicle was recovered with the engine and transmission. A close look at the transmission revealed that a key number had been removed. After further investigation, I identified the transmission and engine as stolen and belonging to a different vehicle. Had the insurance company sold this vehicle at auction, they would have been liable down the road for inadvertently selling stolen property. The insurance company would then have to buy back the vehicle or replace the engine and transmission. Had the officers identified the stolen components during the initial inspection, they would have discovered the stolen items and learned that their insured was also the suspect, which could have saved the insurance company from paying off this fraudulent claim by their insured.

Engines, transmissions, and other components are swapped frequently because the thief assumes no one will check. Thus, an engine stolen from a vehicle would never be listed as stolen and the thief would not have to worry about being caught. We have had dishonest body shops do the same scam with bumpers and fenders, replacing the stolen parts with salvaged parts in hopes that law enforcement will not report the items as missing. Follow-up should always be completed on all high-theft items, including airbags. An additional benefit to a thorough investigation and part identification is that it will frequently lead to a chop shop – or at least to the identification of more suspects – and the recovery of additional stolen vehicles and property.

Another example of the importance of component identification occurs during the recovery of a total burn vehicle. When a fully involved car fire is reported, very little remains of the typical vehicle identification numbers. The responding fire or police department may recover the vehicle based upon the license plates or tags and perhaps the owner's statements. Unfortunately, this scenario is ripe for fraud. A vehicle should NEVER be recovered by its license plate or tag solely. Other identifying information must be used. A qualified auto theft investigator should be contacted to determine the identity of the vehicle, including verifying that the engine and transmission belong in the car.

Some thieves and dishonest owners' acquire a non-operating salvaged vehicle of the same year, make and model as their personal car. They will take the license plates off their matching car and put them on the salvaged car then set it on fire and report it stolen. They are hoping the vehicle will be recovered based on the license plates and their statements alone. After the insurance company pays off the total loss claim, which includes the lien holder, they bring their car out of hiding, and now possess a vehicle free and clear. Insurance companies can help prevent this type of fraud by crushing un-repairable cars that are ripe for fraud.

Generally, when you see numbers missing, as in photo 21, you should assume that the part is stolen and investigate further. For this particular year, make and model the transmission should look like photo 22.

Photo 21

Photo 22

Honda/Acura has been marking the engine and transmission with the VIN on certain high-theft models such as the 1997 and newer Civic and Integra as pictured in photo 22. These markings are required by the National Highway Traffic Safety Administration (NHTSA) because of the Motor Vehicle Theft Law Enforcement Act. For a list of vehicles requiring parts marking through 2006, go to http://www.nhtsa.dot.gov/people/injury/enforce/PartsMarkingYear2006/PartsMarking.pdf

It should be obvious when numbers are missing or altered. If you are not sure what a particular component should look like, contact your local auto theft task force, send us a photo, or contact a knowledgeable automobile dealership. Do not let these red flags go; you may be letting stolen property slip away, settling a claim that should not be settled, and missing an opportunity to identify a chop shop.

There are additional methods used to identify a component further, but that information should be kept protected and not be in print. Simply contact your local auto theft detective or us for further guidance. Just because the numbers have been removed does not mean the part can no longer be indentified. If you are not sure, identify the driver and vehicle, photograph the components from a variety of angles, and email the photos to us or your local auto theft detective.

When stolen components are identified and recovered, the officer should insure that the various systems are updated with the current information so that in the future, the component will be in the clear if it resurfaces in another vehicle. If a component has been recovered with the numbers removed and it is later identified through secondary means, that part should have an assigned number attached by the appropriate law enforcement agency if it is going to end up back in commerce. Too often, we inspect, or seize, component parts that have had the numbers removed only to find out that they had previously been identified and released. If the part cannot be properly numbered by your agency, perhaps it would be wiser to dispose of the property so it cannot be reinstalled in a vehicle, costing new owners, law enforcement, and the insurance industry time and money to reinvestigate its origin and status.

Swapped Engine Identification

Identifying these component swaps and stolens are critical in stopping further destruction and death involving illegal street racers. Historically, Civic and Integra VTEC engines have been very popular to steal and swap. We have created an engine guide containing some of the more popular Honda and Acura engine prefixes to use when inspecting vehicles; this guide is located in Appendix B. A sample of this guide is pictured in photo 23.

B18C	Integra	Japanese		Y80, S80	94-00	VTEC
B18C1	Integra GSR	DB8	DB859 = Leather	Y80, S80	94-01	VTEC
B18C1	Integra GSR	DC2	DC239 = Leather	Y80, S80	94-01	VTEC
B18C5	Integra	DC2	DC231 = Type-R	S80	97-01	VTEC
H22A1	Prelude	BB1		M2F4	93-97	VTEC
H22A4	Prelude	BB6		M6HA, M2Y4, M2U4, MP1A	97-01	VTEC
H23A1	Prelude Si	BB2		M2S4, MP1A	92-96	VTEC

Photo 23

Photo 24

For example, an Acura Integra VTEC engine could start with the prefix of B18C1, whereas an Integra Type-R would start with a B18C5 prefix. If you saw an H22A4 engine prefix in a Honda Civic, you could look at our guide and see that H22A4 (photo 24) belongs in a Prelude, not the Civic you were inspecting. If you were inspecting a Honda Civic in North America and saw the engine prefix of B18C1, you should know that it is a swap based on our engine guide.

All swapped engines should be checked to make sure that they are not stolen. Remember, we are looking for *current stolen vehicles* that this engine is part of, or for *stolen engines and transmissions* that were missing when the vehicle was recovered. If you are not sure if the engine is a current stolen, ID the driver and conduct follow-up later when you are sure. Sometimes it takes weeks to verify if the components are stolen.

Even if a swap is not in the system as stolen, it can lead you to a stolen by inspecting the vehicle the swap came from when appropriate. For example, let's say we inspect a Civic that has B18C1 Integra engine in it. We run that engine number through the system to get the associated VIN. We then run that VIN through the system to see if it is currently registered. If it does have current registration then we know that vehicle also has a swapped engine because the car we are inspecting has its original engine. Follow-up should be done to insure this newly identified swapped engine is not stolen.

In addition to checking for stolen component parts during these inspections, some states require monitoring of engine swapping to ensure emission standards are upheld. The Bureau of Automotive Repair (BAR) in California is a good example of such a program. Since one of the goals of enforcement is to stop the illegal racing, enforcing any applicable modification and smog laws can help in this effort. While you are in the process of verifying the stolen status of the engine, you will be determining if the engine belongs to that car. If it does not, then consider local or federal smog laws (see Engine Modifications in Chapter 5 for additional resources and information).

Additionally, by following through on emissions requirements, you may uncover perjury and additional crimes. Frequently the engines that are swapped into these street racing vehicles won't pass emissions tests and the vehicles owner, along with a dirty inspection facility representative, will falsify documents indicating the vehicle passed when in fact it did not. We worked a case in which a 1987 Honda CRX with a JDM ZC engine was inspected at a facility. The inspection records were obtained and the first test showed the vehicle failed the test and labeled a "gross polluter." The vehicle was then taken to another inspection facility three days later and it again failed the test and labeled a "gross polluter," even though the tests did improve slightly. Approximately four hours – and 15 miles – later, it was re-inspected and passed with flying colors, as if it were a new car. Obtaining these types of records can help to identify fraud, identify dirty shops, and get another illegal street racer off the streets. Contact your local air resources officer or us for more information.

Similar swaps are easily identified, such as a SR20DET engine instead of a KA24DE in a Nissan 240SX, but due to the numerous possibilities, we have just listed Honda/Acura's most common in our guide. For guidance and a good starting point for other makes and models, start with Wikipedia or Google and search for that model's engine codes using search phrases such as "Supra engine codes" or

"Nissan engine codes." You can use similar search engine techniques to locate hard to find engine and transmission number locations.

Most major component parts on vehicles are identifiable via their serial, component, or tracking numbers. If a suspect removes any of those numbers, the part (including the entire car) may be seized for further investigation. Transmission identification based on serial number prefixes can be a little more difficult, as some prefixes are installed in a variety of makes and models. However, putting all the numbers together can lead to an exact identification.

Running Numbers

In running Honda and Acura engine numbers through national databases, there may be several factors to consider. For example, if you had an engine number of H22A1 0123456, you should first try and run it with all 12 numbers. If you don't get a hit, then run the last seven digits, 0123456. If you still don't get a hit, you should try running the last digit of the prefix followed by the seven-digit sequential: 10123456. In running a partial engine number, you may get a return of 40 hits. Use the same engine cheat sheet found in Appendix B to narrow it down to the correct VIN. For example, an H22A1 engine is a Prelude. The Prelude VIN may have **BB6** for the 4, 5, & 6th VIN positions, (JHMBB6). Looking at your list of 40 possible VINs, you should only see one VIN with the BB6 VIN positions.

Most engine numbers are stamped into the block of the engine. Other components such as transmissions may have a label with the number. Honda and Acura use labels to identify their transmissions. Newer transmission labels generally have the serial number barcoded as well as printed. Older transmissions may not have the barcode and may have a foil identification label only.

Various records through third party databases may have component numbers that were entered incomplete. Never accept a "no record" response. Contact the manufacturer or us for verification in cases like these. If you don't have time to run the numbers during an operation, write down the VIN, license number, and engine and transmission number on a field card and forward to auto theft or to us. If the vehicle is being impounded, then add the engine and transmission number to the impound report for auto theft detectives to run later.

Illegal Street Racing Operations

Enforcing illegal street activity will save lives and prevent injuries, damage to property, theft, and fraud. In order for the enforcement to be effective, it needs to be a team effort involving multiple agencies working together for additional resources, expertise, and solutions. This team needs to include all of those involved, including prosecutors, judges, and parents.

Part of the problem in effective enforcement is a lack of awareness in the scope of the problem and the consequences it is having. Because job assignments and trends change, continual, comprehensive, and current training is imperative for successful resolutions. California's Dragnet programs, funded by the Office of Traffic Safety (OTS), have provided training to traffic officers throughout the state. Once trained, these officers have been able to prevent countless accidents through continued enforcement.

There has been a 1200% increase in ticket issuance for unlawful vehicle modifications in some cities after a Dragnet training class. Prior to the classes, officers were not aware, or they were unsure, of which violations they could enforce to help prevent the illegal activity that was a precursor to the related injuries and deaths.

To increase the availability and effectiveness of this training, we founded a nonprofit organization to provide training to law enforcement, the insurance industry, and the public focusing on theft and fraud. F.A.S.T., The Foundation for Automotive Safety and Trends, has several components, one being the training series *"The Fast and the Fraudulent"*™. This training covers emerging trends, auto theft, and fraud as it relates to the illegal street activity. Training in this area further prevents deaths, injuries, property damage, and economic losses (for more information go to www.ProtectOurStreets.org).

In Chapter 3, we discussed the various types of events, including the car shows and illegal street racing. In addition to what we mentioned in those sections, we will expand as to how investigators safely and effectively work these events in an effort to locate stolen vehicles, components, and chop shops. This type of enforcement activity saves lives by removing the problems (illegal cars or racers) from the equation.

The illegal eighth or quarter-mile drags, drifting, and some freeway racing can all be worked in the same manner. Enforcement operations targeting illegal street racing can provide incredible results due to the volume of vehicles involved and potential for stolen vehicle and component recovery.

Determining where this illegal activity is occurring is not too difficult. Local web sites, informants, dispatch, businesses, and local traffic enforcement officers are great sources. I have seen aerial photographs in which the starting line of a favorite illegal drag spot on city streets is visible due to the heavy burnout marks left by the tires.

Several cities have street racing task forces operating against this illegal activity, and they already have operational plans in place and know where the favorite areas are to race. Enlisting their support is necessary. Many times the traffic enforcement officers are not aware of the theft and fraud aspects involved in this scene. A patrol-briefing version of "The Fast and the Fraudulent™" presentation generally gets them interested and up to speed. Even if the traffic officers are aware of the theft and fraud aspects, they are generally too busy with the enforcement aspects of the detail and need an auto theft investigator's help. The illegal street-racer enforcement details with whom I have worked have the expertise and resources to corral hundreds of street racers at a time in one area. This allows us to easily go through the vehicles and look for the theft and fraud aspects while they concentrate on enforcement.

In many cities, there are several areas where participants and spectators go to race. A nice straight section of highway, generally industrial, with room for all of the spectators to line the street is optimal. There may be several scout vehicles driving to these locations to determine if there is a police presence. If police are not present, they put the word out and the racers flock to that location. They may be waiting at a nearby parking lot or hamburger joint, or could be roaming in their vehicles in the area.

During the planning stages of an enforcement action, several factors need to be discussed. In agencies where the number of available personnel or money is a problem, there may be assistance from neighboring agencies. California Dragnet officers routinely bring officers from other agencies (including myself) to assist, as this problem is mobile and affects everyone. Pre-planning can make effective use of limited resources. You should have some idea regarding what to expect number-wise if you have been scouting the areas or receiving reports the weeks prior to the operation. If your resources are insufficient to handle all of the racers and spectators, consider blocking in a smaller amount of participants. Pre-assigning all of the duties outlined here will help to streamline the event.

Cars involved in this scene generally have several occupants. Stopping just 20 vehicles can lead to 80 detainees. If your city has an anti-spectator law, or utilizes unlawful assembly sections, then you may have up to four arrestees per vehicle. Curfew violations need to be considered for juveniles. As soon as practical, the juveniles' parents should be contacted to pick up their children so officers do not have to wait long after the operation for their arrival.

Some agencies utilize offsite or mobile booking vehicles to streamline arrest processing and have a large supply of flex cuffs with several cuff cutters, so handcuffs don't get lost or have to be tracked. If the booking area is off-site, then bus transportation can be of great assistance. Other considerations involve separating juveniles and females and having bathroom access.

Another consideration for a successful operation is confidentiality. I have seen several operations ruined because word got out beforehand that an enforcement action was going to take place on a particular date. Internal police memorandums discussing the plans have made it onto street racer Internet sites, innocent leaks in which an employee happens to mention the pending action to their teenager who quickly spreads the word even though sworn to secrecy. Internal training materials have also made it onto the Internet. One agency that was a victim to this advised the webmaster that they were displaying protected material and a suit would be filed against them if they did not remove the material immediately, which they did.

Leaks have come from people inside the department who unlawfully engage in street racing themselves (several officers and deputies have been fired because of this). However, finding a young officer that can walk the talk when it comes to street racing and has a honest passion for legal vehicle modifications will be a great asset to your enforcement team and be better equipped to research the Internet and gather great intelligence as to what is happening.

Some agencies will not advise the rotational tow truck companies to be on standby out of fear that employees of one of the companies will let the word out of a pending police operation involving the towing of cars. If your laws allow for impounding vehicles involved in illegal street racing and related activities, you can have your impound forms partially completed regarding location and primary violation to help streamline the process.

To help guide the racers to the location you want to conduct the operation in, have marked units visibly patrolling the other areas frequented by racers. On-duty personnel need to be aware of where the operation will be taking place and avoid enforcement in that area. The racer scouts will see that the area is clear of law enforcement and guide the racers to your location. They may use a cell phone or text their observations to get the word out while listening to police frequencies for any possible police intervention. Enforcement agencies should use private channels to communicate, but a better choice would be to use cell phones until the area is contained. If your agency has set up a text tip line, ensure that it is being monitored in case text messages come in regarding race locations and related activity.

If you have a choice, the best location is the one that has the fewest escape routes. There should be a location or two nearby where the majority of the enforcement detail can lay in wait without being detected – close enough to prevent racers from escaping but far enough away so as not to be detected. Sometimes racers will drive through race areas to make sure that law enforcement is not staging somewhere. You may be able to prevent this by closing gates behind you or setting up temporary barricades.

It is best to have police operatives on the ground in an undercover (UC) capacity. These impromptu races happen so fast that by the time you send the signal to swoop in and stop the illegal drags, several races would have most likely already occurred. The undercover police on the ground should video these races and the entire scene. This video can show who is actually driving the vehicles and many other violations, including who the flagger is. The UC observations can also note whether innocent bystanders are trapped in the round up so they are not inadvertently cited for being at a street race (see Chapter 3, "Illegal Street Racing," for more on flaggers and other participants).

Video cameras are very common at all of these events and the UC officers generally will not attract attention by videoing the events themselves. Be aware that if they think you are undercover at their race, they will burn you and your vehicle at the scene and on the Internet. Be careful never to use the undercover officer or his car as part of the enforcement detail. If he is caught up in the enforcement activity, he should be treated like all of the other violators until away from the area.

Once the illegal activity has been observed, a signal should be given to have the enforcement detail block all of the roads and possible escape routes. This portion of the enforcement needs to be well planned and well executed. Utilize motor officers if your department has them. Drivers caught in these blockades have driven over and through many obstacles to get away and this part of the plan needs to be particularly attentive to safety. The vehicles will be driving in all sorts of directions trying to escape. A "no pursuit" policy is usually a good policy regarding escaping racers. Have a plan that will eventually guide them in one direction. The vehicles can be safely driven to an inspection area once the dust settles.

Before the enforcement starts, all of the vehicles should be stopped and facing in the same direction, two to four vehicles across if possible. Keeping all of the vehicle's occupants inside the vehicle helps with officer safety issues. Placing the keys on the roof and immediately marking the driver's hand with a "D" helps prevent occupants from switching positions to confuse the officers or avoid detection from violations such as driving on a suspended license or warrants. In addition to immediately identifying the driver, officers first on the scene could mark their initials on each occupants arm in case questions arise as to who made the initial observations (when applicable). Several video cameras rolling from different angles can also be used for later identification.

While the vehicles are being inspected by traffic enforcement, the auto theft investigators will inspect the vehicles for theft and fraud. The most common mistake made in this type of enforcement action is not having enough officers to inspect and cite depending on the amount of vehicles stopped. We have had operations that went from midnight to 5:00 a.m. An operation that takes this long can generate unlawful detention accusations. You should know your resources and implement your plan accordingly. To control the numbers, you can initiate the round up early on, before too many street racers come to the site.

Having two auto theft investigators and traffic enforcement officers for each lane is optimal. Start at the top and systematically work your way down. The auto theft investigation is separate from the traffic enforcement detail. If you see a vehicle that has altered or stolen numbers, mark the windshield with a predetermined mark to advise other officers and insure it is not let go. Traffic officers should also make a different mark indicating that they are finished with the vehicle.

If questionable components are observed, initial statements should be obtained at the scene to properly identify the vehicle and determine if the owner/driver has knowledge of the theft or component. Casually asking if the driver works on the car, how long he has owned it, or when he installed the engine can be all that you need to make a case. If the driver indicates that he installed the engine last year, but you know that it was stolen three months ago, that statement is a good indicator of guilty knowledge. Other inconsistent or implausible statements should be documented and can be evidence of guilty knowledge. If the driver does not own the car, inquire about the owner's knowledge of the vehicles location and use. Statement such as "this is my Dad's car but he lets me drive it" can help in showing control and use.

Get through all of the vehicles as quickly and safely as possible. It is best to have the questionable vehicles towed for inspection on the following day. Be aware that there could be some fresh, unreported stolens at these events. Pay attention to the key and the ignition areas, as well as potential points of entry. Look for fresh collision damage as unreported hit and runs do occur.

In addition to towing vehicles with stolen component parts, vehicles will be towed for racing and significant traffic violations. In California, they impound the vehicle for 30 days for illegal street racing. All owners of impounded vehicles should be interviewed. This is one of the best opportunities for the auto theft investigator to gain information on chop shops and fraud rings. I have found that our best informants come from this type of interview. The drivers love their cars and want them back, so they will do almost anything to get them.

The participants love to talk about their plans and our enforcement actions. Favorite web sites used by the area racers should be visited periodically before the operation and daily after the operation to gain intelligence that will help your tactics and future plans. After some operations, specific websites may try to keep their members from talking about the incident, as they know law enforcement monitors such chat. Invariably someone will let the cat out of the bag or leave a reference as to what sites have the chat about an event.

Using the Internet can also help to prevent illegal street racing, as well as its related unlawful activity. In March 2008, I assisted the Riverside County Dragnet program in California during a successful anti-street racing operation. Riverside County was experiencing up to 400 street race and show cars that were gathering at a Hooters restaurant. For several weeks, this group of street and show cars would take over the parking lot and show off by doing burnouts and donuts and exhibitions of speed as well as low riders hopping and scrapping with their hydraulics.

I was sitting in my vehicle in the parking lot away from the main group of spectators and participants observing the chaos just prior to the enforcement operation. Two drifters parked next to me and I overheard one of them say he wanted to park far enough away from the action so that if the police came they could get away. During this time, a news helicopter flew over and spooked a few of the participants, as they thought it was a police helicopter.

When Dragnet moved in, approximately 200 vehicles were trapped in and inspected resulting in 150 citations issued and 20 vehicles impounded. This led to six stolen engines located and three chop shops identified and busted. In researching the Internet for chat regarding this operation, I discovered that this Hooter's meet had been ongoing for over one year. Several sites discussed the details of the meet and even included professionally made flyers describing the meets. Some of them pleaded for participants to behave stating, "Please let's not ruin it this time with Burnouts, Drifting, Revving, Alcohol, Drugs, Weapons or Fighting." This type of plea shows that the group's initial intentions were good, but it is nearly impossible to control hundreds of youth with modified sport compact cars, particularly at night.

Many different website forums offered additional information, which assisted in research regarding this operation and how to improve future operations. I also learned that Hooters throughout the country is a popular gathering place for car enthusiasts, particularly our Fast and Fraudulent crowd.

Because these gatherings, and many others like it, are continually written about and occurring on a frequent basis, we can nip them in the bud before they bloom into trouble. Too frequently, we take action only when things get out of hand. I hate to harp on the fact that youth plus fast cars equal trouble in large gatherings, but history has proven this for decades. We cannot wait for the problem to materialize; we need to act as soon as the problem starts to develop. As soon as you hear or read about nighttime gathering places for these Fast and Fraudulent groups, you need to enforce immediately all laws regarding vehicle code violations and large gatherings. If participants know that there will be a law enforcement presence, one that actually enforces the laws, the flagrant violators will not show up and drugs and alcohol will not be an issue. Zero tolerance can lead to zero deaths and injuries.

These enforcement activities can actually be good for public relations. After the Riverside operation, a concerned citizen sent an email to the Riverside Police Department complaining about the use of public resources. This citizen was responding to some of the typical blog headlines that occur after such an event. In this case one headline was, "California: Police Raid Car Enthusiast Gathering

, Generate Revenue" and went on to describe the event as, "Owners of imported sport compact cars had gathered at the Canyon Crossing shopping center on Friday night to swap stories, talk about their passion for cars, and show off the latest enhancements to their rides...." What the citizen wrote regarding this headline or chat is a typical response. What the department's public information officer wrote in his response was thought provoking and elicited a great reply.

The citizen wrote:

"Hello. I am contacting you based on news articles I have seen on the Internet surrounding the incident of a Friday Night Raid your department helped organize and execute in the Canyon Crossing shopping center. I am not sure if you have received anything else related to this incident, but I hope this message does not go unread. I could just as easily as everyone complain that those people should not have gotten tickets, committed no crime, and were not street racing, but I have learned from previous cases that it is completely and utterly useless.

Today, I stand to ask you one question and one question only: How many women were raped, how many places were robbed, how many drug deals were executed, and how many lives were lost while over 100 of the areas officers were busting a legal social gathering for profit? It sickens me to think that your department and the others involved would commit warrant-less searches and write tickets for ridiculous reasons without any merit for monetary reasons.

Congratulations Riverside Sheriff's department, congratulations."

Riverside's response to email:

"Dear Mr. [Name Witheld],

Thank you for your comments directed to the Riverside County Sheriff.

The March 28 street racing enforcement operation you refer to was actually organized and conducted by the City of Riverside Police Department, with the assistance of allied and neighboring agencies, including the Riverside County Sheriff's Department.

In response to your comments, I must caution that it does not make sense to question crimes that may occur while other criminal activities are occurring. Police must enforce more than one section of the legal code, and the purpose is public safety. The reasons for enforcement are not ridiculous, and the motive is not money.

Street racing is a reckless and dangerous entertainment, in which participants and fans always describe it as a harmless good time - until someone gets hurt. It's often innocent parties who pay the price.

Riverside is a city that has suffered at least two relatively recent street racing-related fatalities, in October 2006 and February 2007, the result of speed and young drivers showing off. One victim was a wheelchair-bound mother of two who was killed on a city sidewalk, in front of her young children, when a teen street racer lost control. The second victim was a teenage passenger in a crowded car.

These are the scenarios that sicken law enforcement officers, not the enforcement of laws placed on the books for legitimate public safety reasons. Street racing and public demonstrations of speed are dangerous and illegal, and departments here take the risks very seriously. 'Social gatherings' around such activity encourages reckless show-off behavior and makes spectators culpable, though none were cited as such.

The gatherings at Canyon Crossing were not innocent social gatherings. There are plenty of events in this and other cities that qualify as social events, such as the well-known Route 66 Rendezvous in nearby San Bernardino, or controlled and legal amateur race days at Irwindale Speedway, for example. Canyon Crossing is a busy family-oriented shopping and restaurant center where business owners and their patrons have expressed concern about the crowds, dangerous driving, burning rubber, noise, reckless behavior, and the resulting threats to safety that occurred at that same location week after week. Traditional patrol enforcement activity, including moving momentary offenders along, did nothing to deter the ongoing street racing and demonstration of speed activity.

Further, this was not a 'legal' gathering. Its occupants and managers did not invite the car crowd to the shopping center for any sort of car show. Quite the contrary. The Canyon Crossing parking lot is private property maintained for the convenience of legitimate business customers. The repeat gatherings of persons laying down skid marks on the pavement, and those cheering the action, constituted trespass.

Those cited were in violation of the California Vehicle Code, the same kinds of offenses that trigger many routine traffic stops. On this occasion, it happened that there were more than 100 vehicles that were in violation, or appeared to be in violation of one section or another, gathered in one spot. Those in compliance with the CVC were warned of the street racing safety concerns at the site, and sent on their way. Those in violation were cited accordingly. Your contention that the motivation for this enforcement action is profit," is ludicrous. The costs of conducting enforcement, investigation and related judicial action related to offenses far outweighs the monetary penalty leveled on those cited. Many of the citations issued that evening were "fix-it tickets," directing the owners to remedy citable vehicle code violations within a reasonable period of time. Those that comply pay only a nominal administrative fee to government, after proving their repair and compliance.

Likewise, most of the overtime manpower and costs of the multi-agency enforcement action were borne by a state Office of Traffic Safety grant that the Riverside, Ontario and Irwindale police departments administer specifically to deal with street racing issues in Inland Southern California.

This enforcement operation was conducted almost entirely by officers working on grant-funded special assignment, which did not impact regular police patrol funding, staffing or activities. In contrast, the repeated calls for service to respond to the street racing at a shopping center and on surrounding roadways, here and elsewhere, does have the impact of drawing patrol and traffic officers away from other important policing activity elsewhere in our jurisdictions.

I'm sorry that this has been a lengthy reply, and I have so far neglected to answer your one and only real question: other crimes.

There were no homicides during the period of this enforcement action in any one of the agencies' jurisdictions. In the City of Riverside, the burglary, two drunk driving and four domestic violence incidents that occurred elsewhere in the city during the operational period all resulted in arrests of the perpetrators.

We appreciate your concern, and sharing your perspective, and allowing us to share our perspective on an issue important to all of us.

Sincerely,

Steven Frasher
Public Information Officer (civilian)
Riverside Police Department
Riverside, California"

Reply:

"I would just like to you thank you deeply for your response, and hope you can place my first email in the past. After sending my message, I decided to do some more research on the subject and incident, which I admit should have occurred before hitting the send button. The online articles I had read made your department look like the bad guys, and I'm a bit ashamed to say I let the media rule over reason.

I apologize for what might have been some insulting comments, and congratulate you, without the sarcasm, for the work you and your department is done. I in no way enjoy hearing the stories of deaths due to street racing, I myself had a friend who killed himself, age 19, his 3 passengers, all of whom were under 17, and severely injured two elderly people in another car while he was street racing.

Again, I thank you for your reply, and I am ecstatic to think that my comment, as ludicrous as it was, was not only read, but concerned and replied to, something I find happening less and less in this world. I would also like to apologize again for any accusations that we're made against the departments involved, and hope that you keep up the work our communities need to stay safe."

Preventive Enforcement

Favorite dance clubs, parking lots, burger joints, or the restaurants where these Fast and the Fraudulent vehicles gather should not be ignored. These frequently end up being a staging ground for several races and illegal activities, and they are good locations to conduct operations. Business owners frequently complain about the traffic and vandalism that these groups cause and request law enforcement to take action. Conducting operations at these locations helps the businesses and can prevent deaths and injuries due to the racing that typically takes place later. As mentioned in Illegal Street Racing in Chapter 2, some cities that have known areas of racer gatherings have been notified by the property owners that they do not condone or want this activity. They have also posted "No Trespassing" or "No Loitering" signs between midnight and five a.m. to further define boundaries. Some cities have the property owner sign a victim's complaint form and keep it on file; when the potential racers gather illegally, the police can take immediate action through arrest and vehicle impounds. I know this sounds a little harsh but the purpose is to STOP illegal street racing and related activities and to save lives. There is a huge difference between an organized car show and the "let's meet at Hooters every Wednesday night" crowd.

We have conducted operations at local hamburger restaurants where hundreds would gather late in the evening. Most parking lot operations come about because the business owners have had enough and are at their wits end with the trash, noise, burnouts, and loss of legitimate business. Some enthusiasts do gather just to look at the cars while others are there to line up their next street race. They will mill around these spots until a scout tells them where to race or egos flare and bets are made.

To effectively work these operations, traffic and auto theft enforcement details lay in wait until the parking lots are full. They move in and set up a cone pattern for cars as they exit, while a mobile command post and vehicle checkpoint is set up at the end of the cone pattern. Cars with vehicle code violations or probable cause are sent to the checkpoint for further investigation. *All cars with violations are sent through to avoid profiling accusations.* A mobile command post may be set up for computers and other functions depending on the weather. Mobile lighting helps at the inspection area.

The inspections at these operations are the same as the illegal race operations. Typically, cars are fed through the inspection lane two abreast. Traffic enforcement checks for illegal modifications, and the auto theft investigator should be looking for engine and transmission swaps, fresh stolens, fraud signs, and VIN switches. If the engine was not stolen, and does not belong to that vehicle, obtain the VIN that belongs to the engine number and run the VIN for current registration information. If there is current registration, then you know that vehicle has a different engine, as you just inspected the original engine in another car. Inspect that vehicle later to determine if it contains legitimate equipment. In addition to looking for stolen component parts, some states require inspections when engines are swapped to insure they conform to emissions laws as mentioned previously in this chapter under Swapped Engine Identification. We have found stolen engines and transmissions, which can lead to chop shops, in similar cases many times using parking lot enforcement operations.

Open Highway Racing Enforcement

As mentioned in Chapter 3 under Highway Racing, impromptu highway racing has gained in popularity in the mid- to late-2000s. Deaths and injuries seem to occur more to the innocent third-party victims than to those directly involved in this type of illegal activity.

Highway racing may involve just two vehicles, packs of several vehicles, and in extreme cases, cannonball type runs. Although they may be spontaneous, there are still sections of highways that consistently have this type of activity happening on them. If you haven't seen what this looks like, conduct a Google search for "illegal freeway racing." This will return about a quarter of a million hits with lots of video.

Spotting violators can be as easy as listening for the unique sounds of modified engines or looking for racing signals at night. It is common for participants to use their emergency flashers or horn to signal the start of a race or run. On the third honk of a horn, the race is on; at the beginning or end of a race the emergency flashers may be used to signal others. The flash of a shift light may be seen at night, along with hearing the high-revved shifts. Cars or motorcycles, weaving in and out of traffic at nearly twice the speed limit, combined with the above actions, make it easy to see the racing and to call in a possible intercept location a few miles up the road. Many agencies have successfully caught and stopped this type of activity, even if it was not planned, by working the overpasses in popular areas. Police in Ohio and other states successfully use planes and helicopters to catch dangerous drivers and speeders making the program very cost effective. Other cities have the advantage of utilizing speed cameras or other remote cameras to monitor several sections of highways and identify violators.

Enlisting the public's help is imperative. Public ad campaigns that make people aware of the problem, discuss the dangers, and let the community know they should call 911 when they witness such activity can help curb the problem (Chapter 8 has more information on prevention).

Educating the dispatchers and responding officers about how to intercept the violators will help make sure they don't get away to race again. When I call 911, I try to give a good description of the vehicles, their speed, and an estimate where the cars will be in the next few minutes. By the time dispatch puts the call out over the air, several minutes and miles will have passed. Approximately 80 miles per hour equals 1.3 miles per minute; 100 miles per hour equals 1.6 miles per minute; and 120 mph equals 2 miles per minute. Our Fast and Fraudulent crowd travel between 80 and 130 miles per hour, which means if it takes five minutes to get the call out, the dangerous drivers will have traveled between 6 and 10 miles. Responding officers need to factor in the speed, last location, and their response time to head the racers off. Overpasses several miles forward of the direction of travel are the best location from which to respond.

Sanctioned Race Operations

Sanctioned events are those events generally held at racetracks and can have several hundred competing cars with several thousand spectators attending. I have worked many of these throughout the years, and more times then not, I have found stolen component parts in some of the participating as well as some of the spectator's vehicles.

A good relationship needs to be developed with the racetrack director before developing an operational plan. Some promoters and track officials are hesitant about having any type of law enforcement presence at the tracks. Find out ahead of time if the track is law-enforcement friendly. It has been my experience that neither the track officials nor the promoters promote or encourage all of the theft and fraud that is occurring in this scene and will be more than happy to assist in your operation as long as you do not interfere with their operations in any way.

If you want to ensure a successful operation, make sure that the promoter or officials can be trusted so word does not get out that a pending operation will take place. The promoters and track officials should be reassured that no officer will interfere or impede at any stage of their event. Contact the track well in advance of the race event; you need to get a complete understanding of how the event is run. Many tracks have video from past events to give the officer an idea of manpower and logistics. In past events, the race director has allowed officers to sit in the tower with their computers so VINs and component numbers can be checked if officers do not have wireless access for ISO records.

Ask the race official about additional rules that may assist you. For example, at one raceway we had the option of confiscating any film or video we needed or reviewing tech inspection cards. Use caution, however, in creating potential controversy and losing the opportunity in the future to come back to a particular track.

An area should be set aside to inspect the recovered stolen vehicles that allow enough room for the tow trucks to come take the vehicles away. The general inspection area should be within view of spectators and press, making a statement about auto theft and fraud. This can be accomplished without compromising any confidential inspection processes.

Competitors and spectators arrive early. The largest races are generally held on weekends, and gates can open as early as 7:00 a.m. Officers should already be at the track. The larger races will attract competitors from around the country. Most cars are driven in with very few being trailered. Having an officer viewing the cars driving in may give additional PC to inspect a vehicle later, since these cars are generally in violation of the vehicle code. However, a very low profile should be maintained so as not to interfere with the event or spook away potential auto thieves and the stolen property.

Once the competitors enter the facility, they go to the safety "tech" inspection area. This area generally will be two to five cars across and hundreds deep, depending on the event. Up to 600 racers can attend some of these races. *During the peak season, some tracks have turned away hundreds of racers because they were already at capacity by 8:00 a.m.* Once the cars are in the tech inspection lanes, they are a captive audience and cannot get out. Starting at the front of the line, racetrack inspectors open the hoods and inspect the vehicles. This is the best and least intrusive time for the officer to inspect the vehicle. Officers can just act as if they are part of the Tech Inspection so as not to arouse suspicion. They should be looking for engine and transmission swaps, as well as VIN-switches (see Chapter 3 for the tech inspection process).

Depending on the number of vehicles, the officer(s) may only want to make note of engine numbers that were not factory installed. Using the Engine Swap Guide can assist you in this process. We have gone to races, written down and run **all** engine numbers, and still only recovered stolens that were engine swaps. Two officers per car/row work well if you have the manpower. One reads the number and the other writes it down. If a barcode scanner is available, the barcoded VIN should be scanned to automatically track the vehicle's attendance (VINtrack.com). Pay attention to the key and the ignition areas, as there may be some fresh, unreported stolens at the track.

Once again, care must be given not to impede the track's process. If you can't get to a car, let it go. One officer should be stationed at the end of the inspection line, watching for any activity indicating that the competitors know there is a police inspection occurring. If a vehicle makes a U-turn to flee the track, a unit should be waiting outside to stop him for a vehicle inspection. Once again, keeping a low profile is imperative.

After the inspection is completed, the cars may drive to a staging area to prepare their vehicles for the quarter-mile run. This will provide an additional opportunity to inspect any missed vehicles. At the large events, the vehicles generally will make several passes at the quarter-mile. This will allow ample time to run the VINs without losing the vehicles or impeding the tracks progress.

At this same event, there may be "Show" only cars on display. They are judged for best paint, interior, wheels, and stereos among other things. We have found stolen components at these areas also. Be sure to check the spectator's cars also at these events if you have a sufficient work force.

Business Inspections and Officer Safety

Business inspections are necessary to identify chop shops and decrease auto theft. Auto theft investigators frequently conduct business inspections of repair facilities and performance shops. Most states have a regulation that allows these types of inspections for locating stolen vehicles or component parts. To see a sample regulation you can view California's vehicle code section 2805 on the Department of Motor Vehicles website at http://www.dmv.ca.gov/pubs/vctop/d02/vc2805.htm

Business inspections also provide the opportunity to learn about current trends and issues that effect local business owners and the community. Some of the best sources of information come from shop owners who are tired of being undercut by dishonest business owners involved in the same industry. Inspections should occur randomly throughout the community to ensure businesses are not being targeted and a complete picture of industry trends and issues are revealed.

Throughout this book, I have mentioned numerous chop shops that have been identified based upon information that led to a repair facility or speed/performance shop. By conducting business inspections, many of those chop shops could have been identified sooner with fewer victims being targeted.

Several times per year, we learned after the fact that the performance shop or body shop we were just inspecting also had ties to a larger, organized crime ring involved in extortion, fraud, drugs, gangs, and theft.

One performance shop that I visited frequently, I later learned was funded by money laundering and credit card fraud unrelated to the auto thefts I was investigating. Another time we had just left a repair facility only to learn that just days prior a professional rival crime syndicate had visited that shop with assault rifles apparently to carry out a hit.

Officer safety needs to be in the forefront, as it can be easy to get complaisant when working the "street racer" type cases. As long as I have been investigating this scene, there have been incidents of shootings and gang activity. Within the vehicles themselves, guns have been found in various hidden compartments, and both street racers and spectators that I have interviewed have been involved in shootings.

Gray-Market Vehicles

Identifying Gray-Market cars will prevent future problems. Gray-Market cars can be unsafe, illegal, and prone to claims and damage due to warranty issues. In the United States, a Gray-Market vehicle is one that is manufactured for sale in a country other than the U.S. and later is imported into the U.S.

Each country has different laws as they relate to safety and emissions. For a vehicle to be imported legally from one country to another, it must meet those standards. If the importer does not follow the proper procedures, the vehicle may be considered a non-conforming Gray-Market vehicle. In the United States, it is illegal to import a vehicle that does not meet the U.S. Environmental Protection Agency (EPA) emission standards (see Title 49, United States Code, section 30112).

Most times, these vehicles are not covered under warranty, as they are Gray-Market and do not conform to the country's laws. This lack of warranty and "illegal" status can become theft and fraud problems when the owner cannot maintain or sell the vehicle. Insurance companies and motor vehicle departments many times unknowingly register and insure them, giving the owner a false sense of security.

There has been an influx of Gray-Market vehicles in the United States due to the American desire for Japanese vehicles without the heavy smog equipment the U.S. and California vehicles must conform to. These Japanese Domestic Market, or JDM cars, (see Chapter 5 for more on JDM) can cost more to conform to a different country's standard than the vehicle itself. This is one reason why so many illegal Gray-Market cars exist in the United States currently.

Insurance companies and departments of motor vehicles have been wrongly insuring and registering these illegal vehicles. Popular Japanese vehicles such as the Nissan Skyline and Silvia have inundated the United States without going through registered importers or customs, and they do not comply with NHTSA, DOT, or EPA. These vehicles are not legal and can be seized, even if DMV/MVD has registered them. Some of the importers whom law enforcement has investigated, particularly those importing Skylines and Silvias, were not properly bringing the vehicles into compliance. One such company in Gardena, California was not bringing the vehicles into compliance with such things as failing to install airbags. The owner was sued by several unhappy customers and was subsequently arrested and charged with attempted extortion, attempted kidnapping, and assault with a deadly weapon in addition to his importation issues.

Another Skyline import group was importing Gray-Market vehicles in pieces from Puerto Rico, through Florida and into Kentucky to try and circumvent the import laws. While in

Kentucky, they would reassemble the vehicle to make it complete again. This action is illegal as the vehicle is being reassembled in its entirety.

Honda/Acura JDM vehicles do not have a public VIN plate on the dash, nor do they have a federal safety sticker on the door or pillar post with the full VIN as North American cars do. The primary number that Japan uses to register cars is the firewall VIN, which is stamped into the metal consisting of the model code followed by the serial number, such as **DC2-1300245**.

A North American Integra VIN for the same car would look something like JH4**DC2**390TS**300245**, and have this full VIN stamped in the firewall, displayed on the dash public VIN plate, and printed on the federal safety label on the door or pillar post.

Several officers have reported that when stopping a JDM Honda/Acura, they were told by the drivers that these JDM vehicles have no firewall VIN. It has been my experience that these suspects most likely stole the vehicle and removed the identifying VIN numbers, then lied to the officers trying to confuse them regarding whether the vehicle came with a firewall VIN. Officers should consider impounding the vehicle for further investigation if this fits within their procedures and guidelines. At minimum, it warrants further follow up. Suspects that deal in illegal vehicles are counting on the officer's lack of knowledge in this area to get away with their possession of an illegal or stolen vehicle.

We receive many calls from insurance companies regarding theft and collision claims involving a vehicle in which the VIN does not conform to U.S. standards (Gray-Market). Further investigation reveals that these vehicles were imported illegally and that the vehicle itself does not conform to U.S. standards. My first question to them is, "Why did you insure an illegal car"? I can understand how a few cars would slip through if the VIN conforms, but when the non-conforming VIN is provided, many questions should be asked to ensure the vehicle is legal. Some insurance companies have policies requiring the vehicle be U.S. legal, but that is in the fine print and used as something to fall back upon. However, insurance companies beware: If the signs were obvious that the vehicle was a Gray-Market car, and you were accepting their premium for quite some time, the fine print may not matter.

The following information from NHTSA highlights some of the main issues regarding assembling a vehicle from parts:

If a business imports an "assemblage of motor vehicle parts" (i.e., a vehicle without its drive train), the business may be operating within the laws/regulations administered by the National Highway Traffic Safety Administration (NHTSA). At the time of importation, the importer's obligation for "assemblages of motor vehicle parts" is to declare the equipment items on a United States Department of Transportation (U.S. DOT) HS-7 form. New and used equipment items that are covered by Federal Motor Vehicle Safety Standards (FMVSS) must comply with those FMVSS at the time of importation. Examples include lighting equipment, brake hoses, glazing, and others. The U.S. Department of Homeland Security (Customs) inspectors are responsible for reviewing the U.S. DOT HS-7 declarations and authorizing entry of the equipment items into U.S. commerce.

If a vehicle is assembled with the used parts of the assemblage along with certain new parts, the NHTSA Office of Chief Counsel (OCC) interpretative letters state that the vehicle becomes a new vehicle and the assembler of the vehicle becomes its manufacturer. As the manufacturer, the assembler must certify at the time of delivery to the distributor/dealer/purchaser that the vehicle complies with all applicable FMVSS in effect at the time of production. The assembler must also affix a U.S. certification label to the vehicle, and the vehicle must display the assembler's 17-character VIN. The assembler/manufacturer must abide by regulations that require registration with NHTSA as a manufacturer, as well as other manufacturer's requirements under the motor vehicle safety act, such as recalls. If, however, the vehicle is reassembled from old parts, NHTSA OCC interpretative letters state that this is a used vehicle. NHTSA does not regulate used vehicles being offered for resale, but other regulations relating to emissions may apply.

Furthermore, NHTSA does not have authority over titling and registration matters; these are the purview of the effected states. Some states require the assembled vehicles to be registered as specially constructed vehicles. These vehicles are issued a state-assigned VIN, while others will register them under the original manufacturer's name with the original manufacturer's VINs.

When an FMVSS is in effect under federal law/regulations, a state or a political subdivision of a state may prescribe or continue in effect a standard applicable to the same aspect of performance of a motor vehicle or motor vehicle equipment only if the standard is identical to the standard prescribed under the federal law/regulation.

NHTSA does not regulate the operation (i.e., on road use) of motor vehicles, which is generally under the jurisdiction of the states. A state is not required to impose operational requirements that are "identical" to the FMVSS, but many states incorporate the FMVSS into their state requirements for vehicle safety.

If your state has a requirement that vehicles be inspected at the time of registration to ensure compliance with state safety regulations, and those state regulations mirror the FMVSS, you may be able to find deficiencies in the vehicle presented for inspection. By experience, we find that vehicle headlamps found on foreign vehicles do not comply with the requirements of FMVSS No. 108, because the headlamps do not display the required "DOT" marking. Several Gray-Market vehicles do not have the required side marker lights. Many other readily apparent deficiencies may apply to the vehicle for you to consider.

To properly bring a Gray-Market non-conforming vehicle into the United States the owner must use a Registered Importer (RI) to ensure that the vehicle conforms to all applicable Federal Motor Vehicle Safety Standards issued by NHTSA. Independent Commercial Importers (ICI) ensures that the vehicle conforms to emissions standards and they are regulated by the EPA. Not all non-conforming vehicles are eligible for importation, and ICIs are not required to accept vehicles for which they have qualifying certificates of conformity.

The importer must declare the vehicle to the United States Customs on a form HS-7. These forms are great sources of information during an investigation as there are common tactics fraudulent importers uses when completing this forms regarding the vehicles intended use or modifications. Additional crimes of perjury may be applicable depending on how the HS-7 is completed. Additional information can be obtained from NHTSA at http://www.nhtsa.dot.gov/cars/rules/import/ or from the Customs link site at http://www.customslink.com.

There are several factors involved in bringing a car into compliance depending on the manufacturer of the vehicle. Factors can include safety glass, side impact beams, bumpers, tires, and airbags. Even the key fob frequencies may be different, which can create problems with our key fobs and immobilizer systems, particularly when key replacements are needed. It is possible for a right-hand drive vehicle to be manufactured in compliance with the FMVSS. If a motor vehicle was manufactured to comply with all applicable FMVSS, and bears a label certifying such compliance that was permanently affixed by its original manufacturer, there is no need for NHTSA approval before the vehicle is imported.

Once in compliance, the ICI will place a certification label on the door or striker post. The certification label must meet the requirements of Title 49 CFR Part 567 (Code of Federal Regulations) that, among other things, identifies the vehicle's manufacturer (the actual assembler of the vehicle), states the vehicle's date of manufacture (month and year), and contains the following statement: "This vehicle conforms to all applicable Federal motor vehicle safety standards (FMVSS) in effect on the date of manufacture shown above." This type of label exists currently on all cars that are made for North America. The lack of a certification label is not grounds for the vehicle's seizure under federal statutes and regulations.

In addition to the certification label, NHTSA requires that the motor vehicle manufacturer must assign to each motor vehicle manufactured for sale in the U.S. a 17-digit VIN that uniquely identifies the vehicle. The VIN must be correctly formatted and include a check digit in the ninth position that is mathematically correct under a formula that is included in the regulations.

Section 565.5 of the Code of Federal Regulation indicates that motor vehicles imported into the United States shall utilize the VIN assigned by the original manufacturer of the motor vehicle. Part 592 states that the VIN plate or VIN label shall contain the following statement with the identification number assigned by the original manufacturer provided in the blank: SUBSTITUTE FOR U.S. VIN: _____ SEE PART 565. This plate or label shall be permanently affixed inside the passenger compartment. The plate or label must be readable, without moving any part of the vehicle, through the vehicle glazing under daylight lighting conditions by an observer having 20/20 vision (Snellen) whose eye-point is located outside the vehicle adjacent to the left windshield pillar. It shall be located in such a manner as not to cover, obscure, or overlay any part of any identification number affixed by the original manufacturer.

In other words, if a manufacturer produces a motor vehicle for a country other than the United States, the vehicle's VIN does not have to conform to the Federal regulation's content requirements. When such a vehicle is lawfully imported into the United States by a registered importer (RI), the RI is required to use the original manufacturer's VIN and affix to the vehicle the "substitute VIN plate" which alerts U.S. law enforcement that the vehicle's VIN does not conform to our regulations (49 CFR 565.5). This includes vehicles manufactured for the Japanese market that have chassis numbers rather than VINs. The RI would affix the substitute VIN plate to the dash that displays the vehicle's chassis number that was assigned by the OEM. In order for the Integra in the previous example to conform to U.S. standards, the public VIN plate should read **DC2-1300245.**

There are other rules that apply when importing Gray-Market cars. Non-residents may import a vehicle for personal use for a period not to exceed 1 year. If the vehicles do not conform to the U.S. safety and emissions standards within 1 year, they may not be sold and must be exported. In addition, vehicles imported for testing, demonstrations, or competition may be exempt, providing the vehicle is not driven on public roads. If the vehicle is less than 25 years old and was not originally manufactured to comply with all applicable FMVSS, or was not so certified by its original manufacturer, it cannot be lawfully imported into the U.S. on a permanent basis unless NHTSA determines it eligible for importation.

Title 49, United States Code, section 30112, lists prohibitions on manufacturing, selling, and importing non-complying motor vehicles and equipment, when such vehicle is either new or used. Exemptions to the prohibition are stated under 30112(b). In short, NHTSA's authority covers new and used vehicles at the time of importation. Once imported, NHTSA has limited authority, especially when the vehicle is used based on the exemptions stated in 30112(b). Civil penalties are not more than $6,000 for each violation. A separate violation occurs for each motor vehicle or item of motor vehicle equipment and for each failure or refusal to allow or perform an act required by any of the sections. The maximum penalty under this subsection for a related series of violations is $ 13,375,000.

More information on Gray-Market regulations and laws can be found at the NHTSA and EPA websites: http://www.nhtsa.dot.gov/cars/rules/standards/chapt301.html; http://www.epa.gov/otaq/imports/; http://www.nhtsa.dot.gov/cars/rules/import/.

Chapter 8: Laws, Legislation, Suggestions and Prevention

Cities all over the globe are enforcing existing laws and implementing new ones in an effort to control this illegal and dangerous activity. Too often cities and states do not take action until a problem appears out of control and lives have been lost. There is no need to reinvent the wheel when it comes to saving lives. Street racing and similar activities have been, and will continue to be, a part of society, and strict enforcement has proven to curtail the most dangerous of these gatherings, saving untold lives, injuries, and destruction of property.

Most states already have a variety of laws on the books sufficient to control the illegal activity regarding dangerous street racing. Taking a hard enforcement stance on pre-existing laws may be sufficient to control this problem. I know of several areas within the city where I live that have strict traffic enforcement on certain sections of the local highways. This knowledge of strict enforcement keeps most people from speeding even the slightest.

Cities can set the tone for what is allowed. For years, we have seen groups of street racers who have a policy of staying out of cities or ensuring that they obey the laws of that city, because they know (from prior enforcement) that such activity will not be tolerated. In the mid-90s, street racers would not drive through the city of Fremont, California, for they knew they could be exposed to a ticket sending them to the Bureau of Automotive Repair. They instead started gathering in a neighboring city that was more lenient. It did not take very long before the city had a problem that was very difficult and dangerous to control. Working together as cities, counties, and states to enact laws or ordinances that are universal and are implemented simultaneously will avoid this cat and mouse game. Strict enforcement of traffic laws with our youth will save lives. Education is great, but enforcement can be easily measured as to how effective it is.

One of the biggest mistakes many cities or states make is that they are not aware of the problem or its potential severity because it has not gotten "out of control" or lives have not been lost. Secondarily, they believe that it is not *their* problem but an adjacent city's problem. Once they do realize there are problems and the serious consequences they are having on their citizens, they enact some laws. Unfortunately, many of these new laws have very little teeth or effect because they are not strict enough. The time it takes to get a new law introduced, passed, and implemented has frustrated many communities. These "baby steps" in legislation slow down the process of saving lives and making a difference. To speed up this legislative process, use the data contained throughout this book. Contact other agencies who have already experienced the problems your city may now be facing. Contact victims of street racing as well as cities who have become victims to determine what finally helped to curtail the problem and save lives and property. Starting out with tough legislation and a no tolerance policy will prevent problems and saves lives, guaranteed. At the conclusion of this section are some highlights of legislation that has had an impact when consistently and continuously enforced.

Review the various laws presented here and compare them with your current statutes to see if they need improvement. Cities that are unsure about the severity of the problem may enact a new law or municipal code that is an infraction. The real goal here is to save lives and protect property. Cities should not be shy about implementing the strictest laws presented here in order to avoid the mistakes others have made before them. They soon learn that infractions are ignored and then they have to escalate them to a misdemeanor. Other more serious violations have gone from misdemeanors to felonies. These laws were enacted because things got out of hand in cities across North America and something needed to be done to stop them. Don't wait until it's too late. Implement laws and regulations that have been proven to save lives and prevent illegal and unsafe activity.

For cities across the globe that are at their wit's end and initiating legislation to curb this dangerous activity, take note from cities like the ones mentioned here that have had to introduce more strict legislation than originally sought. In 2007, many parts of Canada were seeing an increase in deaths and injuries related to illegal street racing or other aggressive driving obsessions. Some provinces imposed what they believed to be stricter laws, such as seven-day impounds and license suspensions. As you will read in this book, even 30-day impounds have not been sufficient by themselves. Before you spend the time and money seeking new legislation, make sure it will have an effect that will curb this illegal activity and save lives.

Speed humps have been a 99% solution to stop illegal street racing in remote areas not heavily traveled by the general public and with a low posted speed limit. They are lower profile than speed bumps and less annoying to the public. They are great for chronic problem areas and allow law enforcement to concentrate on other problem areas. Since most street racers like at least an eighth-mile to race, one hump every 300 feet could keep the racers away.

Legislative Examples

Even with a 30-day impound already in place for those caught street racing, California needed to take it a step further to help save lives and protect property. In 2007, California State Senator Darrell Steinberg introduced Senate Bill 266. The bill provided that, when a person is arrested for reckless driving, reckless driving in a parking facility, exhibition of speed, or a speed contest, the officer may seize and impound the vehicle for 30 days. The bill also allowed for forfeiture of the vehicle if a person convicted of one of these offenses has two prior convictions for speed contest.

The 30-day impoundment statutes had not provided authorities in Elk Grove California with sufficient tools to deter these crimes. Recidivism had been extremely high in illegal and unsafe street racing or drifting type activities, despite participants being ticketed or having previous 30-day impounds. The City Council enacted a zero-tolerance ordinance that doubled the state guideline of impounding street racing vehicles from 30 to 60 days. The ordinance also targeted spectators of speed contests by imposing up to a six-month jail sentence and $1,000 fine for those within 200 feet (many illegal races would not occur if there were no spectators watching). Forfeiture and crushing most certainly prevents this repeat activity and sends a strong deterrent message.

Before you propose or pass legislation, look at what has and has not worked. Florida had a statute that addressed two forms of racing: illegal street drag racing and more general, spontaneous racing. It defined drag racing as a race from one fixed point to another in which vehicles attempt to outdistance each other, or a race in which competitors try to reach the highest speed or fastest acceleration within a fixed time or distance. Spontaneous racing sought to address impromptu, high-speed races on major highways. In September 2007, Florida's Fourth District Court of Appeals upheld a lower court's decision to declare the state's statute governing racing on public roads unconstitutional. The courts took issue with the definition of general racing, indicating that the language was so vague that anybody who accelerated through a green light or changed lanes to pass another vehicle could be violating the statute.

Don't limit yourself to defining racing; instead make sure that gross negligent activity with vehicles is defined and think of all applicable terms such as "reckless driving", "exhibition of speed", "unsafe speed", "speed contest", "race", "stunt", "contest", "drift", "burnouts" and other "showboating" activities.

In January 2009, after another street racing fatality in Orlando Florida, State Representative Darren Soto said he plans to introduce a bill that would increase drivers' license suspensions for street racers. The bill would also make the third offense a felony with a five-year license suspension. Due to economic issues, the bill would reduce jail time for the first offense but would double the license suspension to two years.

Rhode Island State Senator Walter Felag and State Representative Raymond Gallison sponsored bills S-783 and H-6014, making it illegal to race vehicles on any public road, whether or not there was an agreement to race. This bill was named the Justin Nunes Law, memorializing a 17-year-old Bristol teenager who was a passenger in one of two cars involved in a fatal street-racing crash on Route 136 in Bristol on April 19, 2003 (Steven Botelho was also killed and another, David Arruda, was severely injured). Laws such as these have been important due to the increase in impromptu races on our streets and highways.

In these bills the first violation is a misdemeanor, while second and subsequent offenses are classified as felonies. A first-time violator would be subject to imprisonment of not more than a year, incur a fine of $500 to $1,000, be subject to 10 to 60 hours of community service, and face license suspension of 90 days to six months. For a second offense, a violator would spend not less than a year in prison, pay a fine of at least $1,000, perform 60 to 100 hours of community service, and incur a license suspension of at least six months. Those guilty of third or subsequent offenses would face two to five years in prison, a $2,500 fine, at least 100 hours of community service, and loss of license for at least a year.

The legislation also contains sentence enhancements for violators with one or more passengers in the vehicle, or those who were under the influence of alcohol or drugs. Street racing resulting in death, serious bodily injury, and personal injury would carry penalties ranging from imprisonment of from 5 to 15 years, fines from $1,000 to $10,000, license suspension and, under certain circumstances, impoundment or forfeiture of the vehicle involved. This bill passed the Senate in June of 2007.

On December 15, 2006, in Canada, Bill C-19 became law, making street racing a crime and provided for stiffer penalties for those convicted of the offense. Bill C-19 provides for a mandatory lifetime driving prohibition. This would occur when an offender has at least two street racing convictions, which have caused bodily harm or death and at least one of those convictions involved street racing causing death.

Under Ontario legislation, drivers caught speeding in excess of 50 km/h (approximately 30mph) over the speed limit can have their vehicle impounded for one week and be fined a minimum $2,000 to a maximum $10,000 Canadian dollars. Police can also suspend the violator's license immediately for a week with a maximums suspension for 2 years. Over 300 violators were charged after the laws first year in 2008 (Bill 203 September 2007).

Between September 2007 and September 2008, about 8,500 drivers across the province of Ontario had been charged under the legislation. While the average age of offenders is 30, officers have also charged two 75-year-olds under the law. Nearly 84% of the drivers charged have been male.

During the 2005 California legislative session, AB1325 established a jail term of 30 days to six months for persons found guilty of engaging in motor vehicle speed contests if the driver causes bodily injury to someone other than himself or herself. In 2006 AB2190 passed, which made reckless driving and engaging in a speed contest of some type (street racing or drifting) that results in Great Bodily Injury (GBI) a felony for first-time violators. Previously, only those with prior convictions of this offense would be charged with the felony. Conducting an Internet search for "AB 2190 California" will bring details of similar laws.

On June 6' 2003, in conjunction with the release of the movie *2 Fast 2 Furious*, in an effort to slow down the inevitable spike in street racing activity due to the movie, the City of Los Angeles advised it would enforce a city ordinance allowing cars used in illegal street racing to be confiscated and sold. It was also reiterated that being a spectator at one of these illegal events is a misdemeanor punishable by $1,000 fine and/or jail.

When citations for driving faster than 100 mph increased more than 25% between 2000 and 2003 in California, Assembly Bill (AB) 2237 was passed, which increased the fines associated with driving over 100 mph from $500 to $750 ($1000 for the 2nd and 3rd convictions).

Spectator laws are imperative in order to have impact on curbing street racing. In Los Angeles, a 22-year-old man was sentenced to 18 months probation, 10 days of community service, a $300 fine, and ordered to stay away from street-racing venues for being a spectator at an illegal racing event. The city passed the stricter law on December 1, 2002. Before that, watching an illegal race was an infraction that was punishable by a small fine only. Google "Spectators prohibited at speed contests or exhibitions" to see a variety of spectator ordinances.

In Hawaii, the Senate passed a bill (SB 85) to allow law enforcement officials to seize the vehicles of repeat racing offenders (or their parents' cars). It would have allowed courts to confiscate the vehicles of offenders who have had a previous racing conviction within the past five years. Under the bill, "racing" would mean exceeding the speed limit by 30 mph. If the offender is a minor and used his or her parents' vehicle in the racing offenses, that vehicle could be confiscated as well.

Current law allows for the forfeiture of a vehicle on the third offense, and forfeiture is limited to vehicles owned by the offender.

In New South Wales, a new message is being sent with the passage of the Road Transport Legislation Amendment (Car Hoons) Act 2008. Police have the power to confiscate street racing or stunting vehicles. They then return the vehicle to the offender's house with the wheels clamped. The car stays in this immobilized state for three months. This serves as a daily reminder of their actions. On a second offense, the vehicles can be confiscated for good as well as nine months in jail for the violator.

Although many states and cities are enacting new laws to combat this problem, there are usually laws already on the books that, if enforced, would slow the theft and fraud problem as well as save lives. Many times at illegal or sanctioned events, we find vehicles being driven by drivers that were excluded on their parent's policy. Additional charges or actions can take place regarding uninsured drivers, particularly in these unsafe venues.

In August 2008, Readers Digest put together a comprehensive report on teen driving, including a listing of effective laws by state. Regarding prevention, the article stated, "An ideal law would set the minimum age for a permit at 16, limit passengers to one, ban cell phones, prohibit driving between 10 p.m. and 5 a.m., and not allow a full license until age 18." The article also stated that a recent study by Johns Hopkins University for the AAA Foundation for Traffic Safety found that a tough phase-in law could decrease deaths among 16-year-old drivers by 38%. States with the toughest driving laws tended to have the lowest fatality rates. For more information go to www.rd.com and search for "The Dangers of Teen Driving."

Legislative Solution Summary

Fines have not been nearly as effective as jail time, vehicle seizures, forfeitures, and crushing. An ongoing, comprehensive enforcement policy is necessary to save lives and prevent injuries. Based on the trials and tribulations of other cities around the world, a model to consider would be the following:

- Zero-tolerance enforcement
- 30-day impound first offense
- Misdemeanor charge with five days in jail, six month license suspension, a fine and community service
- 60-day impound for second offense, felony charge and a minimum one year license suspension
- Curfew enforcement at 10:00 p.m.
- Provisional drivers licenses for minors restricting passenger transportation (many illegal street race vehicles have three passengers in their vehicles)
- Forfeiture of the vehicle for third offense, increased fines, license suspension and community service
- Stiff penalties for violation of probation/parole

- Sentence enhancements for violators with one or more passengers in the vehicle, or while under the influence of alcohol or drugs, and/or increased the fines associated with driving over 100 mph
- Street racing resulting in death or great bodily injury should carry penalties ranging from imprisonment from five to 15 years, fines from $1,000 to $10,000, license suspension and, under certain circumstances, impoundment or forfeiture of the vehicle involved
- Misdemeanor for spectators of speed contests, a six month jail sentence and $1,000 fine for those within 200 feet of a race or related event such as drifting or stunting
- Known areas of racing and gathering should be posted as "no parking, stopping, or standing" between 10:00 p.m. and 4:00 a.m.
- Flagging, starting, organizing, directing, assisting or contributing to a race, stunt or illegal related vehicular event carry's its own penalty for each instance
- For states that have smog and illegal modification laws, mandatory Bureau of Automobile Repair state referee visit mandating the vehicle be returned to stock at the owner's expense
- Probation terms requiring GPS vehicle and speed tracking and/or restraining orders keeping violators away from known street racing and show venues.
- If the vehicle contains stolen parts such as the engine and transmission, crush it!
- If the vehicle is used in a life-threatening manner, crush it!

The escalation of enforcement and zero-tolerance is necessary to save lives. For the states and cities that took baby steps to get to strict laws and enforcement, several more lives had to be lost before more stringent laws were enacted. Avoid needless loss of lives by jumping straight into the most successful solutions proven effective by other cities and states.

A 30-day impound and five days in jail may seem harsh to those that have had no significant legislation to begin with, but there is a reason for this first step. Too many reports come across the wire indicating that the collision or fatality was a result of the driver's first impromptu race. Strict legislation coupled with a strong advertising public awareness campaign can prevent many of these first (and fatal) races.

Addressing the Culture

The street-racing problem needs also to be addressed towards the culture. The next generation needs to grow up knowing that it is never acceptable to engage in exhibition of speed or related stunt activity unless on a track or in a sanctioned controlled location. A cultural shift such as this could breaks this long standing cycle of illegal racing on our highways. Parents can be invaluable in helping change this mindset; parental discipline (taking away the car keys, the driver's license, etc.) for teens who don't drive safely and making teens pay for their own insurance can help them be more responsible, safer drivers.

In June 2007 the Roads and Traffic Authority (RTA) in New South Wales, Australia launched one of the cleverest ad campaigns and videos to stop street racing I have seen. The video "Speeding: No One Thinks Big of You" featured spectators of vehicular exhibition of speed wiggling their pinkie fingers at the driver insinuating that he has a small appendage. The campaign was very successful and given credit to addressing the problem before it occurred.

New South Wales statistics had shown that speeding was a factor in about 40% of road deaths each year, killing more than 200 people. In addition to those killed, more than 4,000 people were injured in speed-related crashes each year. They also estimated the cost to the community of speed-related crashes at approximately $780 million a year.

Educational and public awareness programs, along with community involvement, must be coordinated with legislative efforts. There are family members of victims as well as violators who have set up blogs and websites in their own words and experiences regarding the consequences of street racing and its ripple effect throughout the community. Go to www.ProtectOurStreets.org for links to their sites.

Once you have programs in place that have successfully slowed down the illegal activity and saved lives, cities *must* allow the anti-street racing programs to continue. Too often administrators disband successful programs thinking they have done their jobs and the problem does not exist any more. This type of attitude has been responsible for many subsequent increases in street racing-related activities, which have tragically ended in deaths and injuries. As mentioned in Chapter 1, San Diego's results in stopping illegal street racing and saving lives were impressive. Year 2006 data showed a reduction in organized illegal street racing activity in San Diego and a 98% improvement in illegal street racing deaths and injuries. However, San Diego Police Department's Dragnet team was disbanded, and in 2007, they had 12 fatalities and 4 street racing-related injuries.

Continued Involvement and Evolvement

Prevention was discussed throughout every chapter, but there are additional aspects we need to consider. We can all work together to harden the target and minimize theft and fraud as a community while at the same time saving lives and protecting property. Some of the more successful programs involved multiple organizations. If an individual in the community is passionate about making a difference, they should solicit the help of others involved in the various disciplines in that same community, city, county, and state. Through education and training of the other disciplines, a coordinated effort will bring about the most effective results. Using the information provided in the various chapters of this book, you can present the cause and effect of the various forms of modified vehicle theft and fraud to key people involved in your enforcement and safety efforts.

Officers assigned to illegal street racing, fraud, and auto theft detection and prevention units may start generating many citations, arrests, and vehicle impounds. All of this activity will affect other departments, including courts, judges, probation, city and district attorneys, smog referees, local racetracks, aftermarket parts companies, insurance companies, and outlying agencies. Enforcement is just part of the solution. Before launching an attack on the auto theft and fraud problem associated with the illegal modified vehicles scene, meet with the various departments to educate them on the problem and find out how to best work with them so as not to overwhelm them. Failure to do so can make enforcement activities ineffectual.

Citing violators for one particular section of the law will not do much good if the courts will not hear the case or the judges do not understand why that particular section was used. Since the violators are frequently juveniles, bringing a probation officer on board may help future efforts, as they can be your advocate in the juvenile system and assist with probation searches when necessary.

If civil hearings are going to be involved in cases where vehicles are seized, parted-out, or crushed, make sure the city or county attorneys understand the importance of your actions. Refer them to other attorneys and cities that have had success.

Speed cameras, red light cameras, and sound cameras for the loud music, tire squealing, and exhaust, are all being implemented to try to combat the many problems inherent with this scene. In Britain, they are testing cameras that will record ten seconds of audio and video of the violations. (One such system has been developed by Acoustic Research Laboratories in the U.K). Arizona has deployed approximately 60 of the speed cameras, set to activate when a vehicle exceeds the speed limit by 10 mph, catching twenty to thirty thousand speeders per month the first three months in operation (Utilizing Redflex Traffic Systems out of Australia). For a list of cities in the United States that use speed and red light cameras go to http://www.iihs.org/research/topics/auto_enforce_list.html.

Social Networking sites such as MySpace and Facebook, as well as video-sharing sites such as YouTube, can provide evidence and tools necessary to prosecute offenses. Several successful prosecutions have occurred based on the video posts alone. This MySpace/Facebook generation communicates through technology, sending on average 4,000-6,000 text messages per person each month and posting their lives online. Instead of "dropping a dime," we now ask them to "send a text."

Proactive police agencies have set up texting "tip lines" where our youth can send a text message regarding illegal racing and related activity. Having a law enforcement presence on sites like these can also provide another outlet for concerned youth to access help or notify police of unsafe and illegal activity.

Auto Theft Prevention

Starting with the basics should be everyone's first line of defense. Vehicles are stolen every day with the owner's key, not "hot-wired." The majority of them are stolen while parked at the owner's home or while left running in front of a convenience store.

Protecting yourself can be inexpensive and easy by starting with the basics. The first line of defense is to lock your car, windows, sunroof, and cargo window; take all keys with you and park in well-lit areas within public view. To help slow down the illegal towing of vehicles, point your tires toward the curb, lock the steering wheel, and engage the emergency brake. Make sure there are no visible enticing items that would lure a thief into your car. Make sure no one is watching you "hide" that purse or property in the trunk before you leave (but it would be better if you took your valuable property with you).

Many of today's thefts occur during the winter or summer when people are warming up or cooling down their unattended cars before leaving for work. They also occur at locations where the owner leaves the car running, like at convenience stores or ATMs. Car burglaries may occur just to access the glove box to see if there is a valet key available or if keys to your spouse's cars are in your car. If a suspect locates the keys to your other car, he may then access papers in your vehicle such as mail or registration to locate your home address. Armed with the second set of keys, he will come to your house for the other car. Surfers frequently park their cars and "hide" their key while they surf. Guess what? Car thieves stake out such spots or know the common hiding places and take your car as soon as you are out of site. Humans are creatures of habit, and we are not as unique as we think when it comes to hiding keys.

Anti-theft devices, aftermarket immobilizers, kill switches, tracking units, and other such devices can be beneficial. Just like anything else, some systems are better than others are, and frequently, you get what you pay for. However, no system is unbeatable, so you must still follow all precautionary steps. Car owners need to do their homework before they invest in an anti-theft system or deterrent. Even though many steering wheel lock devices can be easily defeated; if there are two cars side-by-side and one has a lock and the other doesn't, the thief will most likely take the car without the lock. If the vehicle has an alarm, the owner should consider having a hood lock, because many thieves are very proficient in getting under the hood and disabling the alarm before anyone notices. Due to the high number of false alarms that we hear everyday, alarms have become somewhat ineffective (refer to Alarms in Chapter 4).

We recommend immobilizers and tracking devices for owners of high theft cars. Many of the sport compact cars that are on the nation's top ten stolen vehicle lists do not have immobilizers (see Chapter 1). The more creative you are regarding the use of an immobilizer or kill switch, the safer your car is.

Several dealerships sell aftermarket anti-theft devices because they generate a great income for the dealership, not because they are effective. Thieves know many dealerships only disable the starter with a flat-plug type immobilizer system. It can be very easy for them to re-enable the starter with just a jumper wire or a similar method. Many systems will disable the starter, fuel pump, or ignition. If you can find a system that will disable multiple points, your car can be harder to steal, taking more time, which is something thieves do not want.

Some enthusiasts will install their own kill switches in very creative ways. Experienced thieves know that if there is an owner-installed kill switch that it will be conveniently located so they can get to it. The thief will run his fingers around the most convenient places, looking for the switch to bypass it. The creative installers may make it so the seatbelt must be engaged and the cigarette lighter has to be out or they may use touch-sensitive switches and magnets. The combinations can be endless.

Tracking devices like LoJack and OnStar can assist in getting your car back before it is stripped and ruined. With LoJack's Early Warning Recovery System, you will be notified as soon as your vehicle moves without permission. This gives you time to notify the police in case of a theft and your vehicle may be recovered before it is stripped of its parts (disclaimer: since I believe in LoJack, I own 500 shares of LoJack stock, so take my opinion with that in mind).

OnStar can do the same thing, but thieves frequently and easily disable On Star, making it an ineffective choice for security (although it is still great for the other services offered). We have interviewed many professional auto thieves who are worried that a car they stole might have LoJack. Instead of driving the fresh stolen directly to their chop shop, they will park it for a 24-

hour cooling-off period. If the police don't pick it up, they assume it doesn't have LoJack and they will then strip it. Many smaller aftermarket-tracking companies have similar products.

We also recommend parts marking, such as etching of vehicle glass with the VIN to prevent theft or aid in the recovery of a stolen vehicle. The Pennsylvania Auto Theft Prevention Authority has a great website with tips on how to protect your vehicular investment (www.WatchYourCar.org).

Track Alternatives

Several programs exist throughout the nation to help get kids off the streets and onto the safer environment of a track. Track alternatives can help diminish illegal street racing activity and provide a safe outlet to race. In cities where there were alternative legal venues for street racers that were subsequently closed, illegal street racing did increase on the city streets. Cities with available tracks have noticed a decrease in illegal street racing activity.

RaceLegal.com implemented a temporary track at Qualcomm Stadium in San Diego California. Armed with a grant from the California Office of Traffic Safety, they coordinated with law enforcement, city and county government, the City Attorney, the District Attorney, the Superior Court, probation, and the Bureau of Automobile Repair. Their target group is 16-30 year old male racing enthusiasts. They routinely drew 250 racecars and 2,000 spectators per event, which were held in the parking lot of San Diego's Qualcomm Stadium about 24 times per year. They set up an eighth-mile temporary track each Friday night when in season. This entire coordination of efforts resulted in a 98% reduction in street racing-related deaths and injuries.

Texas-based programs such as "Beat the Heat" also address other youth orientated problems such as drugs and alcohol as it relates to driving. Additional information and resources can be found on their website at www.beatTheHeatInc.org; "Street Racing is NOT Drag Racing."

Chapter 9: Insurance Company Issues

Throughout previous chapters, we have discussed the most common types of theft and fraud related to sport compact vehicles and have discussed what insurance companies can do to minimize their losses. Insurance companies can, and do, play a major role in theft and fraud prevention. Establishing clear policies and proper training of claims investigators saves companies millions of dollars. Through proper underwriting, adjusting, investigations, and training, insurance companies can also help curb illegal street racing and related activities, which in turn helps prevent injuries and saves lives.

Insurance companies can take simple steps to reduce their exposure to fraud, starting with the policy. Make sure the policy language is current regarding today's trends. Does the policy address the abuses that are being claimed which occurred from racing, exhibition of speed, excessive or illegal modifications, or nitrous oxide? Are there exclusions or limitations for Show, Drift, Drag, Stunt, and Street related modifications and abuses? Does the policy differentiate between performance driving schools for safety and those that may entice our youth to push their cars to the limit? What is the company's policy on insuring vehicles that have been imported illegally, as discussed in the previous Gray-Market section? If the policy does not limit liability for vehicles that are seized by the government, then the company may have to pay off a total loss to the insured for vehicles that are being seized and crushed due to stolen or illegal components. As simple as it sounds, just having a policy that prohibits insuring illegal cars, modifications, and racing activity can save companies millions of dollars each year. Remember the example we used in Chapter 1, under Modified Vehicle Theft and Fraud Costs? One insurance company discovered 12 vehicles participating in a race event and those 12 vehicles had cost their company nearly a quarter of a million dollars in the previous 18 months. Conversely, they looked at 12 vehicles of similar years, makes, and models that were not involved in the scene and they had only cost their insurance company $6,000.

During the past decade there appears to be no middle ground on what should be tolerated on our streets when it comes to illegal street racing and the related modifications. Our ignorance of a "fad" can allow dangerous trends to persist and grow. This same principal applies to insurance companies. Companies should evaluate what they will allow. If a company knowingly insures a 22-year-old male driving a street legal vehicle, modified to run 10 seconds in the quarter-mile, what message is the company sending?

This scene has some of the highest risk factors of any group. As reported under Deaths and Injuries in Chapter 1, motor vehicle crashes were the leading cause of death among 15-20 year-old males and females in the United States. The crash rate per mile driven for 16-19 year-olds was four times the risk of that for older drivers, and speeding is one of the most prevalent factors contributing to traffic crashes. Because of this and other factors, males under the age of 25 (the majority of our street racing enthusiasts) are already at risk and pay the highest insurance rates. Add to the mix a vehicle modified for increased speed and the risks skyrocket. The cars we are seeing on this scene are the cars that also have the highest injury, collision, and theft losses.

If the policy excludes racing for time, make sure it also addresses events such as Drifting, Touge (canyon racing), Stunting, and other forms of exhibition of speed that are not timed. Policy language should not be vague but should be written to cover future trends that involve similar principals. Drifting on public highways was not a significant problem in the United States in the mid 90s. However, if the policy was written to exclude "Exhibition of Speed," "Speed Contest" and other forms of "Showing Off," "Stunting" or "Displaying Dangerous or Imprudent" actions while operating a motor vehicle, trends such as Drifting or "Ghost Riding the Whip" would be covered now even though those terms did not exist when the policy was written.

The same holds true with modifications that significantly increase the vehicles horsepower or modify its design. Insurance companies base their premiums on risk determined in their Underwriting Guidelines. Sports cars generally have a higher premium because the risk to the insurance company is greater. A Honda Civic that was insured with a 160-horsepower engine is not at the same risk level as the same Civic that has been modified to produce 500 horsepower, but if the policy does not exclude such modifications without notification, then the insurance company's risk exposure is greater than what the premiums were based upon.

I have witnessed several collisions involving a vehicle street racing or drifting that lost control and collided with a spectator or another car. Does the policy address spectators at these illegal events? Spectators who expose themselves and their vehicles to an avoidable or illegal risk may not be covered for the loss, depending on how their insurance policy is written (in some cities being a spectator is illegal).

When the claims come in (and they will) ensure that the "proof of loss" or "affidavit of theft" form is completely filled out. Insureds have a tendency to avoid answering a question if it implicates them. Questions such as, "Was this vehicle ever used for street racing or exhibition of speed?" must not be left blank. The claims process should stop until all questions have been answered or explained.

The idea in this section is not necessarily to exclude everything, but it certainly should focus on disclosure and responsibility, so the appropriate risk can be determined. Many classic car enthusiasts have a separate policy covering the classic vehicle and its unique requirements. The same could be true with a sport compact enthusiast, as there have been companies that specialize in these types of vehicles. We have seen them advertising at sanctioned drag races and car shows. However, insurance companies should be ready to defend their actions in insuring, thus contributing, to some of the unfortunate incidents that arise from this scene.

Inside the Suspect's Mind

We have interviewed thousands of people involved in auto theft and fraud. Whenever possible we re-interview and video tape suspects after their convictions to learn from their perspective what we can do to prevent theft and fraud.

One thief gave us some insight, after admitting to his involvement in hundreds of thefts and fraudulent claims. For the purposes of anonymity, we will call him "Scott." Scott's perception of the dark side of the Fast and the Fraudulent scene is consistent with many other suspects, law enforcement officers, insurance investigators, and my own observations. Scott said, "Insurance companies pay good and everyone knows it." Scott and his friends would make sure they had the coverage before committing fraud, and if they had to increase coverage, they would wait a month or two before making a claim to avoid suspicion (adding additional questions during coverage queries may help to prevent this type of fraud). He said they would get a quote for $5,000 for a paint job and after the insurance company paid them, they would have the car painted for $1,500, pocketing the extra money or using it to do additional upgrades.

I asked Scott to describe some of the more common scams he and his friends would perpetuate to get the insurance companies to cover their expenses. If their paint was fading, they wanted a color change, or they just added a body kit that needed to be painted, they would "key" the car. When they defrauded the insurance company to have their vehicle painted, they made sure every panel of the car was keyed because if it was just the fender, they would have to pay more for the deductible then the repair, and there was a chance that the insurance company would not pay. When Scott and his friends keyed a vehicle, they made sure that they scratched the fenders, doors, quarter panels, trunk lids, and roof. Scott said most reported key vandalisms he knew about were false, particularly when every panel was keyed (See Chapter 2, Keying Vandalism, for more information on this problem affecting the insurance industry).

Blown engines due to aggressive driving and tuning practices are also commonly repaired or replaced by insurance fraud money. Scott said blown motors happen often due to racing, and that they would commit insurance fraud every time a motor blew. If Scott blew his motor, he would remove the engine as quick as possible and call the car in as stolen. The motor would be in his garage – or a friend's garage if he were worried about the insurance company stopping by. He would get $6,000 - $8,000 per claim and Scott called it "free money," stating it was very easy to do. He said, "*It's pathetic how easy it is.*"

Scott continued, "You would steal your own car. You blow your motor; you steal your car. You drop your motor; you strip it down for what you want replaced. You want a body kit; you take your bumpers. You want a carbon fiber hood; you take the hood as well. You want your interior replaced; you steal that. Or you even strip your car down completely; you take the wiring harness and motor so it is totaled. Then you can go back and buy your car back for [a lower] price when they just give you a low bluebook price on it. Make $12,000 on your car when you already have everything for it. So you just made $12,000 and you still have your motor and parts." Scott continued saying, "But on the other hand, we will steal friends' cars for the parts, because they want a new car, and they will get paid off for it. If you have a payment, and we steal your car, you don't have a payment anymore. Especially if you have gap coverage, because they are going to pay for that new car, and we got the parts we wanted."

Scott believed the majority of the sport compact cars in this scene are funded by fraud. He said, "You get in a little fender bender you have them pay for your new paint job or pay for your conversion. You find a shop that is willing to work with you to do the extra mile. You know, I want a headlight conversion, but they will only pay me for a paint job. You take it to someone else to get a higher bid. A lot of the dealerships get used that way. You take your car to a dealership and something you could get at another shop for $1,200 a dealership will charge you $3,500. So you just go to your local distributor ...for the cheaper parts and then have them paint it. That way you have the money to do that."

When asked how he got away with it, Scott said, "You get to be a good liar. Insurance companies usually don't follow up too much. One of the insurance fraud cars we had done, it was the second or third time, and they just never really investigated it. I guess they don't have the time or the money to deal with it. It is cheaper for them to pay out."

Since there is so much continual fraud involved in the sport compact scene, Scott said many would switch over to stealing replacement parts from others to avoid insurance company suspicion surrounding multiple claims. If they became concerned with too many insurance claims, they would steal the parts they needed from other enthusiasts. Scott said, "It was easier to get stolen parts, because you don't have to deal with insurance. Dealing with insurance it's always easy to slip up, or you don't know if they are going to send someone over. Or you don't know who wants to get back at you for something you did. They call your insurance company and say, 'Hey its fraud.' And then you don't want to do it too many times with insurance because your rates go up, so it's just easier to steal it. I would say 75% of the parts we get are stolen." *In our investigations, we certainly see this to be true. Law enforcement is continually recovering stolen component parts from these hard-core street racers.*

Scott summarized by saying, "Everybody I have ever dealt with, any friends who don't want to really break the law, they have all committed insurance fraud; I'd say 60-70%. It's pretty high. I remember a kid wanted a paint job; we keyed his car. Kid wanted a new stereo; we broke into his car and stole a bunch of stuff. He had all his stuff back, but the insurance company is going to pay. So I'd say it's pretty high. Especially in car clubs or on the import scene, insurance usually don't investigate." *Unfortunately, Scott represents many of the suspects we have interviewed over the last decade.*

When I asked Scott what the insurance industry could do to stop this type of fraud, he said, "They should have before and after pictures of the vehicles they are insuring." Insurance companies should require the vehicles to remain stock color, with no upgrades such as body kits. If the suspects could not get a color change nor have their body kits painted, then they would not be keying their cars. If the suspects knew there would be an inspection after the repairs, they would be less willing to try to get away with the fraud.

Scott also thought that if the insurance company could pick the repair facility that the car was taken to for repairs, then a lot of fraud would be avoided. "If you have to take it to the insurance company's shop, they would not be able to get away with getting what they want – the conversions, color changes, and other enhancements".

Scott's advice can't always be followed, as anti-steering laws prevent most states from dictating where an insured should have his car repaired. However, most insurance companies have some form of Direct Repair Program (DRP) with certain repair facilities. These DRPs have a working relationship with the insurance company and have generally agreed to cut their labor costs and discount the cost of any parts needed. They may also assist in the claims process and in authorizing repairs to help expedite the claims; in return, they get referrals and more business. Insurance companies can suggest these facilities to the consumer, however, many consumers are worried that insurance companies don't have their best interest in mind and will repair their car based on cost not quality.

During my career in investigating insurance fraud, there have been many reports of adjusters and estimators working too close with repair facilities. Some allow for pricing to be inflated, while others have accepted kickbacks for bumping up the claim. One adjuster involved in the Fast and the Fraudulent sting mentioned in Body Shop Fraud in Chapter 2 fled the country after the arrest warrants were served. Being on a preferred list of shops is very profitable and every year reports surface of lavish gifts between repair facilities and their insurance company representatives in hopes to remain a DRP. Insurance companies need to monitor these relationships and have strict policies regarding gifts, gratuities, and other favors, particularly around the holiday seasons.

There is no easy answer, but establishing clear policies with proper training can save insurance companies (thus consumers) millions of dollars. Just because a shop has qualified as a Direct Repair Facility, and works closely with the insurance company, does not mean that shop is above suspicion. The largest body shop fraud sting I participated in involved several DRPs. Fraud has no boundaries, and insurance companies need to have periodic inspections and audits to make sure that their customers and assets are not being taken advantage of by both the repair facility and their company's shop representative.

Photographs and Fraud Prevention

There was a time when pre-insurance inspections occurred on new policies and photographs were taken of the vehicle to be insured. This helped to reduce fraud by avoiding insuring "paper cars" (cars that exist on paper only; salvaged or junked vehicles), and to verify the condition of the vehicle. I was able to prove fraud on many cases because of the existence of these photographs. In one case, the suspect had insured her vehicle and then reported it stolen 45 days later. The insurance company she used had inspected the vehicle and taken three photographs of the car, one facing the left front, one facing the right rear, and one of the public VIN plate. When the insurance company received the claim, they noticed the vehicle had a previous salvage history and that the insured had purchased it just 30 days earlier. They contacted the previous insurance company that had salvaged the vehicle and learned that it had been involved in a total burn and only a shell remained. The insurance company provided photos of the burned salvage, which I compared to the pre-insurance inspection photos. The likelihood of purchasing this completely burned vehicle and rebuilding it to the near perfect condition pictured in the pre-insurance inspection photos (in 30 days) was highly unlikely.

When I reviewed the picture of the VIN plate, I could tell that the wrong rivets were used to attach it to the dash, indicating that this vehicle was VIN-switched and most likely stolen. When these photos were presented to the insured during questioning, we were able to prove that the car represented in the photographs was not the insured car and that it was a VIN switch. The claim was denied and the insured was arrested for felony insurance fraud.

Today's insureds are computer savvy with graphics programs and heavily involved in sharing photos and files on social networks as well as various Internet car forums. This can work towards bringing pre-insurance inspection photos back into play before insuring any vehicles, without costing additional time or money for the insurance companies. For insureds that have young drivers still living at home or on their policy, the insureds could email a digital photo of the vehicle at the policy's inception.

The insured could have their child email the photos of the vehicle, which will give the insurance company a very important investigative edge later if a suspicious claim comes in. *To avoid emailing altered photos the parents should be involved in the process.* Having an insurance representative take a pre-insurance inspection photo is still the best protection from false claims. As mentioned in Chapter 6, Internet Investigations, having access to a suspect's email can lead to verifying a story regarding the condition of a vehicle as well as other important data and this would be one way to capture it.

Physical vehicle inspections, before, during, or after a claim, can lead to much useful information. Decals and license plate frames can offer important information. In addition to the modifications mentioned in Chapter 5, a decal spouting, "No Speed, No Life" or "Life begins at 100 mph" could be used as intent or motive regarding speed-related incidents. Decals frequently list the names of car clubs, components, or activities of interest. License plate frames can list the same useful type of information. Sometimes these decals or clues can be seen from photographs that the insured supplies. These types of leads frequently lead to the information necessary to make a complete evaluation of a claim's veracity.

Assigned Risks

It is difficult to prevent the novice driver from having the occasional accident, but where does our responsibility lie with habitually bad drivers? Insurance companies provide coverage based on risk. They are able to calculate loss potential and spread that risk out, adjusting premiums when justified and minimizing risk for themselves and customers as a whole. Most states will require drivers with poor driving histories to be insured, but perhaps there should be a modification to mandatory insurance relating to poor driving habits.

Since it is mandatory for private passenger vehicles in many states to maintain automobile liability insurance, most states have required that even risky drivers be allowed insurance, also known as Assigned Risks. These high-risk drivers have generally been denied insurance because of their poor driving history, resulting in speeding tickets, accidents, driving under the influence, and other related violations. Since the incurred losses on assigned risks may exceed the premiums collected, these risks may be assigned to an insurance company to spread the incurred loss ratio.

Problems can arise in this system depending on what is allowed to continue. The Asbury Park Press did a story regarding a triple fatality involving street racing that had occurred March 14, 2007 in

Neptune, New Jersey. The driver of one of the vehicles had three passengers who were killed. The 19-year-old driver reportedly had more than three dozen motor vehicle violations. The online paper reported, "The drivers in the two other cars involved in the street racing had a combined 35 motor-vehicle points against them. One had his license suspended nine times. The other, whose list of motor vehicle violations included doing 105 mph in a 65 mph zone, lost his license five times."

One of the issues in this report was that although there were laws in place that would escalate the fines and punishment of violators, most sentencing is discretionary and jail time is uncommon. Another issue that could arise would be at what point does forcing an insurance company to insure an assigned risk become a contributing factor. The more responsible approach would be denying insurance to persons proven incapable to drive safely, seizing or crushing their car, or mandating a GPS tracking device that can also set maximum speed. Several insurance companies currently incorporate the use of GPS devices aimed at teens to assist in this area. Instead of parents worrying about children and cars racing or driving in areas they shouldn't be, they could check their GPS log for the vehicle's activity while enjoying an insurance discount for implementing such a device. Such devices can send an email to parents, law enforcement, and even the insurance company if approved.

Prevention and Detection

In addition to the many preventative procedures mentioned throughout this book, several other simple steps can be taken to protect an insurance company's exposure to unnecessary risk without compensation. Make sure those involved in the underwriting process pay attention to vehicles that fit the Fast and the Fraudulent profile, (or other high target vehicles). Knowing that an older Nissan 240SX vehicle may be favored by those involved in Drifting should raise concerns and warrant scrutiny prior to insuring. The value of the vehicle and premium may be small, but the potential for injury and loss of life can be great if they are involved in illegal drifting.

Personalized license plates, also known as vanity plates, can be a first clue to increased exposure to liability. The following plates should raise a red flag: "TooFast," "YBLEGL" (why be legal), "V8KILLR" (4 cylinder car beating an 8 cylinder car), or any personal plate with JDM (Japanese Domestic Market) or references to time as in "10SEC" (meaning a 10 second car in a quarter-mile race), "1320" (quarter-mile racer), combinations or abbreviations of Drift, combinations of VTEC (commonly used to reference Honda/Acura VTEC engines, particularly interesting if used on a different make vehicle), H22EQPD (referring to a possible engine swap of a prelude engine), B18C (indicating an Integra engine and possibly an engine swap), combinations or abbreviations for speed, including "SPD," "IMPTRCR" (Import Racer), and "RACEME" indicate interest in the race scene. Some plates can be cryptic or meaningless to someone not involved in this scene. The important aspect to protecting risk is to ask what a plate means. License plate searches can be a fast, easy, and a practically cost-free way to protect unnecessary exposure and losses.

As mentioned in Gray-Market cars in the previous chapter, Vehicle Identification Numbers that do not conform to normal standards need to be scrutinized. This practice can protect a company from insuring an illegal car or one that is prone to risky or illegal activity.

Simple computer programs and data mining can minimize risk by searching computer data for the above three factors: high target cars, vanity plates, and VINs that do not conform to standards. VINtrack.com Software can run thousands of VINs at a time and instantly sort out questionable, bad, and non-conforming VINs to make this process easier.

Training, Education and Awareness

Continuous and current training and education continues to be the most efficient and effective method to prevent and identify sport compact related fraud. The majority of these types of fraudulent claims go undetected because of a lack of awareness as to what trends and scams are being perpetrated. Through proper knowledge, one can prevent, discover or verify a fraudulent claim.

During my training seminars and workshops, attendees suddenly become aware that claims they are working contain fraud. The attendees can be heard in the hallways at break time calling their offices trying to flag a claim. I am continually hearing from investigators during breaks that they had a similar claim I presented during training but did not recognize the fraudulent factors until presented with our data. To minimize losses due to job reassignments, new hires, and changes in trends, it is imperative for insurance companies to maintain comprehensive and contemporary training on a continual basis. Through our workshops and seminars, and newsletters we have helped many proactive companies become aware of the current trends that are costing them millions of dollars in fraudulent and deceptive claims.

While educating our fellow employees, we also need to work on the public at large, with emphasis on the parents of this Fast and Fraudulent group. Being unaware of all the negative factors involved in this scene allows them to continue. Many of these vehicles are initially paid for and insured by the parents. Most of them are also kept and modified at the parent's house. Making the parents and public aware of the costs involved in modifying or customizing these cars can help control many of the abuses that are occurring.

As mentioned throughout this book, the parents should be the first line of defense when it comes to the actions of their children.

One solution would be to mail educational brochures to insureds that have pictures of vehicles that are prone to racing or heavy modification. This would give parents a visual on what to look for and inform them as to what is occurring. Make them aware that the costs of such modifications can exceed the child's income by tens of thousands of dollars as well as make the vehicle unsafe for their child and unsafe to be on the road. Make them aware that there are heavy fines associated with the illegal activity and that the car may be impounded for 30 days if caught racing in some states. Also, inform them that some cities are crushing cars involved in this illegal scene, their insurance will not reimburse them for this loss, and they will still have to make payments on a crushed car if they owed money. Educating them on how keeping these preventable claims from arising can keep insurance premiums down and save theirs and other children's lives.

Parents can be advised of tools such as GPS tracking that will assist them in preventing unsafe activity. Parents do not want their kids hurt any more than the insurance companies want the exposure to risk. Parents can be made aware of common terms and practices of illegal street racers, including text messages or Internet site activity.

Insurance investigators and law enforcement need to be aware of all the typical insurance frauds not necessarily related to the street racing and modified vehicle scene such as staged accidents. Refer to the Appendices for additional factors to consider.

The day this book was sent to publication several more street racing fatalities, injuries, arrests, indictments and sentencing's took place…

Appendices

Appendix A: Indicators of Modified Vehicle Fraud

No one indicator by itself is necessarily suspicious. Even the presence of several indicators, while suggestive of possible fraud, does not mean that fraud has been committed. Indicators of possible fraud are "red flags" only, and not cause by themselves to take action.

The Fast and the Fraudulent Indicators of Modified Vehicle Fraud; the more boxes checked, the more the claim should be scrutinized.

Claims
- ☐ Claim involves damage or circumstances discussed in The Fast and the Fraudulent book.
- ☐ Previous claims history with similar losses.
- ☐ Vehicle was reported stolen after it was recovered at an illegal street-racing scene.
- ☐ Neighbors, friends or family are not aware of loss or of modifications.
- ☐ Claims are phoned into police department with no on-scene investigation where generally available.
- ☐ Verify all receipts and compare them to the invoices.
- ☐ Ensure items on receipt were not returned for credit or a chargeback occurred after investigation.
- ☐ Are the reported items counterfeited or knock-offs? (Many tires are look-a-likes which effects the value)
- ☐ Friend "loans" tires to insured after reported tire theft (check tire date codes to match year of vehicle).
- ☐ Loss occurs at friends.
- ☐ Insured claims he was backed into during a hit and run.
- ☐ If a multiple party collision is involved, does the insured know the other parties?
- ☐ Is the collision or incident site frequented by the modified vehicle scene?
- ☐ Insured's income does not support value of accessories.
- ☐ Insured has a driving history of exhibition of speed and/or unlawful modification tickets from law enforcement.
- ☐ Insured's driver's license has recently been suspended.
- ☐ Driver was cited to the Bureau of Automotive Repair or similar program (California BAR requires car put back together as stock vehicle).
- ☐ In theft cases involving major component strips, the owner insists on retaining the salvage.
- ☐ Insured is behind in payments, has financial or marital problems.
- ☐ Insured owes more than the car is worth.
- ☐ Did anyone see flashing hazard lights prior to the collision? (Flashing hazards are an invitation to race).

- ☐ What driving patterns were observed prior to the collision?
- ☐ Were there other vehicles that appeared to be associates of one of the parties?
- ☐ Did the insured fill out the Proof of Loss or Affidavit of Theft completely?
- ☐ Did you conduct an Internet search for insured's scene involvement?

Claim Questions
- ☐ What is your email address?
- ☐ Are you into the sport compact scene?
- ☐ Has the vehicle been listed for sale?
- ☐ What related Internet sites do you recommend to understand the scene?
- ☐ What forums do you use for advice or information?
- ☐ What performance shops do you know of, or go to?
- ☐ Have you ever participated in, or been to, a sport compact event?
- ☐ Was your vehicle ever used for street racing, drifting, or related activity?
- ☐ Has anyone recently had possession of your vehicle?
- ☐ What does your friend/witness drive? (They may have made the same claim or supplied the same false receipts).
- ☐ Are your friends involved in the sport compact scene?

Vehicle
- ☐ Vehicle was not seen for an extended period of time prior to the reported theft.
- ☐ Insured's friends, witnesses, or associates have made similar claims. (Cross-reference all phone numbers and addresses).
- ☐ Similar claims coming from the same neighborhood.
- ☐ Vehicle shows signs of interest in the sport compact scene such as modification or decals (if you don't know what a certain modification is for, ask someone or Google the part name).
- ☐ The engine has modifications such as intake, exhaust, nitrous, or turbo charger.
- ☐ The vehicle has an engine swap such as an Aura engine in a Honda or from a different model. (This action may void manufacturer warranty).
- ☐ Engine damage shows signs of racing.
- ☐ The engine was reported stolen and stripped, but vehicle computer is still in vehicle.
- ☐ Engine or transmission number missing or altered.
- ☐ Emissions label under the hood is damaged.
- ☐ The vehicle was recovered burned but there were no personal items in vehicle.
- ☐ The battery is moved from under the hood to the trunk.
- ☐ The vehicle is stock looking vehicle before claim, and after repairs it has custom paint and/or ground effects.
- ☐ Stock front and/or rear bumpers and lights damaged, and the repair features an aftermarket body kit.
- ☐ Vehicles paint was "keyed" or similarly vandalized on most major sections of the vehicle. (Frequently a word is scratched into one of the body panels).
- ☐ Were lenses or lights scratched?
- ☐ Insured claims expensive tires and wheels were stolen and vehicle was recovered with stock tires and wheels.

- ☐ If it is recovered with tires, what condition are they in and what were they manufactured for
- ☐ Passenger seat and rear seats are reported stolen or cut.
- ☐ "Stolen" items appear to have been carefully removed from vehicle for later reinstallation.
- ☐ There were other items of value in the car that were not taken.
- ☐ The vehicle was pushed or towed to the scene of recovery (not drivable)
- ☐ "Stolen" items are those that are frequently bet (in lieu of cash) during an illegal street race, i.e. air bags, tires, or wheels.
- ☐ No signs of forced entry or ignition defeat on thefts.
- ☐ The vehicle was recovered with damage consistent with racing abuse, i.e. damaged drivetrain or body panels.
- ☐ The vehicle was listed "for sale" prior to the theft or claim.
- ☐ The costs involved in modifying the vehicle cannot be recovered by selling the car.
- ☐ The vehicle was purchased with cash and there is a questionable bill of sale.
- ☐ The vehicle has a previous salvage history.
- ☐ The vehicle was registered as special construction.
- ☐ The vehicle has a history of mechanical problems.
- ☐ The VIN does not conform with your countries standards or has a questionable history.
- ☐ Any identifying VIN labels are missing, altered, or seem questionable.
- ☐ Who installed the components?
- ☐ Who tunes or modifies your car?
- ☐ What modifications have been done to the vehicle?
- ☐ Who services the car?
- ☐ When was the vehicle last serviced?
- ☐ Why did you choose this body shop?
- ☐ Who referred you?
- ☐ Have you had recent mechanical work?
- ☐ Has any dealership denied work due to warranty issues?
- ☐ Are they legal?
- ☐ Do you have Adjustable cams?
- ☐ Did you modify the intake or exhaust?
- ☐ Do you have nitrous oxide installed?
- ☐ Do you have an aftermarket turbo?
- ☐ Did you modify the ECU?
- ☐ Who installed the modifications?
- ☐ Who supplied the parts?
- ☐ How much did you pay for them?
- ☐ How much did you pay for your car?
- ☐ How much have you put into it?
- ☐ How much more do you want to put into it?
- ☐ How much could you sell it for?
- ☐ What are the current trends?
- ☐ Where is this trend going?

- [ ] What decals did you have on the car?
- [ ] Follow up on any decals from website or performance shops or license plate frame information
- [ ] Verify any mileage discrepancies via service records, DMV histories, etc (mileage may be determined even if dash is missing).
- [ ] Is the vehicle modified for teenage children and not appropriate for the age of the insured

Internal Clues or Causes of Racing and Modification Damage:
- [ ] Air intake and exhaust modifications
- [ ] Improper ECU modifications or management systems exceeding engine design for power and/or speed
- [ ] Camshaft modifications
- [ ] Body modifications that restrict air flow
- [ ] Ignition system modifications including plugs
- [ ] Relocation of components that could effect engine management systems
- [ ] Damage related to excessive speed or torque such as transmission gear teeth missing or stripped, or burnt transmission clutches
- [ ] Pressure plate broken or over heated
- [ ] Differential gear damage
- [ ] Sheared axel shafts

Performance and Repair Shops
- [ ] The same performance or repair shop is frequented by many insureds with similar claims.
- [ ] Insured drives vehicle to far away shop for repair.
- [ ] Insured obtains receipts from far away shop.
- [ ] Receipt number is out of sequence with other receipts from that time or tax rate is off for that county.
- [ ] Does the performance shop stock the reported stolen items?
- [ ] Invoice for receipt show that the item was returned to the manufacturer after insurance inspection.
- [ ] Receipt for "stolen" wheels indicate 5-lugs and insured has a 4-lug vehicle, or vice versa (check to see if the insured had a lug conversion).
- [ ] Shop has small inventory and high sales/receipt volume.
- [ ] Does the shop personally know the insured?
- [ ] Who referred the insured to the shop?
- [ ] Insured uses a shop that charges the highest hourly rate.
- [ ] Performance shop has one price for the insured and a higher price is billed to Insurance.
- [ ] Signs of increased damage occurring at body shop. Fresh key marks continuing from old key marks. Paint flakes or broken glass on ground at body shop.
- [ ] Shop has many used parts (such as bumpers and engines) stockpiled with no apparent damage
- [ ] Same estimator's name appears consistently on similar losses from same shops and is at high end of estimate.

Insurance Industry Suggestions:

☐ Pre-Insurance inspection photos of all target cars.

☐ All target accessories that are added later must be submitted to the carrier with a receipt and photo. (The photo must be of the items while they are installed on the insured's car and not computer generated).

☐ Include a statement that if the vehicle needs to be repainted or repaired, only stock items will be used and only the original stock paint color will be applied.

☐ Monitor estimator's relationship with shop in conjunction with high estimates (rotate).

☐ Mandatory completion of "Proof of Loss" statement. Any blank lines left on form should be rejected until form is completely filled out. Add line "was vehicle used in racing, stunting, speed contest, or any other exhibition of speed."

☐ Examine all vehicles with previous salvage history or extensive driver history.

☐ If Pre-Insurance Inspection photos exist, compare them to the insured's recent photos. Insist on obtaining recent photos showing modifications.

☐ Do not allow owner retained salvage.

☐ If case warrants, determine who purchases the subsequent salvage to ensure the insured does not surreptitiously buy back the salvage and install the "stolen" parts.

☐ Re-inspect after repairs. Were used parts supplied when you were charged for new? Were the old ones put back on? Does the car look completely different?

☐ If new tires and wheels are reported stolen, ask for location of stock tires.

☐ Certain modifications, like Nitrous Oxide, should void insurance.

☐ Conduct personalized license plate searches for flags such as JDMRCR (JDM racer).

Appendix B: Engine Swap Table

The engine table that follows is for Honda and Acura. This chart should be used as guide only and lists the most popular numbers; there are many more that are not listed. All data should be verified with the manufacturer. Use this chart to assist you in determining if the vehicle you are inspecting has had an engine swap. See Chapter 5, Engine Identification and Swaps, for more information. Contact VINtrack.com if you have any questions or concerns.

One of the more desirable engine swaps is the Acura Integra engine into a Honda Civic. The B18C1 engine is a very desirable Acura engine and can be found in an Integra that would have a VIN with the fourth, fifth, and sixth characters of DC2 or DB8, (see Vehicle Description Section in below table). For example, if you were inspecting a vehicle with the VIN of JH4**DC2**38XSS123456, the fourth, fifth, and sixth characters (DC2) would indicate that the vehicle was manufactured with an engine type of B18C1. If you were inspecting a Honda and it had a B18C1 engine in it, you should know that it is a swap. All too often, a swap of this type is from a stolen vehicle.

Engine	Model	Vehicle Description Section	Trans	Year	Type
A18A1	Prelude	BA6	AB15, AS	84-87	
A20A1	Accord	CA5, CA6 DX LX	E2R6, E2Q6, A2Q6, A1B5, AS, F4	87-89	
A20A3	Accord	CA5 LXI SEI fuel injection	A2K5, A2Q5, E2R5, F4	87-89	
A20A3	Prelude	BA3	A2K5, F4	87-89	
B16A	Civic/CRX/Integ	Japanese RXi/XSi/SiR	S1, J1, Y1, YS1, (S4C (92-95))	89-01	VTEC
B16A	Del Sol	Japanese Si-R		93-97	VTEC
B16A1	Del Sol	Japanese EE8	Y2	89-92	VTEC
B16A2	Civic Si	EM1	S4C	99-00	VTEC
B16A2	Del Sol	EG2	S21	97	VTEC
B16A3	Del Sol	EG2	Y21	94-95	VTEC
B16A4	Civic Si	Asian version	Y21	96-00	VTEC
B17A1	Integra	DB2	YS1	93	VTEC
B18A1	Integra	DA9 (Integra RS, LS, GS, LSSP)	YS1, MPRA, A1, S1, RO	90-93	
B18A1	Integra	DB1 RS, GS, GSL	YS1, SS0, MPRA, A1, S1, RO	90-93	
B18B	Integra	Japanese		90-91	
B18B1	Integra	DB7, DC4 (LS, GS)	Y80, S80, MP7A, S4XA, SKWA, SP7A	94-01	
B18C	Integra	Japanese	Y80, S80	94-00	VTEC
B18C1	Integra GSR	DB8 DB859 = Leather	Y80, S80	94-01	VTEC
B18C1	Integra GSR	DC2 DC239 = Leather	Y80, S80	94-01	VTEC
B18C5	Integra	DC2 DC231 = Type-R	S80	97-01	VTEC
B20A3	Prelude	BA4	D2J4, D2M4, PY8A, K4	88-90	
B20A5	Prelude Si	BA4	D2A4, D2J3, D2J5, PY8A, MY8A, K4	88-91	
B20B	CR-V	Japanese		96-98	
B20B4	CR-V	RD1, RD2	M4TA, SBXM, MDLA,	97-98	
B20Z2	CR-V	RD1, RD2	MDMA, M4TA, SBXM, MDLA	99-01	VTEC
B21A1	Prelude Si	BA4	D2A4, PY8A	90-91	
BS	Accord	BA5, BA7 DX/LX	A2Q6, A2Q5, F4	86	
BT	Accord	BB5, BB7, BA5, BA7, DX/LX	A2K5, A2Q5, F4	85-86	
C25A1	Legend	KA2	C3P4, G4	86-87	
C27A1	Legend	KA3, KA4	C3F4, G3T4, PL5X, L5	87-90	
C27A4	Accord	CE6, V-6	MPZA	95-97	
C30A1	NSX	NA1, NA2	MR9A, J4A4, SR8M,	98-05	VTEC
C32A1	Legend	KA7, KA8	SY5, MPYA, K4F6,	91-95	
C32B1	NSX	NA2	SR8M	00-05	
D15A2	Civic	EC1, EC3, EC4, EC5, EC6, EY1	CA, GW,	87	
D15A3	Civic	EC1, EC3	GW	87	
D15B	Civic/CRX	Japanese		92-95	VTEC
D15B 1	Civic	ED6	L3	88-91	
D15B2	Civic DX LX	ED3, ED6, ED8, EE2, EY3	L3, L4, ML4A	88-91	
D15B6	CRX HF	ED8	L3	88-91	
D15B7	Civic	EG1, EG8, EH2, EH8, EJ2	S20, A24A, M24A, S24A	92-95	
D15B8	Civic CX	EH2	S20	92-95	
D15Z1	Civic VX	EH2	S20	92-95	VTEC
D16A1	Integra	DA1, DA3	CG, CA, P1	86-89	
D16A3	Civic	Australia		86-89	
D16A6	Civic	ED4, ED7, ED9, EE4, EE7	L3, S5, ML4A, MPSA,	88-91	
D16A8	Civic	Japanese		88-91	
D16A9	Civic	Japanese		88-91	
D16B5	Civic	EN1	BDRA	98-00	
D16Y5	Civic HX	EJ7	S40, M4VA	96-00	VTEC-
D16Y7	Civic	EJ6	S40	96-01	106HP
D16Y7	Del Sol	EH6		96-98	

Engine	Model	Vehicle Description Section	Trans	Year	Type
D16Y8	Civic	EH6, EJ8	S40, S8G, B4RA, S4RA, M4RA, A4RA	95-00	VTEC
D16Z6	Civic	EH3, EH6, EH9, EJ1,	S40, S20, S8G, A24A, S4RA, M24A	92-95	VTEC
D17A1	Civic	EM2, ES1	SLW, SLXA, BMXA	01-05	
D17A2	Civic	EM2, ES2	SLW, SLXA, BMXA	01-04	VTEC
D17A6	Civic	EM2	SLW, SLYA, MLYA	01-04	VTEC
D17A7	Civic	EN2	SLYA	01-05	
F20B	Accord	Japanese	T2T4	98	VTEC
F20C1	S2000	AP1	SCYM	00-05	VTEC
F22A1	Accord	CB7, CB9	H2U5, H2A5, PX4B, APXA,	90-93	VTEC
F22A1	Prelude S	BA8	MP1A, M2L5,	92-96	
F22A4	Accord	CB7	H2U5, PX4B	90-91	VTEC
F22A6	Accord	CB7, CB9	H2A5, H2C4, APXA, MPXA, MPWA,	91-93	
F22B1	Accord	CD5 CD7, CE1, YA1	A0YA, A6VA, P2A4, P2U5, BOYA, S2A4,	94-97	VTEC
F22B2	Accord	CD5 CD7, CE1	A0YA, P2A4, P2A5, B0YA, P2C4, MPOA	94-97	
F22C1	S2000	AP2	SCYM	04-07	VTEC
F23A1	Accord	YA3, CG3, CG5	MAXA, BAXA, B6VA, P2A8, S2A8,	98-02	VTEC
F23A4	Accord	CG3, CG6	MAXA, BAXA, P2A8	98-02	VTEC
F23A5	Accord	CF8	MAXA, BAXA, P2A8	98-02	
H22A1	Prelude	BB1	M2F4	93-97	VTEC
H22A4	Prelude	BB6	M6HA, M2Y4, M2U4, MP1A	97-01	VTEC
H23A1	Prelude Si	BB2	M2S4, MP1A	92-96	VTEC
J30A1	Accord	CG1, CG2, YA2	B7XA, M7ZA	97-02	VTEC
J32A1	3.2	UA5, YA4	BGFA, B7WA, B7VA, MGFA, M7WA	99-03	VTEC
J32A2	3.2	UA5, YA4	B7WA, YZC6, BGFA, MGFA	01-03	VTEC
J35A1	Odyssey	RL1	BYBA, B7TA	99-01	VTEC
J35A4	Odyssey	RL1, YF1	BVGA, BYBA	02-04	VTEC
J35A5	MDX	YD1	BDKA, MDKA	03-06	VTEC
K20A	Civic	Japanese		02-05	VTEC
K20A2	RSX	DC5(30)	X2M5	02-04	I-VTEC
K20A3	Civic Si	EM2	NRH3 / SLW	02	I-VTEC
K20A3	RSX , Civic 3D	DC5(38-5M)(48-5A), EP3	PTD6, W2M5, MRMA, NRH3,	02-06	I-VTEC
K20Z1	RSX Type S	DC530	NSN4	05-06	I-VTEC
K20Z2	Civic	Japanese, Europe, Canada		06	iVTEC
K20Z3	Civic Si	FG2, FA5	PNN3, PNN4	06-07	iVTEC
K23A1	RDX	TB1	BWEA	07	iVTEC
K24A1	CR-V	RD6, RD7	PSA4, MKZA, MRVA, MCVA, GPLA, GP	02-06	iVTEC
K24A2	Acura TSX	CL9	MCTA, ASU5	04-07	iVTEC
K24A4	Accord Element	CM5, CM7, YH1, YH2	BCLA, BZKA, APG6, MCLA, ZGM3, ZFJ	03-06	iVTEC
K24A8	Accord Element	CM5, CM6, CM7, YH1, YH2	BCLA, MCLA, APG6, MNZA, ZFJ3, ZGM	06-07	iVTEC
K24Z1	CR-V	RE3, RE4	MZHA, MZJA	07	iVTEC
L15A1	Fit	GD3	SMMA, SMJM	07	i-DSL
LDA1	Civic Hybrid	ES9	SZB, SZCA,	03-05	
LDA2	Civic Hybrid	FA3	SPSA	06-07	
R18A1	Civic	FA1, FG1,	SPFM, SPCA,	06-07	iVTEC
R18A4	Civic GX	FA4	SPCA	06-07	iVTEC
ZC	Civic/CRX	Japanese		88-91	130hp
ZC16	Civic Si-R	Japanese		<90	VTEC

Appendix C: Fast Facts

Costs:

- The FBI estimates that non-health related insurance fraud costs the average U.S. family $400-700 per year with a total yearly cost of $40 billion (Chapter 1, Theft and Fraud Costs). The Coalition Against Insurance Fraud (CAIF) estimates that the cost of fraud in the industry is as high as $80 billion each year.

- The average return on sport compact total investments can be as little as 30 cents on the dollar (Introduction).

- The majority of the sport compact car participants of the street, show, stunt, drift and drag scene are 16-27 year-olds driving heavily modified vehicles that are often times paid for and insured by their parents (Introduction).

- A record $38.11 billion worth of specialty automotive products were purchased in 2007 (Introduction; Aftermarket Parts Industry and New Trends).

- In Car Entertainment (ICE) is a huge industry. The primary consumers of these systems are once again our 16-24 year-old sport compact enthusiasts. According to SEMA, electronics and software represent more than 20% of the cost of today's vehicles. It is estimated that auto electronics sales will reach more than $50 billion by 2012, up from $38 billion in 2006.

- Daily insured vehicles involved in racing at sanctioned tracks, have cost some insurance carriers more than 37 times as much in claims payouts then the same make vehicle not involved in this scene (Chapter 1, Theft and Fraud Costs).

- Another insurance company took a proactive stance in identifying sport compact insurance fraud. They initiated training and education of their employees and customers and their claim losses dropped from over $4 million to $1.6 million (Chapter 1, Theft and Fraud Costs).

- One sting we were involved in showed that 76% of the body shops that we contacted were either willing to commit fraud or referred us to a shop that would commit fraud when it came to having our car repainted through fraudulent means.

- Additional fraud costs information can be found at the Coalition Against Insurance Fraud's website, www.insurancefraud.org; the Insurance Information Institute, www.iii.org, and at the National Insurance Crime Bureau www.nicb.org

- Speeding is one of the most prevalent factors contributing to traffic crashes. The economic cost to society of speed-related crashes was estimated by NHTSA to be $40.4 billion per year. In 2004, NHTSA estimated that highway crashes cost our society more than $230 billion a year (Chapter 1, The Fast and the Fatal).

Fatalities:

- In April 2007, the World Health Organization reported that road traffic injuries are the leading cause of death worldwide among young people aged 10-24 years. Out of the 1.2 million people that die in car crashes each year, nearly 400,000 people under the age of 25 die on the world's roads, an average of more than 1,000 deaths a day. More than 5,000 teens die every year in the United States (Chapter 1, The Fast and the Fatal).

- According to the Insurance Institute for Highway Safety, Highway Loss Data Institute (HLDI), the crash rate for 16-19 year-olds is four times the risk of that for older drivers, with 16 year-olds being the highest risk. The crash rate for 16 year-olds is twice as high as it is for 18-19 year-olds (Chapter 1, The Fast and the Fatal).

- According to AAA Foundation for Traffic Safety, more 16-18 year-olds die in car crashes then the next six leading causes of death combined: homicides, suicides, drowning, poisonings, cancer, and heart disease; with 18 year-olds being at the highest risk. Two additional people die for each teenager involved fatal collision; such as other drivers, passengers, or pedestrians (Chapter 1, The Fast and the Fatal).

- The US Department of Transportation's Fatality Analysis Reporting System (FARS) reported that 84% of teenage motor vehicle crash deaths in 2005 were passenger vehicle occupants. Of all motor vehicle crash deaths among teenagers in 2005, 54% occurred on Friday, Saturday, or Sunday. Midnight to 3 a.m. on Saturdays and Sundays proved to be the deadliest three-hour periods throughout 2004 (Chapter 1, The Fast and the Fatal).

- According to NHTSA, 31% of the 15-to 20-year-old drivers who were killed had been drinking (Chapter 1, The Fast and the Fatal).

- RaceLegal.com reported that for every 1,000 people participating in illegal street racing in California, 49 were either killed or seriously injured; in contrast, the national fatality rate due to drunk driving was 15 per 100,000 (Chapter 1, The Fast and the Fatal).

- RaceLegal.com commented that racers were 100 more times more likely to be killed while street racing in San Diego than they were to die in an alcohol related crash.

- San Diego Police Department's Dragnet team used innovative tactics to nearly stop illegal street racing. In 2002, San Diego was faced with an "epidemic" of illegal street racing activity. They documented 16 deaths and 31 serious injuries directly attributed to illegal street racing. Due to Dragnet's proactive and innovative operations, no lives were lost the first eight months of 2003, and in 2005, they had an unprecedented 94% improvement with only three serious injuries and no deaths. This decrease took place when the rest of the state and country were having increases. *In 2007, Dragnet disbanded, and there were subsequently 12 street race related deaths and four injuries.* (Chapter 1, The Fast and the Fatal).

- In 2008 Maryland experienced a street race in which eight spectators died from one incident; the ages of the victims of this tragedy ranged from 20-61.

- The National Highway Traffic Safety Administration said that connecting fatal crashes to illegal drag racing is difficult, but the year the first *Fast and the Furious* movie came out in June 2001, at least 135 people died in accidents from possible races. That was almost double the number recorded the year prior (Chapter 1, Movies Blamed for Street Racing Deaths).

- Motorcycle deaths are rising while traffic fatalities overall have declined. For the last nine years, NHTSA has seen an increase in motorcycle deaths. The average age for sport bike fatalities is 27. The death rate for sport bikes is four times higher than other motorcycles, and they have the worst overall insurance losses among all types of motorcycles based on registrations. Sport bikes made up less than 10% of the registered motorcycles in 2005 but accounted for 25% of the fatalities. (Chapter 3, Motorcycles).

- Laurence Steinberg and others have found that the mere physical presence of peers increases the likelihood of teens taking risks and Flaura Winston reported findings indicating that the ability to control impulses is not fully formed in the teenage years (Chapter 1, The Fast and the Fatal).

Vehicle Theft

- With approximately 1.2 million thefts per year for the last five years running, auto theft is the largest and most expensive property crime committed. Additionally, theft from motor vehicles and theft of motor vehicle accessories occurs, and costs more, than any other property crimes including robbery, burglary, and shoplifting. (Chapter 1, Theft and Fraud Costs).

- According to the most recent report from the National Crime Information Center (NCIC), the top ten cars stolen in the United States for 2007 were dominated by sport compact cars (Chapter 1, Vehicle Theft Statistics).

    1. 1995 Honda Civic
    2. 1991 Honda Accord
    3. 1989 Toyota Camry
    4. 1997 Ford F-150 Series Pickup
    5. 1994 Chevrolet C/K 1500 Pickup
    6. 1994 Acura Integra
    7. 2004 Dodge Ram Pickup
    8. 1994 Nissan Sentra
    9. 1988 Toyota Pickup
    10. 2007 Toyota Corolla

- **Top five stolen sport bikes**
    1. Suzuki GSX-R
    2. Yamaha YZF-R
    3. Honda CBR
    4. Suzuki Hayabusa
    5. Kawasaki ZX-R

Made in the USA
Lexington, KY
06 June 2015